PRACTICE MAKES PERFECT™

Complete German Grammar

Premium Second Edition

Ed Swick

Mc Graw Hill Education

New York   Chicago   San Francisco   Athens   London   Madrid
Mexico City   Milan   New Delhi   Singapore   Sydney   Toronto

6 7 8 9   LHS   23 22 21

ISBN   978-1-260-12165-0
MHID   1-260-12165-8

e-ISBN   978-1-260-12166-7
e-MHID   1-260-12166-6

Trademarks: McGraw-Hill Education, the McGraw-Hill Education logo, Practice Makes Perfect, and related trade dress are trademarks or registered trademarks of McGraw-Hill Education and/or its affiliates in the United States and other countries and may not be used without written permission. All other trademarks are the property of their respective owners. McGraw-Hill Education is not associated with any product or vendor mentioned in this book.

McGraw-Hill Education books are available at special quantity discounts to use as premiums and sales promotions or for use in corporate training programs. To contact a representative, please visit the Contact Us pages at www.mhprofessional.com.

McGraw-Hill Education Language Lab App

Extensive audio recordings, vocabulary flash cards, and review quizzes are available to support your study of this book. Go to the Apple app store or the Google Play store (for Android devices) to download the free Language Lab mobile app. A web version is also available online at: mhlanguagelab.com.

Note: Internet access required for streaming audio.

Contents

Preface v
Acknowledgment vi

1 Pronunciation and gender 1

2 Definite and indefinite articles 7

3 Pronouns, plurals, and the verb **sein** 17

4 Titles, locations, and interrogatives 26

5 The verbs **haben** and **werden** and negation 37

6 The present tense and numbers 47

7 Direct objects and the accusative case 56

8 Irregular verbs in the present tense 64

9 Separable and inseparable prefixes
and imperatives 74

Review 1 85

10 Accusative case prepositions and interrogatives 93

11 Regular verbs in the past tense and word order 103

12 Indirect objects and the dative case 112

13 Irregular verbs in the past tense 120

14 Modal auxiliaries in the present and past tenses 128

15 The accusative-dative prepositions 137

16 Regular verbs in the present perfect tense
and more imperatives 144

17 Genitive case, the comparative, and the superlative 152

18 Irregular verbs in the present perfect tense and adjectives 159

Review 2 169

19 Past perfect, future, and future perfect tenses 177

20 Relative pronouns 184

21 Modifiers, adverbs, reflexive pronouns, and conjunctions 191

22 Double infinitive structures 199

23 Infinitive clauses 207

24 The passive voice 213

25 The subjunctive 220

Final Review 231

Appendix A: The principal parts of irregular verbs 239
Appendix B: Prepositions and their required cases 247
Appendix C: Summary of declensions 251
Answer Key 253

Preface

This book can serve as a reference for the complete German grammar. It is designed to provide detailed explanations of the various aspects of German grammar as well as numerous examples that illustrate how the grammar functions in practical sentences. Each chapter contains a variety of exercises for practice with the covered grammar topics.

The explanations and example sentences are accompanied by the English translation, which should help you more clearly understand how a specific point in grammar works.

The exercises take a variety of forms. Some are conjugations of an isolated verb in any of the tenses. Some exercises are completions that need a single word or short phrase, and others may require writing a complete sentence. Some chapters have multiple-choice exercises, which require the reader to demonstrate not only the understanding of a grammatical concept but also how that concept is correctly applied in a sentence.

Most chapters have a single major grammatical topic. However, some chapters also include a secondary topic that is often linked in some manner to the major topic. The earliest chapters contain the topics that are appropriate for readers who have limited experience with German, for example, conjugations of verbs and basic declensions. The later chapters introduce structures that require an intermediate level of understanding of German grammar, such as the passive voice or the subjunctive mood.

New to this second edition are three review chapters that will assess your grasp of topics as you progress through the book. In addition, the McGraw-Hill Education Language Lab app contains extensive resources to support your study: flashcards for all vocabulary lists; review quizzes for each chapter; and extensive streaming audio recordings, corresponding to the answers of more than 80 exercises.

Mastery of the chapters in this book will give the reader a greater understanding of the complete German grammar. That mastery will be the result of consistent practice. Remember, practice makes perfect. *Übung macht den Meister.*

Acknowledgment

With much gratitude to Stefan Feyen for all his help and suggestions.

Pronunciation and gender

Pronunciation

Just like English and most other European languages, German uses the Latin alphabet as the basis for its writing. But the letters, in many cases, are pronounced slightly differently from English, and in four instances there are special letters for four sounds unique to German. Let's look at the German alphabet and its pronunciation.

LETTER	PHONETICS	EXAMPLE	
A a	ah	Maler	*painter*
B b	bay	Ball	*ball*
C c	tsay	Cent	*cent*
D d	day	dumm	*stupid*
E e	ay	weh	*sore*
F f	eff	finden	*find*
G g	gay	Garten	*garden*
H h	hah	Haus	*house*
I i	ee	ich	*I*
J j	yawt	ja	*yes*
K k	kah	Kind	*child*
L l	ell	Lampe	*lamp*
M m	emm	Mann	*man*
N n	enn	nein	*no*
O o	oh	Oma	*granny*
P p	pay	Park	*park*
Q q	koo	Quark	*curd cheese*
R r	air	rot	*red*
S s	ess	was	*what*
T t	tay	Tante	*aunt*
U u	oo	tut	*does*
V v	fow	Verbot	*ban*
W w	vay	wo	*where*
X x	ix	fixieren	*fix*
Y y	uepsilon	Gymnasium	*preparatory school*
Z z	tset	zehn	*ten*

German adds an umlaut to three vowels to change their pronunciation. These vowels are **ä**, **ö**, and **ü**. In addition, there is one special letter called ess-tset, which is the combination of an earlier form of an **s** and a **z**, and it looks like this: **ß**.

1

The vowel **ä** is pronounced very much like the German **e**. For example: **spät**, shpate, *late*. The vowel **ö** sounds something like the English sound *er* in the word *her*, but the *r* in that word is muted. For example: **können**, kernen, *can*. The sound of the vowel **ü** is made by pursing the lips to say *oo* but pronouncing *ee* in the mouth. For example: **Tür**, tuer, *door*. Note that the vowel **y** is pronounced in much the same way as **ü**. For example: **Gymnasium**, guem-nah-zee-oom, *preparatory school*.

The consonant sound of **ß** is identical to a double *s* in English. For example: **weiß**, vice, *white*.

Let's look at certain letter combinations that have their own unique sound.

LETTER	PHONETICS	EXAMPLE	
ch	*raspy* ch *as in Scottish* loch	nach	*after*
sch	sh	Schule	*school*
sp	shp	sparen	*save*
st	sht	Straße	*street*
au	ow	Frau	*woman*
äu	oy	läuft	*runs*
eu	oy	Freund	*friend*
ei	aye	mein	*my*
ie	ee	wie	*how*
th	t	Theater	*theater*
v	ff *but* v *in foreign words*	vor	*before*
		Vase	*vase*
tz	tz	Satz	*sentence*

Words that end in *voiced consonants* change to their *voiceless* counterparts.

IF A WORD ENDS IN . . .	PRONOUNCE IT AS . . .	EXAMPLE	
b	p	Leib	*body*
d	t	Bad	*bath*
g	k	Weg	*path*

The final syllable *-er* in a word is pronounced much like the final *-er* in a British English word, or something like *-uh*.

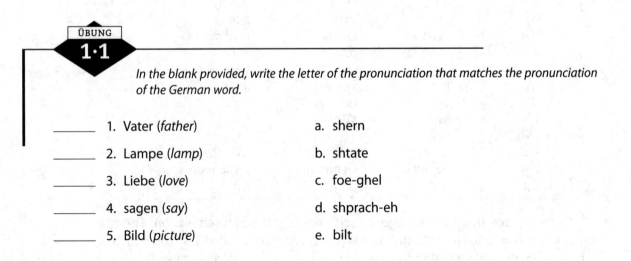

ÜBUNG
1·1

In the blank provided, write the letter of the pronunciation that matches the pronunciation of the German word.

_____	1. Vater (*father*)	a.	shern
_____	2. Lampe (*lamp*)	b.	shtate
_____	3. Liebe (*love*)	c.	foe-ghel
_____	4. sagen (*say*)	d.	shprach-eh
_____	5. Bild (*picture*)	e.	bilt

_____	6. machen (*make*)	f.	lee-beh
_____	7. warten (*wait*)	g.	fah-tuh
_____	8. Sprache (*language*)	h.	tsook
_____	9. Land (*country*)	i.	kahm
_____	10. Leute (*people*)	j.	loy-teh
_____	11. Vogel (*bird*)	k.	lunt
_____	12. kam (*came*)	l.	vahr-ten
_____	13. steht (*stands*)	m.	mahch-en
_____	14. Zug (*train*)	n.	zah-ghen
_____	15. schön (*pretty*)	o.	lahm-peh

Whenever in doubt about how a word is pronounced, refer to a good dictionary or speak to a German speaker. But be aware that just as with English, there are regional differences of pronunciation.

Gender

The gender of a noun can be masculine, feminine, or neuter. In English, the gender of masculine and feminine nouns is primarily determined by whether a living thing is male or female. Inanimate objects are called neuter. Look at these examples of English nouns that illustrate this:

MASCULINE/MALE	FEMININE/FEMALE	NEUTER/INANIMATE
boy	*girl*	*rock*
father	*mother*	*house*
actor	*actress*	*car*

There are some rare exceptions to this concept of gender. For example, ships are often referred to as feminine:

That's Old Ironsides. *She's a fine old ship.*

Or a car might be considered feminine when there is a strong attachment to it:

My old Ford just won't run anymore. But she got me around for years.

The English speaker learning German has to put the English concept of gender aside and accept a different concept of gender—gender in the German language. For German gender is determined in more than one way. The easiest to understand is sexual gender. Most males are considered masculine, and most females are considered feminine. For example:

MASCULINE		FEMININE	
Mann	*man*	Frau	*woman*
Bruder	*brother*	Schwester	*sister*

Often, a suffix is attached to a masculine noun to make it feminine. You should be aware that this is a very common practice in German.

Lehrer	(*male*) *teacher*	Lehrerin	(*female*) *teacher*
Schauspieler	*actor*	Schauspielerin	*actress*

If a German noun is masculine, its definite article (*the*) is **der**. If it is feminine, its definite article is **die**. For example:

der Mann	*the man*	die Frau	*the woman*
der Lehrer	*the teacher*	die Schauspielerin	*the actress*

ÜBUNG
1·2

*In the blank provided, write the appropriate definite article for each noun—**der** or **die**.*

1. _____ Junge (*boy*)

2. _____ Lehrerin (*teacher*)

3. _____ Frau (*woman*)

4. _____ Diplomat (*diplomat*)

5. _____ Diplomatin (*diplomat*)

6. _____ Lehrer (*teacher*)

7. _____ Professor (*professor*)

8. _____ Professorin (*professor*)

9. _____ Schwester (*sister*)

10. _____ Bruder (*brother*)

German, like English, also has a neuter gender. But it does *not* necessarily refer to inanimate objects. The definite article (*the*) used with neuter nouns is **das**. Notice that neuter nouns can include persons as well as objects:

INANIMATE NEUTER NOUNS		ANIMATE NEUTER NOUNS	
das Haus	*the house*	das Kind	*the child*
das Auto	*the car*	das Mädchen	*the girl*

And masculine and feminine nouns can include objects as well as persons. For example:

MASCULINE		FEMININE	
der Garten	*the garden*	die Blume	*the flower*
der Stuhl	*the chair*	die Rose	*the rose*

Perhaps you are now wondering how you determine gender in German. Let's consider some signals to watch for. Masculine nouns:

- *Tend* to be those nouns that describe males

der Mann	*the man*

- Often end in **-er**, **-en**, or **-el**

der Pullover	*sweater*
der Brunnen	*well*
der Mantel	*coat*

Feminine nouns:

- *Tend* to be those that describe females

die Frau	*woman*

- End in **-in**

die Lehrerin	*teacher*

- End in **-ung**, **-heit**, **-keit**, **-ion**, **-schaft**, or **-tät**

die Übung	*exercise*
die Gesundheit	*health*
die Einsamkeit	*loneliness*
die Position	*position*
die Freundschaft	*friendship*
die Majorität	*majority*

- *Tend* to end in **-e**

die Lampe	*lamp*

Neuter nouns:

- End in **-chen** or **-lein** and are diminutives

das Mädchen	*girl*
das Röslein	*little rose*

- End in **-um**

das Gymnasium	*preparatory school*

- *Tend* to end in **-tum**

das Königtum	*kingdom*

These descriptions of gender are not rules; they are signals for determining the *likely* gender of a German noun. There are many exceptions, because often the choice of a noun's gender is based upon the traditional use of that noun. Sometimes the gender used in Germany is different from the gender used in Austria or Switzerland. The newcomer to German has to put up with this in the beginning stages of learning. But in time and with experience, using German gender correctly becomes a reality.

*In the blank provided, write in the appropriate definite article (**der, die,** or **das**) for each of the following nouns.*

1. _____ Kind (*child*)

2. _____ Schule (*school*)

3. _____ Tante (*aunt*)

4. _____ Onkel (*uncle*)

5. _____ Brüderlein (*little brother*)

6. _____ Studium (*studies*)

7. _____ Universität (*university*)

8. _____ Landschaft (*landscape*)

9. _____ Situation (*situation*)

10. _____ Wagen (*car*)

11. _____ Gärtner (*gardener*)

12. _____ Eigentum (*property*)

13. _____ Landkarte (*map*)

14. _____ Sportler (*athlete*)

15. _____ Boden (*floor*)

16. _____ Sängerin (*singer*)

17. _____ Sicherheit (*safety*)

18. _____ Mutter (*mother*)

19. _____ Katze (*cat*)

20. _____ Freiheit (*freedom*)

Definite and indefinite articles

Definite articles

Just as in English, the subject in a German sentence can be a noun or a pronoun. If the subject is a noun, it will illustrate its gender by being accompanied by either **der**, **die**, or **das**, the definite articles in German that all mean *the*. Naturally, to have a sentence, there has to be a verb and perhaps other elements in the sentence besides the subject. Let's look at some simple sentences that demonstrate masculine nouns, feminine nouns, and neuter nouns used as the subject of a sentence.

Masculine nouns

Der Mann ist hier.	*The man is here.*
Der Lehrer ist hier.	*The teacher is here.*
Der Stuhl ist hier.	*The chair is here.*
Der Wagen ist hier.	*The car is here.*
Der Schauspieler ist hier.	*The actor is here.*

Feminine nouns

Die Frau ist da.	*The woman is there.*
Die Lehrerin ist da.	*The teacher is there.*
Die Landkarte ist da.	*The map is there.*
Die Blume ist da.	*The flower is there.*
Die Schauspielerin ist da.	*The actress is there.*

Neuter nouns

Das Haus ist klein.	*The house is little.*
Das Auto ist klein.	*The car is little.*
Das Mädchen ist klein.	*The girl is little.*
Das Kind ist klein.	*The child is little.*
Das Gymnasium ist klein.	*The preparatory school is little.*

*Rewrite each sentence with the nouns provided in parentheses. Add the appropriate definite article—**der**, **die**, or **das**.*

FOR EXAMPLE: _____ ist hier.

(Mann) _____ *Der Mann ist hier.*

_____ ist da.

1. (Kind) _____

2. (Blume) _____

3. (Haus) _____

4. (Garten) _____

5. (Wagen) _____

6. (Stuhl) _____

7. (Auto) _____

8. (Bruder) _____

9. (Schwester) _____

10. (Sängerin) _____

_____ ist klein.

11. (Gymnasium) _____

12. (Katze) _____

13. (Sportler) _____

14. (Mädchen) _____

15. (Boden) _____

16. (Landkarte) _____

17. (Universität) _____

18. (Pullover) _____

19. (Schule) _____

20. (Kind) _____

_____ ist hier.

21. (Auto) _____

22. (Gärtnerin) _____

23. (Frau) _____

24. (Professorin) _____

25. (Junge) _____

The definite articles (**der, die, das**) are called **der**-words. Another word that can be used in place of a definite article is **dieser** (*this*), and it, too, is a **der**-word. Note how similar the ending of this word is to the ending of a definite article used with masculine, feminine, and neuter nouns.

Masculine
der Mann	dieser Mann	*this man*
der Lehrer	dieser Lehrer	*this teacher*
der Garten	dieser Garten	*this garden*

Feminine
die Schauspielerin	diese Schauspielerin	*this actress*
die Schule	diese Schule	*this school*
die Bluse	diese Bluse	*this blouse*

Neuter
das Kind	dieses Kind	*this child*
das Fenster	dieses Fenster	*this window*
das Bett	dieses Bett	*this bed*

ÜBUNG
2·2

*Rewrite each phrase by changing the definite article to the appropriate form of **dieser**.*

1. der Mann _____

2. die Frau _____

3. das Kind _____

4. die Blume _____

5. der Garten _____

6. die Gärtnerin _____

7. die Lehrerin _____

8. das Studium _____

9. das Bett _____

10. der Professor _____

11. der Diplomat _____

12. die Bluse _____

13. der Boden _____

14. das Fenster _____

15. die Schauspielerin _____

*Now supply the appropriate form of **dieser** for each of the following nouns.*

16. _____ Haus

17. _____ Universität

18. _____ Königtum

19. _____ Gärtner

20. _____ Lehrer

21. _____ Schule

22. _____ Mädchen

23. _____ Sänger

24. _____ Sängerin

25. _____ Landkarte

Indefinite articles

The German indefinite articles for the subject of a sentence are **ein** and **eine**, and both mean *a* or *an*. **Ein** is used with masculine and neuter nouns, and **eine** is used with feminine nouns. For example:

Masculine
ein Lehrer	*a teacher*
ein Arzt	*a doctor*
ein Fernsehapparat	*a television set*
ein Schauspieler	*an actor*

Feminine
eine Schule	*a school*
eine Mutter	*a mother*
eine Tochter	*a daughter*
eine Tante	*an aunt*

Neuter
ein Bett	*a bed*
ein Buch	*a book*
ein Restaurant	*a restaurant*
ein Bild	*a picture*

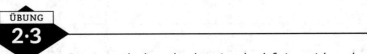

ÜBUNG
2·3

Rewrite each phrase by changing the definite article to the appropriate indefinite article.

1. die Lehrerin _____

2. der Junge _____

3. das Fenster _____

4. das Bett _____

5. die Universität _____

6. die Tante _____

7. das Mädchen _____

8. der Arzt _____

9. das Buch _____

10. der Fernsehapparat _____

11. die Tochter _____

12. das Restaurant _____

13. der Boden _____

14. die Mutter _____

15. das Bild _____

The indefinite articles are known as **ein**-words. Another such **ein**-word is **kein**, which means *not any* or *no*. Notice that its ending in the feminine is identical to the ending required with **eine**.

Masculine
kein Vater	*no father*
kein Bruder	*no brother*
kein Tisch	*no table*
kein Film	*no film, movie*

Feminine
keine Großmutter	*no grandmother*
keine Butter	*no butter*
keine Zeit	*no time*
keine Uhr	*no clock*

Neuter
kein Geld	*no money*
kein Fenster	*no window*
kein Rathaus	*no town hall*
kein Schlafzimmer	*no bedroom*

ÜBUNG
2·4

*Rewrite each phrase by changing the definite article to the appropriate form of **kein**.*

1. die Tochter _____

2. der Tisch _____

3. das Fenster _____

4. das Restaurant _____

5. der Gärtner _____

6. die Großmutter _____

7. der Arzt _____

8. die Ärztin _____

9. das Rathaus _____

10. die Butter _____

*In the blank provided, write the appropriate form of **kein** for each noun.*

11. _____ Junge

12. _____ Schlafzimmer

13. _____ Bild

14. _____ Schwester

15. _____ Tante

16. _____ Bruder

17. _____ Zeit

18. _____ Fernsehapparat

19. _____ Uhr

20. _____ Fenster

21. _____ Mantel

22. _____ Frau

23. _____ Geld

24. _____ Mutter

25. _____ Universität

ÜBUNG
2·5

*Rewrite each sentence twice, once by changing the definite article to the indefinite article and once by changing it to the appropriate form of **kein**.*

FOR EXAMPLE: Der Mann ist hier.

Ein Mann ist hier.

Kein Mann ist hier.

1. Die Frau ist da.

_____

_____

2. Das Restaurant ist klein.

_____

_____

3. Die Schule ist groß. (groß = *big*)

_____

_____

4. Die Mutter ist hier.

_____

_____

5. Der Film ist alt. (alt = *old*)

_____

_____

6. Das Bild ist klein.

_____

_____

7. Die Großmutter ist alt.

_____

_____

8. Der Tisch ist neu. (neu = *new*)

_____

_____

9. Das Restaurant ist groß.

_____

_____

10. Die Landkarte ist hier.

_____

_____

11. Die Tante ist alt.

_____

_____

12. Der Vater ist jung. (jung = *young*)

_____

_____

13. Das Rathaus ist neu.

_____

_____

14. Die Tochter ist jung.

_____

_____

15. Die Uhr ist da.

_____

_____

_____

The subject of a sentence does not occur solely in statements. It is also used in questions. In a German question, the verb precedes the subject, and the rest of the sentence remains the same. For example:

STATEMENT	QUESTION	
Der Mann ist da.	Ist **der** Mann da?	*Is **the** man there?*
Diese Frau ist alt.	Ist **diese** Frau alt?	*Is **this** woman old?*
Eine Katze ist klein.	Ist **eine** Katze klein?	*Is **a** cat small?*
Kein Buch ist neu.	Ist **kein** Buch neu?	*Isn't **any** book new?*

ÜBUNG
2·6

Rewrite each statement as a question.

1. Der Film ist neu.

_____

2. Dieses Kind ist klein.

_____

3. Kein Lehrer ist da.

_____

4. Ein Restaurant ist da.

_____

5. Die Tochter ist jung.

_____

6. Dieser Arzt ist alt.

_____

7. Keine Schule ist neu.

_____

8. Kein Bild ist hier.

_____

9. Eine Uhr ist da.

_____

10. Die Großmutter ist alt.

_____

11. Dieser Professor ist jung.

_____

12. Ein Bett ist hier.

_____

13. Keine Butter ist da.

_____

14. Der Boden ist neu.

_____

15. Dieses Auto ist alt.

_____

ÜBUNG
2·7

In the blanks provided, write the appropriate forms of the definite article, indefinite article,
dieser*, and* **kein***.*

FOR EXAMPLE: _____ *der ein dieser kein* _____ Lehrer

DEF. ART.	INDEF. ART.	DIESER	KEIN	
1. _____	_____	_____	_____	Tochter
2. _____	_____	_____	_____	Ärztin
3. _____	_____	_____	_____	Bruder
4. _____	_____	_____	_____	Bild
5. _____	_____	_____	_____	Uhr
6. _____	_____	_____	_____	Fenster
7. _____	_____	_____	_____	Haus

8. _____	_____	_____	_____	Wagen
9. _____	_____	_____	_____	Gymnasium
10. _____	_____	_____	_____	Rathaus
11. _____	_____	_____	_____	Schlafzimmer
12. _____	_____	_____	_____	Tante
13. _____	_____	_____	_____	Großmutter
14. _____	_____	_____	_____	Mantel
15. _____	_____	_____	_____	Film
16. _____	_____	_____	_____	Schauspielerin
17. _____	_____	_____	_____	Diplomat
18. _____	_____	_____	_____	Restaurant
19. _____	_____	_____	_____	Schule
20. _____	_____	_____	_____	Bluse
21. _____	_____	_____	_____	Mutter
22. _____	_____	_____	_____	Vater
23. _____	_____	_____	_____	Buch
24. _____	_____	_____	_____	Kind
25. _____	_____	_____	_____	Garten
26. _____	_____	_____	_____	Gärtnerin
27. _____	_____	_____	_____	Arzt
28. _____	_____	_____	_____	Bett
29. _____	_____	_____	_____	Junge
20. _____	_____	_____	_____	Mädchen

Pronouns, plurals, and the verb **sein**

In Chapters 1 and 2, you discovered just how great a role gender plays in German. Endings on **der**-words and **ein**-words signal the gender of a noun and follow a consistent pattern. That pattern continues when dealing with pronouns.

Just as in English, specific pronouns are used for certain kinds of nouns in German. Look at the following English nouns and the pronouns required to replace them:

MASCULINE NOUN	PRONOUN REPLACEMENT
the man	*he*
a boy	*he*
this doctor	*he*

FEMININE NOUN	PRONOUN REPLACEMENT
the girl	*she*
a mother	*she*
this lioness	*she*

NEUTER NOUN	PRONOUN REPLACEMENT
the tree	*it*
a book	*it*
this door	*it*

PLURAL NOUN	PRONOUN REPLACEMENT
the women	*they*
five houses	*they*
these workers	*they*

Note that all plurals in English—whether animate or inanimate—are replaced by the same pronoun: *they*. These pronouns, *he*, *she*, *it*, and *they*, are called third-person pronouns and replace nouns.

The German third-person pronouns also replace nouns and like English pronouns conform to the gender of the noun they replace. But remember that German gender is not always determined by the sex of an individual. Let's look at the German pronouns and how they replace nouns:

MASCULINE NOUN		PRONOUN REPLACEMENT	
der Mann	*the man*	er	*he*
ein Bruder	*a brother*	er	*he*
der Garten	*the garden*	er	*it*
dieser Tisch	*this table*	er	*it*

FEMININE NOUN		PRONOUN REPLACEMENT	
die Tochter	*the daughter*	sie	*she*
eine Ärztin	*a doctor*	sie	*she*
diese Landkarte	*this map*	sie	*it*
keine Bluse	*no blouse*	sie	*it*

NEUTER NOUN		PRONOUN REPLACEMENT	
das Mädchen	*girl*	es	*she*
ein Kind	*a child*	es	*he, she*
dieses Haus	*this house*	es	*it*
das Bild	*the picture*	es	*it*

ÜBUNG

3·1

In the blank provided, write the appropriate pronoun replacement for each noun.

1. das Restaurant _____

2. der Arzt _____

3. die Universität _____

4. der Gärtner _____

5. die Lehrerin _____

6. das Rathaus _____

7. das Bett _____

8. die Großmutter _____

9. der Boden _____

10. das Kind _____

11. ein Vater _____

12. eine Schule _____

13. ein Mädchen _____

14. ein Junge _____

15. ein Buch _____

16. kein Gymnasium _____

17. keine Tante _____

18. kein Tisch _____

19. keine Blume _____

20. kein Fenster _____

21. dieser Wagen _____

22. dieser Bruder _____

23. diese Tochter _____

24. dieses Haus _____

25. dieser Fernsehapparat _____

German plurals are formed in a variety of ways. A small number end in **-s**, and some examples are:

SINGULAR	PLURAL	
das Auto	die Autos	*cars*
die Kamera	die Kameras	*cameras*
das Sofa	die Sofas	*sofas*

All plural nouns use the definite article **die**, no matter what their gender is in the singular.

Many masculine nouns form their plural by an **-e** ending or by an umlaut over **a**, **o**, or **u** plus an **-e** ending. For example:

SINGULAR	PLURAL	
der Tisch	die Tische	*tables*
der Schuh	die Schuhe	*shoes*
der Satz	die Sätze	*sentences*
der Stuhl	die Stühle	*chairs*

If a masculine noun ends in **-en**, **-er**, or **-el**, there is no additional ending, but sometimes an umlaut is added. For example:

SINGULAR	PLURAL	
der Boden	die Böden	*floors*
der Wagen	die Wagen	*cars*
der Sportler	die Sportler	*athletes*
der Lehrer	die Lehrer	*teachers*
der Mantel	die Mäntel	*coats*
der Onkel	die Onkel	*uncles*

But many other masculine nouns have their own plural formation and do not conform to simple patterns. For example:

SINGULAR	PLURAL	
der Mann	die Männer	*men*
der Junge	die Jungen	*boys*
der Soldat	die Soldaten	*soldiers*

Many feminine nouns form their plural by an **-n** or **-en** ending. For example:

SINGULAR	PLURAL	
die Blume	die Blumen	*flowers*
die Zeitung	die Zeitungen	*newspapers*
die Lampe	die Lampen	*lamps*
die Decke	die Decken	*blankets*

But many feminine nouns have a plural formation that is based upon what is commonly accepted or tradition. For example:

SINGULAR	PLURAL	
die Wand	die Wände	*walls*
die Mutter	die Mütter	*mothers*
die Tochter	die Töchter	*daughters*
die Wurst	die Würste	*sausages*

Many neuter nouns form their plural by an **-er** ending, often adding an umlaut to **a**, **o**, or **u**. But if the noun ends in **-chen** or **-lein**, no ending is required. For example:

SINGULAR	PLURAL	
das Haus	die Häuser	*houses*
das Land	die Länder	*countries*
das Kind	die Kinder	*children*
das Mädchen	die Mädchen	*girls*
das Röslein	die Röslein	*little roses*

It must be pointed out that there is no clear-cut way to always determine the plural of a noun; there are only *inconsistent patterns* and not always fixed rules. It is wise to check in a dictionary for the correct plural of a noun. Do not be frustrated by German plurals. Give yourself time and plenty of practice, and in due course the plurals will fall in line for you. Remember, practice makes perfect.

With this information about plurals, you are ready to look at the German third-person plural pronoun. And just like the English pronoun *they*, the German third-person plural pronoun is used for all plurals, no matter the gender of the singular noun. For example:

PLURAL NOUN		PRONOUN REPLACEMENT	
die Frauen	*women*	sie	*they*
die Männer	*men*	sie	*they*
die Sofas	*sofas*	sie	*they*
die Bücher	*books*	sie	*they*
die Brüder	*brothers*	sie	*they*
die Zeitungen	*newspapers*	sie	*they*

Let's look at some plurals used in complete sentences:

Die Männer sind hier.	*The men are here.*
Sie sind hier.	*They are here.*
Die Bücher sind alt.	*The books are old.*
Sie sind alt.	*They are old.*
Die Kinder sind jung.	*The children are young.*
Sie sind jung.	*They are young.*

ÜBUNG
3·2

Rewrite each sentence by changing the subject of the sentence to a pronoun.

1. Die Brüder sind jung.

_____

2. Die Frauen sind da.

_____

3. Die Mädchen sind klein.

_____

4. Die Jungen sind groß.

_____

5. Die Zeitungen sind neu.

_____

6. Die Töchter sind hier.

_____

7. Die Lehrer sind alt.

_____

8. Die Soldaten sind da.

_____

9. Die Tanten sind jung.

_____

10. Die Mäntel sind neu.

_____

ÜBUNG

3·3

In the blank provided, write the pronoun that is the correct replacement for the nouns that follow. Note that these nouns are masculine, feminine, neuter, and plural. For feminine singular, write **sie** (sing.). For plural, write **sie** (pl.).

1. das Haus _____

2. die Professorin _____

3. der Onkel _____

4. die Mütter _____

5. die Landkarten _____

6. das Mädchen _____

7. die Mädchen _____

8. die Länder _____

9. der Tisch _____

10. das Rathaus _____

11. ein Buch _____

12. keine Bücher _____

13. ein Bild _____

14. keine Großmutter _____

15. ein Soldat _____

16. kein Geld _____

17. diese Sofas _____

18. dieser Gärtner _____

19. diese Gärtner _____

20. diese Lampen _____

Do not let the similarity between the third-person singular pronoun **sie** and the third-person plural pronoun **sie** confuse you. Usage makes their distinction clear. It's like the English words *its* and *it's*. They sound exactly the same, but their usage avoids any confusion. In German, **sie** (*sing.*) is used with a singular verb, and **sie** (*pl.*) is used with a plural verb. For example:

sie ist	*she is*
sie sind	*they are*

ÜBUNG
3·4

Underline the noun that can be correctly substituted for the pronoun in each sentence.

FOR EXAMPLE: Es ist da.	eine Uhr	<u>das Haus</u>	kein Mann
1. Er ist klein.	der Mantel	ein Buch	kein Geld
2. Sie sind hier.	die Gärtnerin	die Landkarte	die Töchter
3. Es ist groß.	ein Wagen	ein Auto	keine Frauen
4. Sie sind alt.	die Onkel	keine Mutter	ein Junge
5. Sie ist neu.	keine Bücher	die Zeitungen	eine Kamera
6. Er ist da.	ein Arzt	kein Bild	diese Kinder
7. Sie sind klein.	ein Bruder	dieses Rathaus	die Würste
8. Sie sind alt.	die Schulen	diese Landkarte	keine Zeit
9. Es ist jung.	das Mädchen	kein Vater	ein Diplomat
10. Sie ist hier.	keine Mütter	diese Jungen	eine Lampe

There are also first-person and second-person pronouns in German. They are **ich** *I*, **du** *you*, **wir** *we*, **ihr** *you*, and **Sie** *you*. **Ich** and **wir** are first-person pronouns, and **du**, **ihr**, and **Sie** are second-person pronouns. Take a careful look at the following description of the second-person pronouns:

du	Singular and informal. Use with children, family, and friends.
ihr	Plural and informal. Use with children, family, and friends.
Sie	Singular or plural formal. Use with strangers and to show respect.

If you call someone by his or her first name (**Karl**, **Martin**, **Luise**), you should probably use **du**. Use **ihr** if you are speaking to more than one person. Use **Sie** when you address someone with a title (**Frau Braun**, **Herr Schmidt**, **Doktor Schneider**).

ÜBUNG
3·5

In the blank provided, write the pronoun you should use to address the person identified in each line: du, ihr, or Sie.

1. Herr Schäfer _____

2. Frau Bauer _____

3. Angela _____

4. Angela und Johann _____

5. Kinder _____

6. Tante Inge _____

7. Professor Braun _____

8. Onkel Karl _____

9. Frau Schneider und Doktor Benz _____

10. Stefan _____

You have encountered the verb **sein** (*to be*) only with third-person pronouns, but it is used with all pronouns. The changes the verb makes according to those pronouns are the *conjugation* of the verb **sein**.

ich bin	*I am*	wir sind	*we are*
du bist	*you are*	ihr seid	*you are*
er ist	*he is*	Sie sind	*you are*
sie ist	*she is*	sie sind	*they are*
es ist	*it is*		

ÜBUNG
3·6

In the blank provided, write in the missing pronoun or form of the verb sein.

1. es _____

2. ich _____

3. _____ seid

4. sie (*sing.*) _____

5. _____ bin

6. _____ bist

7. Sie _____

8. sie (*pl.*) _____

9. wir _____

10. es _____

11. du _____

12. ihr _____

No matter what pronoun or noun is the subject of a sentence, a question can be formed. And like the questions described in Chapter 2, they are formed by placing the verb before the subject:

Er ist klein.   *He is small.*
Ist **er** klein?   *Is he small?*

ÜBUNG
3·7

Rewrite each statement as a question.

1. Das Haus ist groß.

   _____

2. Die Häuser sind klein.

   _____

3. Er ist jung.

   _____

4. Sie sind alt.

   _____

5. Du bist klein.

   _____

6. Wir sind Töchter.

   _____

7. Die Kinder sind hier.

   _____

8. Ihr seid Brüder.

_____

9. Sie ist Lehrerin.

_____

10. Die Stühle sind alt.

_____

11. Ich bin alt.

_____

12. Dieser Mann ist Professor.

_____

13. Sie ist neu.

_____

14. Es ist groß.

_____

15. Herr Braun! Sie sind Arzt.

_____

Titles, locations, and interrogatives

Titles

The three major titles for addressing a person are:

Herr	*Mr.*
Frau	*Mrs., Miss, Ms.*
Fräulein	*Miss*

The title **Fräulein** is generally not used anymore; it is considered somewhat sexist since it literally means *little woman*. Germans now use only **Frau** to refer to either a married or single woman.

The word **Herr** literally means *gentleman* and politely refers to an unfamiliar male. The word **Mann** means *man* or *husband* and is the more casual term used to refer to a man. Say **mein Herr** when you wish to convey the English meaning of *Sir*.

Mein Herr, ist das Ihr Buch?	*Sir, is that your book?*
Ist der Mann Sportler?	*Is the man an athlete?*
Mein Mann ist Richter.	*My husband is a judge.*

The word **Dame** means *lady* and politely refers to an unfamiliar female. The word **Frau** means *woman* or *wife* and is the more casual term used to refer to a woman.

Diese Dame ist Ärztin.	*This lady is a doctor.*
Diese Frau ist meine Schwester.	*This woman is my sister.*
Meine Frau heißt Angela.	*My wife's name is Angela.*

When addressing both men and women politely, you say **meine Damen und Herren** or **meine Herrschaften** (*ladies and gentlemen*).

If someone has a professional title, **Herr** and **Frau** precede those titles to be polite.

Herr Doktor/Frau Doktor	*doctor*
Herr Professor/Frau Professor	*professor*
Herr Minister/Frau Minister	*minister*
Herr Direktor/Frau Direktor	*principal, director*

When providing someone with your name, you usually say your last name first followed by your first name. An exchange with someone regarding your name would look like the following:

Guten Tag. Ich heiße Braun, Felix Braun.	*Hello. My name is Braun, Felix Braun.*
Guten Tag, **Herr** Braun.	*Hello, **Mr.** Braun.*

Using the name provided in parentheses, write a short dialogue like the one provided in the example that follows.

FOR EXAMPLE: (Tina Benz)

Guten Tag. Ich heiße Benz, Tina Benz.

Guten Tag, Frau Benz.

1. (Martin Schäfer)

_____

_____

2. (Boris Bauer)

_____

_____

3. (Angelika Schneider)

_____

_____

4. (Maria Schulze)

_____

_____

5. (Erik Neumann)

_____

_____

6. (Sonja Kraus)

_____

_____

7. (Heinrich Gasse)

_____

_____

8. (Marianne Becker)

_____

_____

9. (Thomas Schnell)

_____

_____

10. (Gabriele Kiefer)

_____

_____

Locations

Many geographical locations of the world have German names that are identical to their English names. And some are similar but still quite recognizable, and others are completely different in form. Let's look at some of these locations:

Kontinente (Continents)

Europa	_Europe_
Asien	_Asia_
Afrika	_Africa_
Nordamerika	_North America_
Südamerika	_South America_
Antarktis	_Antartica_

Länder (Countries)

Deutschland	_Germany_
die USA	_the U.S.A._
die Vereinigten Staaten von Amerika	_the United States of America_
England	_England_
Frankreich	_France_
Großbritannien	_Great Britain_
Italien	_Italy_
Norwegen	_Norway_
Polen	_Poland_
Russland	_Russia_
Spanien	_Spain_

Städte (Cities)

Berlin	_Berlin_
Hamburg	_Hamburg_
London	_London_
Madrid	_Madrid_
Moskau	_Moscow_
München	_Munich_
Paris	_Paris_
Rom	_Rome_
Warschau	_Warsaw_
Washington	_Washington_

When you wish to say that someone or something is in a certain location, use the German preposition **in** (_in_).

Paris ist **in Frankreich**.	_Paris is **in France**._
Mein Vater wohnt **in Berlin**.	_My father lives **in Berlin**._

Using the names and locations given, write brief sentences that tell where someone is and then where that person lives.

FOR EXAMPLE: Herr Braun/Deutschland

Herr Braun ist in Deutschland.

Herr Braun wohnt in Deutschland.

1. Frau Bauer/Italien

2. die Kinder/Russland

3. der Diplomat/Nordamerika

4. ein Richter/Rom

5. Frau Professor Schneider/München

6. der Direktor/Europa

7. meine Frau/Frankreich

8. mein Mann/Afrika

9. Ihr Bruder/Warschau

_____

_____

10. Ihre Töchter/Spanien

_____

_____

When the location is at a person's home, the phrase **zu Hause** (*at home*) should be used.

Die Dame ist **zu Hause**.	*The lady is **at home**.*
Der Herr ist **zu Hause**.	*The gentleman is **at home**.*

ÜBUNG
4·3

*Complete each sentence with the appropriate form of **sein** and the expression **zu Hause**.*

FOR EXAMPLE: Er _____ .

Er _____ *ist zu Hause* _____ .

1. Meine Tochter _____ .

2. Ich _____ .

3. Diese Frauen _____ .

4. Ihre Brüder _____ .

5. Du _____ .

6. Sie (*sing.*) _____ .

7. Wir _____ .

8. Mein Mann _____ .

9. Ihr _____ .

10. Sie (*pl.*) _____ .

The interrogative word **wo** (*where*) inquires into the location of someone or something. If the answer to such a question uses the German preposition **in** but the location is not a broad geographical name (i.e., continent, country, city), the definite article must accompany the preposition. With masculine and neuter nouns, the form used is **im** (*in the*, the contraction of **in dem**), and with feminine nouns, the form used is **in der** (*in the*).

Wo sind die Kinder?	*Where are the children?*
Sie sind im Park.	*They are in the park.*
Wo ist der Richter?	*Where is the judge?*
Er ist in der Bibliothek.	*He is in the library.*

Using the words given, write a question using the first word in parentheses that asks where someone or something is. Use the second word in parentheses to answer the question with the German preposition **in**.

FOR EXAMPLE: Frau Becker/die Schule

_____ Wo ist Frau Becker? _____

_____ Frau Becker ist in der Schule. _____

1. Ihre Mutter/der Keller (*basement, cellar*)

_____

_____

2. mein Bruder/die Garage (*garage*)

_____

_____

3. Martin und Angela/die Stadt (*city*)

_____

_____

4. ihr/die Kirche (*church*)

_____

_____

5. Thomas/das Café (*café*)

_____

_____

6. wir/das Wohnzimmer (*living room*)

_____

_____

7. ich/das Esszimmer (*dining room*)

_____

_____

8. Herr Doktor Bauer/das Hotel (*hotel*)

_____

_____

9. mein Onkel/der Garten

_____

_____

The interrogative word **wie** (*how*) can be used to ask what someone's name is. The word itself means *how*, and the German expression actually means *How is this person called?* For example:

Wie heißt der Mann?   ***What*** *is the man's name?*
Der Mann heißt Herr Braun.   *The man's name is Mr. Braun.*

ÜBUNG
4·5

*Using the name given in parentheses, ask what the person's name is (use **Mann** or **Frau** in each question), and then answer with the name provided.*

FOR EXAMPLE: (Maria)

Wie heißt die Frau?

Die Frau heißt Maria.

1. (Herr Schulze)

_____

_____

2. (Frau Schneider)

_____

_____

3. (Thomas)

_____

_____

4. (Anna Schäfer)

_____

_____

5. (Martin Neufeld)

_____

_____

6. (Erik Schmidt)

_____

_____

7. (Professor Benz)

_____

_____

8. (Doktor Tina Kiefer)

_____

_____

9. (Wilhelm Kassel)

_____

_____

10. (Angela)

_____

_____

The interrogatives **was** (*what*) and **wer** (*who*) ask what object something is or who someone is. For example:

Was ist das?	**What** is that?
Das ist ein Kino.	*That is a movie theater.*
Was ist das?	**What** is that?
Das ist eine Bäckerei.	*That is a bakery.*
Was ist das?	**What** is that?
Das ist ein Glas Bier.	*That is a glass of beer.*
Wer ist das?	**Who** is that?
Das ist der Polizist.	*That is the police officer.*
Wer ist das?	**Who** is that?
Das ist die Tänzerin.	*That is the dancer.*
Wer ist das?	**Who** is that?
Das ist der Verkäufer.	*That is the salesman.*

If the answer to these questions is a plural noun, the verb becomes the plural form **sind**.

Das sind meine Bücher.	*These are my books.*
Das sind meine Kinder.	*These are my children.*

*If the given word is an object, ask what the object is with **was**. Then answer the question. If the given word is a person, ask who the person is with **wer**. Then answer the question.*

FOR EXAMPLE: ein Haus

Was ist das?

Das ist ein Haus.

1. eine Kirche

_____

_____

2. ein Mantel

_____

_____

3. der Polizist

_____

_____

4. die Richterin

_____

_____

5. eine Bibliothek

_____

_____

6. Frau Schneider

_____

_____

7. die Zeitungen

_____

_____

8. Herr Bauer

_____

_____

9. Karl und Martin

_____

_____

10. die Garage

_____

_____

The interrogative word **wann** asks when something occurs.

Wann ist die Party?	*When is the party?*
Die Party ist heute.	*The party is today.*
Wann ist das Konzert?	*When is the concert?*
Das Konzert ist morgen.	*The concert is tomorrow.*
Wann ist das Examen?	*When is the exam?*
Das Examen ist am Freitag.	*The exam is on Friday.*
Wann ist Weihnachten?	*When is Christmas?*
Weihnachten ist im Dezember.	*Christmas is in December.*

The days of the week are:

Montag	*Monday*
Dienstag	*Tuesday*
Mittwoch	*Wednesday*
Donnerstag	*Thursday*
Freitag	*Friday*
Samstag *or* Sonnabend	*Saturday*
Sonntag	*Sunday*

Use the prepositional contraction **am (an dem)** to say *on* a certain day: **am Montag**.

The months of the year are:

Januar	*January*
Februar	*February*
März	*March*
April	*April*
Mai	*May*
Juni	*June*
Juli	*July*
August	*August*
September	*September*
Oktober	*October*
November	*November*
Dezember	*December*

Use the prepositional contraction **im (in dem)** to say *in* a certain month: **im Oktober**.

Answer each question with the cue words given.

FOR EXAMPLE: Freitag, September

Wann ist die Party?

Die Party ist am Freitag.

Die Party ist im September.

1. Montag, Januar

   Wann ist das Konzert?

   _____

   _____

2. Dienstag, März

   Wann ist das Examen?

   _____

   _____

3. Mittwoch, Mai

   Wann ist die Reise (*trip*)?

   _____

   _____

4. Donnerstag, Juli

   Wann ist die Oper (*opera*)?

   _____

   _____

5. Freitag, September

   Wann ist Ihr Geburtstag (*birthday*)?

   _____

   _____

The verbs **haben** and **werden** and negation

·5·

The conjugations of the verbs **sein** (*to be*), **haben** (*to have*), and **werden** (*to become, get*) are important building blocks for understanding the tenses of the German language. Let's look at the present tense conjugation of these three verbs:

	sein	**haben**	**werden**
ich	bin	habe	werde
du	bist	hast	wirst
er	ist	hat	wird
sie (*sing.*)	ist	hat	wird
es	ist	hat	wird
wir	sind	haben	werden
ihr	seid	habt	werdet
Sie	sind	haben	werden
sie (*pl.*)	sind	haben	werden

Besides telling what someone or something *is*, **sein** is used to describe conditions or qualities. For example:

Das Buch **ist** lang.	*The book **is** long.*
Der Roman **ist** kurz.	*The novel **is** short.*
Der Artikel **ist** langweilig.	*The article **is** boring.*
Das Gedicht **ist** interessant.	*The poem **is** interesting.*
Das Wetter **ist** schlecht.	*The weather **is** bad.*
Die Geschichten **sind** gut.	*The stories **are** good.*
Die Prüfungen **sind** schwer.	*The tests **are** hard.*
Die Fragen **sind** leicht.	*The questions **are** easy.*
Es **ist** kalt.	*It **is** cold.*
Es **ist** heiß.	*It **is** hot.*
Es **ist** kühl.	*It **is** cool.*
Es **ist** warm.	*It **is** warm.*
Es **ist** regnerisch.	*It **is** rainy.*

Haben is used to show what someone possesses. For example:

Ich **habe** das Geld.	*I **have** the money.*
Du **hast** keine Zeit.	*You **have** no time.*
Er **hat** meine Schuhe.	*He **has** my shoes.*
Sie **hat** das Kleid.	*She **has** the dress.*
Wir **haben** viele Zeitungen.	*We **have** a lot of newspapers.*
Ihr **habt** wenig Geld.	*You **have** little money.*
Sie **haben** Ihre Fahrkarten.	*You **have** your tickets.*
Sie **haben** keine Prüfung.	*You **do not have** a test.*

It is also used in some special expressions.

Ich **habe** Sonja gern.	*I like Sonja.*
Er **hat** Durst.	*He is thirsty.*
Hast du Hunger?	*Are you hungry?*

Werden describes what a person becomes or how conditions are changing. For example:

Ich **werde** Zahnarzt.	*I **am becoming** a dentist.*
Du **wirst** krank.	*You **get** sick.*
Er **wird** gesund.	*He **gets** healthy.*
Sie **wird** Krankenschwester.	*She **becomes** a nurse.*
Wir **werden** Politiker.	*We **become** politicians.*
Ihr **werdet** böse.	*You **become** angry.*
Sie **werden** Rechtsanwalt.	*You **become** a lawyer.*
Es **wird** kalt.	*It **is getting** cold.*
Es **wird** dunkel.	*It **is getting** dark.*
Es **wird** hell.	*It **is getting** light.*

ÜBUNG
5·1

*In the blanks provided, write the appropriate conjugation of **sein**, **haben**, and **werden** for the subjects given.*

	1. sein	2. haben
ich	_____	_____
du	_____	_____
er	_____	_____
sie (*sing.*)	_____	_____
es	_____	_____
der Zahnarzt	_____	_____
wir	_____	_____
ihr	_____	_____
die Krankenschwester	_____	_____
Sie	_____	_____
sie (*pl.*)	_____	_____

	3. werden
ich	_____
du	_____
er	_____
sie	_____
es	_____

wir	_____
ihr	_____
Sie	_____
sie (*pl.*)	_____
das Wetter	_____

As with other sentences formed as questions, the verb precedes the subject when posing a question with **sein**, **haben**, or **werden**.

Das Wetter **ist** schlecht.	*The weather **is** bad.*
Ist das Wetter schlecht?	***Is** the weather bad?*
Sie **hat** keine Zeit.	*She **has** no time.*
Hat sie keine Zeit?	*Doesn't she **have** any time?*
Es **wird** regnerisch.	*It **is getting** rainy.*
Wird es regnerisch?	*Will it **get** rainy?*

ÜBUNG
5·2

Rewrite each sentence as a question.

1. Ihr Bruder wird Zahnarzt.

   _____

2. Sie ist Tänzerin.

   _____

3. Ich habe Durst.

   _____

4. Dieser Artikel ist interessant.

   _____

5. Es ist heiß.

   _____

6. Frau Bauer wird Krankenschwester.

   _____

7. Die Kinder haben Hunger.

   _____

8. Es wird dunkel.

   _____

9. Sie haben keine Fahrkarten.

   _____

10. Erik hat Maria gern.

_____

11. Mein Onkel wird Rechtsanwalt.

_____

12. Sonja ist krank.

_____

13. Dieser Roman ist langweilig.

_____

14. Es wird am Montag kalt.

_____

15. Es ist kalt im Dezember.

_____

16. Das Gedicht ist kurz.

_____

17. Die Mädchen haben Karl gern.

_____

18. Wir sind zu Hause.

_____

19. Der Herr heißt Martin Schäfer.

_____

20. Frau Keller wird gesund.

_____

ÜBUNG
5·3

*Fill in the blank with the appropriate form of **sein**, **haben**, or **werden**.*

1. Ich _____ Zeit.

2. _____ die Kinder zu Hause?

3. Es _____ heiß.

4. Thomas _____ Maria gern.

5. _____ du meine Fahrkarte?

6. Mein Geburtstag _____ im Juli.

7. Du _____ krank.

8. Meine Mutter _____ durst.

9. Es _____ regnerisch.

10. Meine Töchter _____ kein Geld.

11. _____ Sie die Zeitung?

12. Ihr _____ jung.

13. Diese Frau _____ Ärztin.

14. _____ diese Dame Ihre Tante?

15. _____ du die Bücher?

You have already discovered that the word **kein** (*no, not any*) is used to add a negative to a sentence. But be aware that **kein** is the negation of **ein**, as well as of any noun that is not preceded by a definite article.

Ich habe ein Buch	*I have a book.*
Ich habe **kein** Buch.	*I do **not** have a book.*
Er ist Zahnarzt.	*He is a dentist.*
Er ist **kein** Zahnarzt.	*He is **not** a dentist.*
Du hast Geld.	*You have money.*
Du hast **kein** Geld.	*You have **no** money.*
Das ist eine Landkarte.	*That is a map.*
Das ist **keine** Landkarte.	*That is **not** a map.*

You have probably noticed that when expressing one's profession or nationality, an article is not used. For example:

Ich bin Arzt.	*I am a physician.*
Er ist Deutscher.	*He is a German.*

Kein is used to negate such expressions.

Ich bin kein Arzt.	*I am not a physician.*
Er ist kein Deutscher.	*He is not a German.*

ÜBUNG
5·4

*Rewrite each sentence by adding the correct form of the negative **kein**.*

1. Er hat Schuhe.

_____

2. Du hast eine Zeitung.

_____

3. Frau Bauer ist Krankenschwester.

_____

4. Herr Schneider ist Politiker.

_____

5. Ich habe Zeit.

_____

6. Das ist ein Kleid.

_____

7. Er ist Polizist.

_____

8. Ein Tourist ist in Berlin.

_____

9. Wir haben am Mittwoch eine Prüfung.

_____

10. Hast du Geld?

_____

11. Das ist eine Bibliothek.

_____

12. Maria ist Tänzerin.

_____

13. Die Männer werden Politiker.

_____

14. Er hat ein Glas Bier.

_____

15. Das ist eine Kirche.

_____

When you answer a question with **nein** (*no*), it indicates that your response is negative. Besides using **kein** as a negative, adding the adverb **nicht** (*not*) is also a form of negation. **Nicht** is placed after a verb such as **sein**, before an adverb or adjective, or before a prepositional phrase.

Ist das Ihr Bruder?	*Is that your brother?*
Nein, das ist **nicht** mein Bruder.	*No, that is **not** my brother.*
Wird es kalt?	*Is it getting cold?*
Nein, es wird **nicht** kalt.	*No, it is **not** getting cold.*

Heißt sie Sonja Keller?	*Is her name Sonja Keller?*
Nein, sie heißt **nicht** Sonja Keller.	*No, her name is **not** Sonja Keller.*
Ist Martin zu Hause?	*Is Martin at home?*
Nein, Martin ist **nicht** zu Hause.	*No, Martin is **not** at home.*

Following the verb **haben**, place **nicht** after the object of the verb.

Wir haben die Fahrkarten **nicht**.	*We do **not** have the tickets.*
Haben Sie Ihr Buch **nicht**?	*Don't you have your book?*
Ich habe das Kleid **nicht**.	*I do **not** have the dress.*

*Rewrite each sentence by using the negative **nicht**.*

1. Die Touristen sind in Deutschland.

   _____

2. Mein Geburtstag ist im Oktober.

   _____

3. Das ist Herr Dorfmann.

   _____

4. Meine Schwester wohnt in der Stadt.

   _____

5. Wir haben am Freitag das Examen.

   _____

6. Ist Frau Benz zu Hause?

   _____

7. Es wird warm.

   _____

8. Das sind meine Bücher.

   _____

9. Sonja hat die Bluse.

   _____

10. Das ist der Lehrer.

   _____

11. Sie haben die Fahrkarten.

   _____

12. Ist das Herr Bauer?

   _____

13. Hast du die Zeitungen?

_____

14. Die Dame heißt Frau Becker.

_____

15. Sind das meine Schuhe?

_____

Fill in the blank with the missing negative word: **kein/keine** *or* **nicht**.

FOR EXAMPLE: Das ist _____ Herr Keller.

Das ist _____*nicht*_____ Herr Keller.

1. Er heißt _____ Erik.

2. Wir wohnen _____ in Italien.

3. Ich habe _____ Geld.

4. Wir sind _____ Politiker.

5. Es wird am Sonntag _____ kalt.

6. Das ist _____ Gedicht.

7. Das ist _____ mein Gedicht.

8. Haben Sie Ihre Schuhe _____?

9. Mein Mann heißt _____ Heinrich.

10. Sind das _____ Ihre Bücher?

11. Das Examen ist _____ im Juni.

12. Ist Ihr Geburtstag _____ am Donnerstag?

13. Erik hat _____ Zeit.

14. Wird es _____ dunkel?

15. Meine Großmutter ist _____ krank.

16. Ich bin _____ zu Hause.

17. Er ist _____ der Verkäufer.

18. Ist die Landkarte _____ da?

19. Meine Tante wohnt _____ in München.

20. Habt ihr _____ Geld?

Answer each question twice, once with **ja** and once with **nein**. Use **kein** and **nicht** appropriately.

FOR EXAMPLE: Ist Herr Braun Ihr Vater?

Ja, Herr Braun ist mein Vater.

Nein, Herr Braun ist nicht mein Vater.

1. Hat sie Ihre Bücher?

2. Ist er Zahnarzt?

3. Wird es regnerisch?

4. Werden die Jungen Sportler?

5. Sind Sie Deutscher?

6. Seid ihr zu Hause?

7. Ist die Tänzerin in Paris?

8. Bin ich krank?

9. Hast du das Kleid?

10. Wird es kühl?

_____

_____

11. Habt ihr Zeit?

_____

_____

12. Wird Erik Student?

_____

_____

13. Ist der Onkel alt?

_____

_____

14. Sind wir in München?

_____

_____

15. Haben Sie Martin gern?

_____

_____

The present tense and numbers

The present tense

You have already encountered the present tense of **haben**, **sein**, and **werden**. Other verbs in the present tense follow a similar pattern; that is, they conform to the same endings used following the personal pronouns. Compare **haben** with two other verbs in their present tense conjugation.

	haben	**lachen** (*laugh*)	**glauben** (*believe*)
ich	habe	lache	glaube
du	hast	lachst	glaubst
er/sie/es	hat	lacht	glaubt
wir	haben	lachen	glauben
ihr	habt	lacht	glaubt
Sie	haben	lachen	glauben
sie (*pl.*)	haben	lachen	glauben

The infinitive form of a verb is its basic form and usually ends in **-en**. English infinitives often appear with the particle *to*. Compare the German and English that follow:

weinen *(to) cry*   **blühen** *(to) bloom*   **lachen** *(to) laugh*

The conjugational endings of the present tense are added to the verb after the infinitive ending has been dropped. Those endings are used with specific personal pronouns and are **-e**, **-st**, **-t**, and **-en**.

Many verbs follow this ending pattern in the present tense. Some are:

brauchen	*need*
decken	*cover/set (the table)*
denken	*think*
dienen	*serve*
fragen	*ask*
gehen	*go*
hoffen	*hope*
hören	*hear*
kaufen	*buy*
kommen	*come*
lächeln	*smile*
leben	*live*
lieben	*love*
machen	*make/do*
probieren	*try*
rauchen	*smoke*
sagen	*say*
schicken	*send*

schwimmen	swim
setzen	place/set
singen	sing
sitzen	sit
spielen	play
stehen	stand
stellen	place/put
suchen	look for/search
wohnen	live/reside
zeigen	show

Any of these verbs will add the conjugational endings in the present tense in the same way as illustrated previously. For example:

	brauchen	**stellen**	**wohnen**
ich	brauche	stelle	wohne
du	brauchst	stellst	wohnst
er/sie/es	braucht	stellt	wohnt
wir	brauchen	stellen	wohnen
ihr	braucht	stellt	wohnt
Sie	brauchen	stellen	wohnen
sie (*pl.*)	brauchen	stellen	wohnen

ÜBUNG
6·1

In the blanks provided, write the correct conjugations for the pronouns given.

1.   machen   gehen   fragen

ich   _____   _____   _____

du   _____   _____   _____

er   _____   _____   _____

2.   sagen   hören   zeigen

wir   _____   _____   _____

ihr   _____   _____   _____

Sie   _____   _____   _____

3.   lachen   setzen   schwimmen

ich   _____   _____   _____

sie (*sing.*)   _____   _____   _____

sie (*pl.*)   _____   _____   _____

4.   decken   probieren   schicken

du   _____   _____   _____

Sie   _____   _____   _____

ihr   _____   _____   _____

5.	denken	hoffen	lieben
ich	_____	_____	_____
du	_____	_____	_____
er	_____	_____	_____
wir	_____	_____	_____
ihr	_____	_____	_____
Sie	_____	_____	_____
sie (*pl.*)	_____	_____	_____

If the infinitive ending of a verb is preceded by the letter **-d** or **-t**, the second-person singular, and the second- and plural and the third-person singular endings become **-est** and **-et** respectively. For example:

	arbeiten (*work*)	**finden** (*find*)
ich	arbeite	finde
du	arbeitest	findest
er/sie/es	arbeitet	findet
wir	arbeiten	finden
ihr	arbeitet	findet
Sie	arbeiten	finden
sie (*pl.*)	arbeiten	finden

ÜBUNG
6·2

In the blanks provided, write the correct conjugation for each of the following verbs with the pronouns given.

	1. wetten (*bet*)	2. senden (*send*)
ich	_____	_____
du	_____	_____
er	_____	_____
wir	_____	_____
ihr	_____	_____
Sie	_____	_____
sie (*pl.*)	_____	_____

	3. meiden (*avoid*)	4. antworten (*answer*)
ich	_____	_____
du	_____	_____
er	_____	_____

wir	_____	_____
ihr	_____	_____
Sie	_____	_____
sie (*pl.*)	_____	_____

5. husten (*cough*)

ich	_____
du	_____
er	_____
wir	_____
ihr	_____
Sie	_____
sie (*pl.*)	_____

If the infinitive ending is preceded by -**s**, -**ss**, -**ß**, **z**, or -**tz**, the second-person singular ending becomes -**t**. For example:

	reißen (*tear*)
ich	reiße
du	reißt
er	reißt
wir	reißen
ihr	reißt
Sie	reißen
sie (*pl.*)	reißen

ÜBUNG
6·3

In the blank provided, write the correct conjugation for each of the following verbs with the pronouns given.

	1. setzen (*set*)	2. heißen (*be called*)
ich	_____	_____
du	_____	_____
er	_____	_____
wir	_____	_____
ihr	_____	_____
Sie	_____	_____
sie (*pl.*)	_____	_____

	3. tanzen (*dance*)	4. sitzen (*sit*)
ich	_____	_____
du	_____	_____
er	_____	_____
wir	_____	_____
ihr	_____	_____
Sie	_____	_____
sie (*pl.*)	_____	_____

	5. schmerzen (*hurt, pain*)	6. reisen (*travel*)
ich	_____	_____
du	_____	_____
er	_____	_____
wir	_____	_____
ihr	_____	_____
Sie	_____	_____
sie (*pl.*)	_____	_____

	7. beißen (*bite*)	8. niesen (*sneeze*)
ich	_____	_____
du	_____	_____
er	_____	_____
wir	_____	_____
ihr	_____	_____
Sie	_____	_____
sie (*pl.*)	_____	_____

Some infinitives end in **-eln** and **-ern**. In such cases, only the final **-n** is dropped when the conjugational endings are added. And the **-en** conjugational ending becomes **-n**. For example:

	paddeln (*paddle/row*)
ich	paddele
du	paddelst
er	paddelt
wir	paddeln
ihr	paddelt
Sie	paddeln
sie (*pl.*)	paddeln

When using **wer** (*who*) or **man** (*one/you*) as the subject of a sentence, the third-person ending is required in the conjugation.

wer	hat	lacht	glaubt
man	hat	lacht	glaubt

In the blank provided, write the correct conjugation of the verb in bold with the pronoun given.

1. **sagen** ich _____

2. **machen** ihr _____

3. **schmeicheln** (*flatter*) wir _____

4. **hören** du _____

5. **schmelzen** (*melt*) es _____

6. **gehen** Sie _____

7. **fragen** sie (*sing.*) _____

8. **sein** ihr _____

9. **schließen** (*close*) du _____

10. **wohnen** sie (*pl.*) _____

11. **glauben** ich _____

12. **pflanzen** (*plant*) er _____

13. **bellen** (*bark*) sie (*sing.*) _____

14. **wandern** (*wander, hike*) ich _____

15. **werden** es _____

16. **rauchen** wer _____

17. **warten** (*wait*) sie (*sing.*) _____

18. **feiern** (*celebrate*) man _____

19. **baden** (*bathe*) du _____

20. **lächeln** ihr _____

21. **haben** er _____

22. **wünschen** (*wish*) du _____

23. **finden** wer _____

24. **kosten** es _____

25. **singen** ich _____

Numbers

There are many similarities between English numbers and German numbers. Look at the following list of German numbers, and consider how much they resemble their English counterparts.

0	null
1	eins
2	zwei
3	drei
4	vier
5	fünf
6	sechs
7	sieben
8	acht
9	neun
10	zehn
11	elf
12	zwölf
13	dreizehn
14	vierzehn
15	fünfzehn
16	sechzehn
17	siebzehn
18	achtzehn
19	neunzehn
20	zwanzig

The numbers 21 to 99 follow a pattern that once existed in English, but is now unique to German. Instead of *twenty-one*, German uses *one and twenty*.

21	einundzwanzig
22	zweiundzwanzig
30	dreißig
33	dreiunddreißig
40	vierzig
44	vierundvierzig
50	fünfzig
55	fünfundfünfzig
60	sechzig
66	sechsundsechzig
70	siebzig
77	siebenundsiebzig
80	achtzig
88	achtundachtzig
90	neunzig
99	neunundneunzig
100	hundert
200	zweihundert
500	fünfhundert
1 000	tausend
10 000	zehntausend
200 000	zweihunderttausend
1 000 000	eine Million
1 000 000 000	eine Milliarde
1 000 000 000 000	eine Billion

Notice that **Milliarde** is used where in English *billion* is said, and **Billion** in German means *trillion*.

The basic arithmetic structures in German look like this:

Addition
Zehn plus drei sind dreizehn.   *10 plus 3 is 13.*
or Zehn und drei sind dreizehn.   *10 and 3 is 13.*

Subtraction
Elf minus neun sind zwei.   *11 minus 9 is 2.*
or Elf weniger neun sind zwei.   *11 minus 9 is 2.*

Multiplication
Drei mal drei sind neun.   *3 times 3 is 9.*

Division
Zehn (geteilt) durch zwei sind fünf.   *10 divided by 2 is 5.*

In division, the word **geteilt** can be omitted.

ÜBUNG
6·5

Rewrite the following equations in German.

FOR EXAMPLE: 2 + 3 = 5 _____ *zwei plus drei sind fünf* _____

1. 6 + 1 = 7 _____

2. 5 × 3 = 15 _____

3. 9 − 7 = 2 _____

4. 20 + 3 = 23 _____

5. 12 ÷ 3 = 4 _____

6. 100 − 50 = 50 _____

7. 88 + 2 = 90 _____

8. 200 ÷ 40 = 5 _____

9. 19 − 8 = 11 _____

10. 60 + 12 = 72 _____

Ordinals

Numbers have another form called *ordinals*. Ordinals function as adjectives and specify the *order* in which someone or something appears in a list. German ordinals from *first* to *nineteenth* end in **-te**. Ordinals from *twentieth* and higher end in **-ste**. Notice the few irregular forms in the following examples.

1	erste	*first*
2	zweite	*second*
3	dritte	*third*
4	vierte	*fourth*
5	fünfte	*fifth*
6	sechste	*sixth*
7	siebte	*seventh*
20	zwanzigste	*twentieth*
31	einunddreißigste	*thirty-first*
76	sechsundsiebzigste	*seventy-sixth*
100	hundertste	*hundreth*

In sentences the ordinals function like other adjectives:

| Heute ist der **vierte** März. | *Today is the **fourth** of March.* |
| Ich habe sein **erstes** Gedicht gelesen. | *I read his **first** poem.* |

ÜBUNG 6·6

*Fill in the blank with the ordinal form of the number provided in parentheses. Add the necessary adjective endings. Use the ending -e after the definite article **der**. Use the ending -en after am.*

FOR EXAMPLE: (4) Heute ist der _____ *vierte* _____ Mai.

(4) Ihr Geburtstag ist am _____ *vierten* _____ Juni.

1. (2) Heute ist der _____ Dezember.

2. (11) Mein Geburtstag ist am _____ Juni.

3. (3) Ist morgen der _____ Februar?

4. (1) Meine Frau ist am _____ gestorben.

5. (12) Dezember ist der _____ Monat.

6. (31) Mein Bruder kommt am _____ Oktober zu Besuch.

7. (21) War gestern der _____ April?

8. (10) Montag ist der _____ August.

9. (16) Der alte Mann ist am _____ Januar gestorben.

10. (7) Der Krieg endete am _____ Mai.

Direct objects and the accusative case

You have encountered nouns and pronouns that have been used primarily as the subject of a sentence. The form of a noun or pronoun used as the subject of a sentence is the *nominative case* of that noun or pronoun. For example, each subject that follows shown in bold is in the nominative case:

Der Mann wohnt in Berlin.	*The man lives in Berlin.*
Eine Lehrerin ist Amerikanerin.	*A teacher is an American.*
Dieses Haus ist alt.	*This house is old.*
Ich bin Rechtsanwalt.	*I am a lawyer.*
Du hast keine Fahrkarten.	*You don't have any tickets.*
Er hat Sonja gern.	*He likes Sonja.*
Sie kauft eine Bluse.	*She buys a blouse.*
Es wird kalt.	*It is getting cold.*
Wir sind zu Hause.	*We are at home.*
Ihr lernt Deutsch.	*You learn German.*
Sie heißen Karl Benz.	*Your name is Karl Benz.*
Sie sind Kinder.	*They are children.*
Wer ist das?	*Who is that?*
Was ist das?	*What is that?*

Another important case in German is the *accusative case*. In many instances, you will find that the accusative case is identical to the nominative case, especially in the case of nouns. If a masculine noun is in the accusative case, the **der**-word or **ein**-word that precedes it changes its form slightly. For example:

NOMINATIVE	ACCUSATIVE
der Arzt	den Arzt
ein Wagen	einen Wagen
dieser Bruder	diesen Bruder
kein Mantel	keinen Mantel
mein Tisch	meinen Tisch
Ihr Computer	Ihren Computer

It should be obvious that the masculine accusative noun is preceded by a determiner that ends in -**en**.

In the blank provided, rewrite each noun and its determiner in their accusative form.

1. der Lehrer _____

2. der Roman _____

3. ein Artikel _____

4. ein Zahnarzt _____

5. dieser Politiker _____

6. dieser Mann _____

7. mein Geburtstag _____

8. mein Onkel _____

9. Ihr Wagen _____

10. kein Sportler _____

It is only with masculine nouns that you have to be concerned about a new ending. Feminine, neuter, and plural nouns are identical in form in both the nominative and the accusative. For example:

	NOMINATIVE	ACCUSATIVE
FEMININE	die Dame	die Dame
	eine Tänzerin	eine Tänzerin
	diese Bluse	diese Bluse
NEUTER	das Buch	das Buch
	Ihr Auto	Ihr Auto
	mein Gedicht	mein Gedicht
PLURAL	die Bücher	die Bücher
	diese Kinder	diese Kinder
	keine Prüfungen	keine Prüfungen

In the blank provided, rewrite each noun and its determiner in their accusative form.

1. der Schauspieler _____

2. meine Schuhe _____

3. Ihre Tante _____

4. ein Stuhl _____

5. das Mädchen _____

6. ein Gymnasium _____

7. keine Schwester _____

8. dieses Wetter _____

9. keine Zeit _____

10. eine Landkarte _____

11. ein Mantel _____

12. ein Kind _____

13. Ihre Prüfung _____

14. das Examen _____

15. mein Garten _____

16. keine Universität _____

17. der Boden _____

18. die Schule _____

19. mein Pullover _____

20. Ihre Schwester _____

21. dieser Garten _____

22. meine Bücher _____

23. das Glas _____

24. dieses Fenster _____

25. eine Schauspielerin _____

The accusative case is used to identify the *direct object* in a sentence. To find the direct object in a sentence, first identify the subject of the sentence. Then find the verb and determine that it is conjugated correctly for the subject. Look at the other elements in the sentence. Then ask *what* or *whom* with the subject and verb of the sentence, and the answer to that question is the direct object. Let's look at some example sentences in English:

SENTENCE FOLLOWED BY QUESTION	ANSWER: THE DIRECT OBJECT
John borrows my car. *What does John borrow?*	*my car*
We help the woman in that house. *Whom do we help in that house?*	*the woman*
I need some extra cash. *What do I need?*	*some extra cash*
Mrs. Jones met Mary's teacher. *Whom did Mrs. Jones meet?*	*Mary's teacher*

The direct object in a German sentence is determined in the same way. Ask a question with **was** or **wen** (accusative form of **wer** = *whom*). For example:

Sentence followed by question and answer

Martin kauft **meinen Wagen**.	*Martin buys **my car**.*
Was kauft Martin?	***What** does Martin buy?*
meinen Wagen	*my car*
Tina kennt **diese Dame**.	*Tina knows **this lady**.*
Wen kennt Tina?	***Whom** does Tina know?*
diese Dame	*this lady*
Mein Bruder liebt **das Mädchen**.	*My brother loves **the girl**.*
Wen liebt mein Bruder?	***Whom** does my brother love?*
das Mädchen	*the girl*
Der Junge hat **keine Bücher**.	*The boy has **no books**.*
Was hat der Junge?	***What** does the boy have?*
keine Bücher	*no books*

ÜBUNG

7·3

Underline the direct object in each of the following sentences.

1. Ich habe keine Zeit.

2. Mein Vater kennt Frau Schneider.

3. Wir hören Radio.

4. Onkel Peter sucht die Kinder.

5. Sie kauft ein Kleid und einen Pullover.

6. Liebst du dieses Mädchen?

7. Werner hat Maria gern.

8. Meine Schwestern kaufen einen Wagen.

9. Wir lernen Deutsch.

10. Der Rechtsanwalt braucht Geld.

11. Sie hat keinen Mantel.

12. Findet ihr den Roman?

13. Wir haben ein Problem.

14. Lieben Sie meinen Bruder?

15. Kennen Sie diese Schauspielerin?

Just as pronouns can be used as the subject of a sentence, so too can they be used as direct objects. Note how the English personal pronouns are different as subjects and as direct objects.

SUBJECT	DIRECT OBJECT
I	*me*
you	*you*
he	*him*
she	*her*
it	*it*
we	*us*
you	*you*
they	*them*
who	*whom*
what	*what*

German does something very similar.

SUBJECT	DIRECT OBJECT
ich	mich
du	dich
er	ihn
sie (*sing.*)	sie (*sing.*)
es	es
wir	uns
ihr	euch
Sie	Sie
sie (*pl.*)	sie (*pl.*)
wer	wen
was	was

ÜBUNG
7·4

Rewrite each sentence with the correct accusative case form of the pronouns in parentheses.

FOR EXAMPLE: Er hat _____.

(es) _____ *Er hat es* _____.

1. Kennst du _____?

   (ich) _____

   (er) _____

   (sie [*sing.*]) _____

   (wir) _____

2. Ja, ich habe _____.

   (er) _____

   (sie [*sing.*]) _____

   (es) _____

   (sie [*pl.*]) _____

3. Doktor Bauer hat _____ gern.

(du) _____

(er) _____

(wir) _____

(ihr) _____

4. Meine Großmutter liebt _____.

(ich) _____

(du) _____

(sie [*sing.*]) _____

(sie [*pl.*]) _____

5. Die Männer suchen _____.

(du) _____

(wir) _____

(ihr) _____

(Sie) _____

ÜBUNG
7·5

*Using the word in boldface as your cue, write a question with **was** or **wen**.*

FOR EXAMPLE: Martin hat **einen Mantel**.

Was hat Martin?

1. Die Frauen brauchen **Geld**.

_____

2. Meine Schwester kennt **diesen Herrn** nicht.

_____

3. Ich liebe **Rosen**.

_____

4. Wir suchen **Ihre Tochter**.

_____

5. Herr Benz kauft **ein Glas Bier**.

_____

6. Werner und Karl finden **einen Pullover**.

_____

7. Ihr habt **die Fahrkarten**.

_____

8. Mein Bruder braucht **Schuhe**.

_____

9. Martin sucht **einen Zahnarzt**.

_____

10. Sie hören **Ihren Vater**.

_____

11. Ich frage **meine Tante**.

_____

12. Die Kinder decken **den Tisch**.

_____

13. Erik liebt **die Amerikanerin**.

_____

14. Sabine hat **ein Problem**.

_____

15. Die Jungen kaufen **einen Computer**.

_____

_____

ÜBUNG

7·6

In the blank provided, write the pronoun that correctly replaces the noun in boldface. Some answers will be in the nominative case, some in the accusative case.

FOR EXAMPLE: Werner hat **das Geld**. _____es_____

1. **Der Junge** ist zu Hause. _____

2. Wir kaufen **einen Wagen**. _____

3. Erik und Tina suchen **ein Restaurant**. _____

4. Wer hat **die Landkarte**? _____

5. Der Zahnarzt liebt **Frau Bauer**. _____

6. Hat **Sonja** eine Blume? _____

7. Kaufen **die Männer** das Haus? _____

8. Meine Schwester hat **Werner Schmidt** gern. _____

9. Ich liebe **diesen Roman**. _____

10. Thomas zeigt **das Fenster**. _____

11. Wer kennt **diesen Mann**? _____

12. Was hat **Herr Schneider**? _____

13. Der Student findet **das Examen**. _____

14. Wir suchen **das Gymnasium**. _____

15. Liebst du **das Kind**? _____

Irregular verbs in the present tense

You have already encountered the present tense conjugation of verbs that follow a regular pattern. For example:

	lernen	spielen
ich	lerne	spiele
du	lernst	spielst
er/sie/es	lernt	spielt
wir	lernen	spielen
ihr	lernt	spielt
Sie	lernen	spielen
sie (*pl.*)	lernen	spielen

You have also been introduced to three irregular verbs that break that pattern:

	haben	sein	werden
ich	habe	bin	werde
du	hast	bist	wirst
er/sie/es	hat	ist	wird
wir	haben	sind	werden
ihr	habt	seid	werdet
Sie	haben	sind	werden
sie (*pl.*)	haben	sind	werden

Several other verbs break that pattern, and they tend to fall into one of two major groups: verbs that add an umlaut in the second-person and third-person singular, and verbs that make a vowel change in the second-person and third-person singular.

The addition of an umlaut

Only the vowels **a**, **o**, and **u** can have an umlaut, and the addition of that diacritical mark changes the pronunciation of the vowel. This can occur in an irregular present tense conjugation, but only in the second-person and third-person singular (**du, er, sie** [*sing.*], **es**), primarily with the vowel **a**, and in one instance with the vowel **o**. Let's look at the form that this irregular conjugation takes:

	fahren (*drive*)	**laufen** (*run*)	**stoßen** (*kick*)
ich	fahre	laufe	stoße
du	fährst	läufst	stößt
er/sie/es	fährt	läuft	stößt
wir	fahren	laufen	stoßen
ihr	fahrt	lauft	stoßt
Sie	fahren	laufen	stoßen
sie (*pl.*)	fahren	laufen	stoßen

Other verbs that follow this irregular present tense conjugational pattern are:

backen, bäckst, bäckt	*bake*
braten, brätst, brät	*fry, roast*
fallen, fällst, fällt	*fall*
fangen, fängst, fängt	*catch*
halten, hältst, hält	*hold*
lassen, lässt, lässt	*let*
raten, rätst, rät	*advise*
schlafen, schläfst, schläft	*sleep*
schlagen, schlägst, schlägt	*beat*
tragen, trägst, trägt	*carry, wear*
wachsen, wächst, wächst	*grow*
waschen, wäschst, wäscht	*wash*

ÜBUNG

8·1

In the blank, rewrite each verb in parentheses with the subject provided.

1. (fahren) du _____

2. (haben) er _____

3. (fallen) wir _____

4. (raten) sie (*sing.*) _____

5. (raten) ihr _____

6. (backen) ich _____

7. (braten) du _____

8. (halten) es _____

9. (lassen) er _____

10. (fangen) sie (*pl.*) _____

11. (waschen) du _____

12. (stoßen) sie (*sing.*) _____

13. (sein) ihr _____

14. (wachsen) er _____

15. (schlafen) Sie _____

16. (tragen) du _____

17. (schlagen) der Mann _____

18. (fangen) die Lehrerin _____

19. (fallen) mein Bruder _____

20. (raten) du _____

21. (schlafen) das Kind _____

22. (werden) ihr _____

23. (halten) du _____

24. (waschen) ich _____

25. (tragen) die Dame _____

Write the full conjugation of each verb with the subjects provided.

	1. wachsen	2. tragen
ich	_____	_____
du	_____	_____
er	_____	_____
wir	_____	_____
ihr	_____	_____
Sie	_____	_____
man	_____	_____

	3. fallen	4. schlagen
ich	_____	_____
du	_____	_____
er	_____	_____
wir	_____	_____
ihr	_____	_____
Sie	_____	_____
man	_____	_____

	5. braten	6. stoßen
ich	_____	_____
du	_____	_____

er	_____	_____
wir	_____	_____
ihr	_____	_____
Sie	_____	_____
man	_____	_____
	7. lassen	**8. schlafen**
ich	_____	_____
du	_____	_____
er	_____	_____
wir	_____	_____
ihr	_____	_____
Sie	_____	_____
man	_____	_____

Vowel change e to i

When a verb has a vowel change in an irregular present tense conjugation, that vowel change occurs primarily with the vowel **e**. An exception is the vowel **ö** in the verb **erlöschen** (*go out, die out*), which forms **erlischst** and **erlischt** in the second-person and third-person singular respectively. Let's look at the form that this irregular conjugation takes:

	brechen (*break*)	**essen** (*eat*)	**nehmen** (*take*)
ich	breche	esse	nehme
du	brichst	isst	nimmst
er/sie/es	bricht	isst	nimmt
wir	brechen	essen	nehmen
ihr	brecht	esst	nehmt
Sie	brechen	essen	nehmen
sie (*pl.*)	brechen	essen	nehmen

Other verbs that follow this irregular present tense conjugational pattern are:

bergen, birgst, birgt	*rescue*
erschrecken, erschrickst, erschrickt	*be startled*
fressen, frisst, frisst	*eat* (*for animals*)
geben, gibst, gibt	*give*
gelten, giltst, gilt	*be valid*
helfen, hilfst, hilft	*help*
melken, milkst, milkt	*milk*
messen, misst, misst	*measure*
schmelzen, schmilzt, schmilzt	*melt*
sprechen, sprichst, spricht	*speak*
stechen, stichst, sticht	*stick, prick*
sterben, stirbst, stirbt	*die*

treffen, triffst, trifft	*meet*
treten, trittst, tritt	*step, kick*
verderben, verdirbst, verdirbt	*spoil*
vergessen, vergisst, vergisst	*forget*
werfen, wirfst, wirft	*throw*

In the blank, rewrite each verb in parentheses with the subject provided.

1. (brechen) du _____

2. (vergessen) sie (*sing.*) _____

3. (sprechen) ihr _____

4. (treten) er _____

5. (stechen) ich _____

6. (messen) wir _____

7. (schmelzen) es _____

8. (werfen) du _____

9. (erschrecken) Sie _____

10. (geben) er _____

11. (helfen) sie (*sing.*) _____

12. (sterben) sie (*pl.*) _____

13. (essen) wir _____

14. (fressen) der Hund (*dog*) _____

15. (nehmen) er _____

16. (treffen) du _____

17. (bergen) die Männer _____

18. (gelten) es _____

19. (melken) ich _____

20. (treten) du _____

21. (essen) mein Freund (*friend*) _____

22. (werfen) ihr _____

23. (geben) Ihre Töchter _____

24. (sterben) er _____

25. (brechen) meine Kinder _____

Write the full conjugation of each verb with the subjects provided.

1. essen   2. helfen

ich   _____   _____

du   _____   _____

er   _____   _____

wir   _____   _____

ihr   _____   _____

Sie   _____   _____

man   _____   _____

3. verderben   4. nehmen

ich   _____   _____

du   _____   _____

er   _____   _____

wir   _____   _____

ihr   _____   _____

Sie   _____   _____

man   _____   _____

5. sprechen   6. sterben

ich   _____   _____

du   _____   _____

er   _____   _____

wir   _____   _____

ihr   _____   _____

Sie   _____   _____

man   _____   _____

7. geben   8. treffen

ich   _____   _____

du   _____   _____

er   _____   _____

wir	_____	_____
ihr	_____	_____
Sie	_____	_____
man	_____	_____

Vowel change **e** to **ie**

Other verbs that have the vowel **e** in their stem change that vowel to an **ie** in the second-person and third-person singular. For example:

	lesen (*read*)	**geschehen** (*happen*)	**empfehlen** (*recommend*)
ich	lese	N/A	empfehle
du	liest	N/A	empfiehlst
er/sie/es	liest	geschieht	empfiehlt
wir	lesen	N/A	empfehlen
ihr	lest	N/A	empfehlt
Sie	lesen	N/A	empfehlen
sie (*pl.*)	lesen	geschehen	empfehlen

Other verbs that follow this irregular present tense conjugational pattern are:

sehen, siehst, sieht	*see*
stehlen, stiehlst, stiehlt	*steal*

ÜBUNG
8·5

Write the full conjugation of each verb with the subjects provided.

1. sehen   **2. stehlen**

ich	_____	_____
du	_____	_____
er	_____	_____
wir	_____	_____
ihr	_____	_____
Sie	_____	_____
man	_____	_____

3. empfehlen   **4. lesen**

ich	_____	_____
du	_____	_____
er	_____	_____

wir	_____	_____
ihr	_____	_____
Sie	_____	_____
man	_____	_____

The verb **wissen**

The verb **wissen** (*know*) has an irregular present tense conjugation, but its irregularities occur not only with the second-person and third-person singular but also with the first-person singular. Let's look at this conjugation:

wissen	
ich	weiß
du	weißt
er/sie/es	weiß
wir	wissen
ihr	wisst
Sie	wissen
sie (*pl.*)	wissen

ÜBUNG
8·6

In the blank, rewrite each verb in parentheses with the subject provided.

1. (brechen) er _____

2. (fahren) wir _____

3. (sein) ihr _____

4. (stehlen) sie (*sing.*) _____

5. (fallen) du _____

6. (fangen) man _____

7. (sehen) ich _____

8. (geschehen) es _____

9. (nehmen) er _____

10. (lassen) Sie _____

11. (stoßen) du _____

12. (werden) es _____

13. (wissen) sie (*sing.*) _____

14. (helfen) sie (*sing.*) _____

15. (empfehlen) wir _____

16. (lesen) du _____

17. (schlafen) er _____

18. (wissen) wer _____

19. (messen) ihr _____

20. (laufen) es _____

21. (stehlen) Sie _____

22. (treten) du _____

23. (raten) ihr _____

24. (wissen) ich _____

25. (sprechen) man _____

26. (raten) sie (*sing.*) _____

27. (geschehen) was _____

28. (lassen) es _____

29. (haben) du _____

30. (wissen) wir _____

Using the word in parentheses as the new subject, rewrite the sentence as a question.

FOR EXAMPLE: (er) Wir lernen Deutsch.

Lernt er Deutsch?

1. (man) Wir sprechen Englisch.

_____

2. (du) Sie läuft nach Hause (*home, homeward*).

_____

3. (er) Ich nehme die Fahrkarten.

_____

4. (ihr) Sie gibt kein Geld.

_____

5. (er) Sie fahren nach Hause.

_____

6. (wer) Wir sehen die Bibliothek.

_____

7. (sie [*pl.*]) Sie isst kein Brot (*bread*).

_____

8. (ich) Ihr empfehlt den Roman.

_____

9. (du) Ich fange den Ball (*ball*).

_____

10. (er) Wir wissen nichts (*nothing*).

_____

11. (Sie) Sie tritt mir auf den Fuß (*steps on my foot*).

_____

12. (Thomas) Ich helfe Sonja und Sabine.

_____

13. (du) Wir lesen die Zeitung.

_____

14. (sie [*sing.*]) Er bricht sich den Arm (*breaks his arm*).

_____

15. (meine Schwester) Ich trage einen Pullover.

_____

See Appendix A for a complete list of verbs with present tense irregularities.

Separable and inseparable prefixes and imperatives

Prefixes

The meaning and use of German verbs are changed by the addition of prefixes. This occurs in English, but not as frequently as in German. Look at a few English verbs and how their meaning is altered by prefixes.

have	*trust*	*believe*	*report*
behave	*entrust*	*relieve*	*transport*

German has three types of prefixes: inseparable prefixes, separable prefixes, and those prefixes that are sometimes inseparable and sometimes separable. The inseparable prefixes are **be-**, **emp-**, **ent-**, **er-**, **ge-**, **ver-**, and **zer-**. They are called inseparable because they remain affixed to the verb in a conjugation. Compare verbs with no prefix and verbs with an inseparable prefix.

	warten	**erwarten** (*expect*)	**hören**	**gehören** (*belong to*)
ich	warte	erwarte	höre	gehöre
du	wartest	erwartest	hörst	gehörst
er/sie/es	wartet	erwartet	hört	gehört
wir	warten	erwarten	hören	gehören
ihr	wartet	erwartet	hört	gehört
Sie	warten	erwarten	hören	gehören
sie (*pl.*)	warten	ewarten	hören	gehören

When a prefix is added to a verb, it is not the conjugation that changes, but the meaning of the verb and, therefore, the use of the verb. If a verb has an irregular present tense conjugation, those irregularities remain intact when an inseparable prefix is added. For example:

	lassen	**entlassen** (*release*)	**halten**	**behalten** (*keep*)
ich	lasse	entlasse	halte	behalte
du	lässt	entlässt	hältst	behältst
er/sie/es	lässt	entlässt	hält	behält
wir	lassen	entlassen	halten	behalten
ihr	lasst	entlasst	haltet	behaltet
Sie	lassen	entlassen	halten	behalten
sie (*pl.*)	lassen	entlassen	halten	behalten

A list of commonly used verbs with inseparable prefixes follows:

bekommen	*receive, get*	besuchen	*visit*	begrüßen	*greet*
empfangen	*receive*	empfehlen	*recommend*	empfinden	*feel*

entdecken	discover	entfernen	remove	entlaufen	run away
ersetzen	replace	erstaunen	amaze	ertragen	bear
gebrauchen	use	gefallen	please, like	gewinnen	win, gain
verstehen	understand	verkaufen	sell	versprechen	promise
zerstören	destroy	zerreißen	tear up	zerschmettern	smash

ÜBUNG
9·1

In the blank, rewrite each verb in parentheses with the subject provided.

1. (erfahren [*experience*]) du _____

2. (entlassen) sie (*sing.*) _____

3. (empfangen) die Dame _____

4. (bekommen) ich _____

5. (empfehlen) ihr _____

6. (verkaufen) Sie _____

7. (besuchen) du _____

8. (gefallen) es _____

9. (erstaunen) er _____

10. (gebrauchen) die Jungen _____

11. (verstehen) wir _____

12. (gelingen [*succeed*]) es _____

13. (zerstören) sie (*pl.*) _____

14. (begrüßen) ich _____

15. (erschlagen [*kill*]) er _____

16. (entlaufen) das Mädchen _____

17. (beschreiben [*describe*]) man _____

18. (empfinden) Sie _____

19. (bekommen) er _____

20. (gefallen) sie (*pl.*) _____

21. (ertragen) der Herr _____

22. (versuchen [*try*]) ich _____

23. (gewinnen) du _____

24. (enlassen) sie (*pl.*) _____

25. (behalten) du _____

Write the full conjugation of each verb phrase with the subjects provided.

Bekommen einen Brief (*Receive a letter*)

1. ich _____
2. du _____
3. er _____
4. wir _____
5. ihr _____
6. Sie _____
7. man _____

Empfangen sie mit Blumen (*Receive, greet her with flowers*)

8. ich _____
9. du _____
10. er _____
11. wir _____
12. ihr _____
13. Sie _____
14. niemand (*no one*)_____

Entdecken eine kleine Insel (*Discover a little island*)

15. ich _____
16. du _____
17. er _____
18. wir _____
19. ihr _____
20. Sie _____
21. der Professor _____

Verstehen kein Wort (*Not understand a word*)

22. ich _____
23. du _____
24. er _____
25. wir _____
26. ihr _____

27. Sie _____

28. die Touristen (*tourists*) _____

Zerreißen die Zeitschriften (*Tear up the magazines*)

29. ich _____

30. du _____

31. er _____

32. wir _____

33. ihr _____

34. Sie _____

35. man _____

The separable prefixes are prepositions and adverbs and form a very large group. They are called separable, because in the conjugation of a verb, the prefix separates from the verb and becomes the final element in a sentence. For example, using the prefixes **mit-**, **fort-**, and **vor-**:

Einen Freund mitbringen (*Bring along a friend*)
Ich bringe einen Freund mit.
Du bringst einen Freund mit.
Er bringt einen Freund mit.
Wir bringen einen Freund mit.
Ihr bringt einen Freund mit.
Sie bringen einen Freund mit.
Meine Eltern bringen einen Freund mit. (*My parents*)

Den Weg zu Fuß fortsetzen (*Continue the journey on foot*)
Ich setze den Weg zu Fuß fort.
Du setzt den Weg zu Fuß fort.
Sie (*sing.*) setzt den Weg zu Fuß fort.
Wir setzen den Weg zu Fuß fort.
Ihr setzt den Weg zu Fuß fort.
Sie setzen den Weg zu Fuß fort.
Sie (*pl.*) setzen den Weg zu Fuß fort.

Die Gäste vorstellen (*Introduce the guests*)
Ich stelle die Gäste vor.
Du stellst die Gäste vor.
Er stellt die Gäste vor.
Wir stellen die Gäste vor.
Ihr stellt die Gäste vor.
Sie stellen die Gäste vor.
Mein Mann stellt die Gäste vor.

If the conjugated verb is irregular in the present tense, the addition of a separable prefix does not alter the conjugation. For example:

Das neue Gemälde ansehen (*Look at the new painting*)
Ich sehe das neue Gemälde an.
Du siehst das neue Gemälde an.
Er sieht das neue Gemälde an.

Wir sehen das neue Gemälde an.
Ihr seht das neue Gemälde an.
Sie sehen das neue Gemälde an.
Man sieht das neue Gemälde an.

A list of verbs with some commonly used separable prefixes follows:

abfahren	*depart*	abspülen	*rinse off*	abreißen	*tear down*
ankommen	*arrive*	anbieten	*offer*	anfangen	*begin*
aufräumen	*tidy up*	aufmachen	*open*	aufstehen	*stand up*
ausgeben	*spend*	aussehen	*look like*	aussteigen	*get off, alight*
beibringen	*teach*	beistehen	*stand by*	beitragen	*contribute*
fortfahren	*continue*	fortbleiben	*stay away*	forteilen	*hurry away*
mitgehen	*go along*	mitnehmen	*take along*	mitsingen	*sing along*
nachdenken	*think about*	nachfolgen	*follow*	nachkommen	*come later*
vorbereiten	*prepare*	vorlesen	*read aloud*	vortragen	*perform*
umbringen	*kill*	umkommen	*die*	umziehen	*change clothes*
weglaufen	*run away*	weggehen	*go away*	wegnehmen	*take away*
zurückgehen	*go back*	zurückbleiben	*stay behind*	zurücknehmen	*take back*
zumachen	*close*	zunehmen	*increase*	zuhören	*listen to*

ÜBUNG
9·3

In the blank, rewrite each verb in parentheses with the subject provided.

1. (ankommen) ihr _____

2. (umbringen) sie (*pl.*) _____

3. (mitnehmen) er _____

4. (zurückgehen) wir _____

5. (vorbereiten) mein Vater _____

6. (umziehen) ich _____

7. (anfangen) sie (*sing.*) _____

8. (weglaufen) ihr _____

9. (zumachen) die Touristen _____

10. (umkommen) sie (*pl.*) _____

11. (wegnehmen) er _____

12. (beibringen) ich _____

13. (aufhören) Sie _____

14. (vorstellen) meine Gäste _____

15. (aufmachen) die Ärztin _____

16. (weglaufen) der Hund _____

17. (mitbringen) wir _____

18. (fortsetzen) Tina und Werner _____

19. (anbieten) du _____

20. (aufräumen) sie (*sing.*) _____

Write the full conjugation of each verb phrase with the subjects provided.

Abfahren um neun Uhr (*Depart at nine o'clock*)

1. ich _____

2. du _____

3. er _____

4. wir _____

5. ihr _____

6. Sie _____

7. man _____

Zumachen die Fenster und die Türen (*Close the windows and the doors*)

8. ich _____

9. du _____

10. er _____

11. wir _____

12. ihr _____

13. Sie _____

14. niemand _____

Beibringen ihnen Deutsch (*Teach them German*)

15. ich _____

16. du _____

17. er _____

18. wir _____

19. ihr _____

20. Sie _____

21. man _____

Aufhören damit (*Stop that*)

22. ich _____

23. du _____

24. er _____

25. wir _____

26. ihr _____

27. Sie _____

28. Martin _____

Ausgeben zwanzig Euro (*Spend twenty euros*)

29. ich _____

30. du _____

31. er _____

32. wir _____

33. ihr _____

34. Sie _____

35. wer _____

A relatively small group of prefixes can be either separable or inseparable. If they are separable, the accented syllable is the prefix itself. If they are inseparable, the accented syllable is the stem of the verb. Let's look at a few examples of these prefixes.

SEPARABLE		INSEPARABLE	
dúrchfallen	*fail*	durchzíehen	*pass through*
überwerfen	*throw over*	übertréiben	*exaggerate*
úmkommen	*die*	umármen	*embrace*
únterkommen	*find housing*	untersúchen	*investigate*
vólltanken	*fill the gas tank*	vollzíehen	*carry out, complete*
wíderrufen	*retract*	widerspréchen	*contradict*
wíederkommen	*come back*	wiederhólen	*repeat*

In the following, compare how the same prefix is used as a separable prefix and then as an inseparable prefix.

Ich komme morgen **wieder**.   *I'll come back tomorrow.*
Ich **wieder**hole den Satz.   *I repeat the sentence.*

Write the full conjugation of each verb phrase with the subjects provided.

Umkommen vor Langeweile (*Die of boredom*)

1. ich _____

2. du _____

3. er _____

4. wir _____

5. ihr _____

6. Sie _____

7. man _____

Unterbrechen die Rede (*Interrupt the speech*)

8. ich _____

9. du _____

10. er _____

11. wir _____

12. ihr _____

13. Sie _____

14. niemand _____

Imperatives

The imperative form is the command form of a verb. In English there is only one imperative form, and it is the base form, or infinitive, of a verb. For example:

> *Sit.*
> *Stand up.*
> *Go away.*
> *Be as quiet as possible.*

Imperatives are directed at the second person (*you*), and since there are three forms of *you* in German, there are three imperative forms, one for each of these pronouns: **du**, informal singular; **ihr**, informal plural; and **Sie**, formal singular or plural.

The **du**-form is derived from the infinitive with the **-en** ending omitted. Sometimes, an optional **e** is added to this imperative form.

Lach! (Lache!)	*Laugh!*	Komm! (Komme!)	*Come!*	Sing! (Singe!)	*Sing!*
Spiel!	*Play!*	Such!	*Search!*	Trink!	*Drink!*
Lern!	*Learn!*	Wein!	*Cry!*	Schreib!	*Write!*

If an infinitive ends in **-eln**, **-ern**, **-igen**, or **-men**, the -e ending is not optional and must be included in the **du** imperative.

Öffne! (öffnen)	*Open!*	Entschuldige! (entschuldigen)	*Excuse!*
Atme! (atmen)	*Breathe!*	Lächele! (lächeln)	*Smile!*
Wandere! (wandern)	*Hike!*	Behandele! (behandeln)	*Treat!*

If the present tense of a verb is irregular and has an umlaut in the second-person and third-person singular, that umlaut does not occur in the imperative. However, if the irregularity is a change from **e** to **i** or **ie**, that form of irregularity appears in the **du** imperative. For example:

Fahr! (*Drive!*)	fahren, du fährst, er fährt
Lauf! (*Run!*)	laufen, du läufst, er läuft
Gib! (*Give!*)	geben, du gibst, er gibt
Sieh! (*See!*)	sehen, du siehst, er sieht

The **ihr** imperative is in most cases identical to the present tense conjugation for **ihr**. The same is true of the **Sie** imperative, except that the pronoun **Sie** accompanies the imperative form. For example:

INFINITIVE	**IHR** IMPERATIVE	**SIE** IMPERATIVE	
lachen	Lacht!	Lachen Sie!	*Laugh!*
arbeiten	Arbeitet!	Arbeiten Sie!	*Work!*
geben	Gebt!	Geben Sie!	*Give!*
helfen	Helft!	Helfen Sie!	*Help!*

ÜBUNG
9·6

*In the blanks provided, write the **du**, **ihr**, and **Sie** imperative forms for each infinitive.*

INFINITIVE	DU	IHR	SIE
1. trinken	_____	_____	_____
2. kaufen	_____	_____	_____
3. nehmen	_____	_____	_____
4. paddeln	_____	_____	_____
5. schlafen	_____	_____	_____
6. gehen	_____	_____	_____
7. sprechen	_____	_____	_____
8. hören	_____	_____	_____
9. stehlen	_____	_____	_____
10. schwimmen	_____	_____	_____

The separable prefixes separate from the verb in the imperative, but the inseparable prefixes remain affixed to the verb. For example:

ausgeben (*spend*)	Gib aus!	Gebt aus!	Geben Sie aus!
verkaufen (*sell*)	Verkauf!	Verkauft!	Verkaufen Sie!

ÜBUNG
9·7

*In the blanks provided, write the **du**, **ihr**, and **Sie** imperative forms for each infinitive.*

INFINITIVE	DU	IHR	SIE
1. abfahren	_____	_____	_____
2. gewinnen	_____	_____	_____
3. bekommen	_____	_____	_____
4. mitbringen	_____	_____	_____
5. zumachen	_____	_____	_____
6. versuchen	_____	_____	_____
7. erschlagen	_____	_____	_____
8. ansehen	_____	_____	_____
9. aufhören	_____	_____	_____
10. ankommen	_____	_____	_____

The verbs **haben**, **sein**, and **werden** always play a special role, and their imperatives are no exception.

haben	Hab!	Habt!	Haben Sie!
sein	Sei!	Seid!	Seien Sie!
werden	Werde!	Werdet!	Werden Sie!

ÜBUNG
9·8

*Rewrite each sentence as an imperative. But take care to use the correct form for **du**, **ihr**, or **Sie**. The words in parentheses are your signal to tell you to whom the imperative is addressed, and you need to provide the form that is appropriate for an informal singular or plural imperative or the form that is appropriate for a formal singular or plural imperative.*

FOR EXAMPLE: Die Kinder spielen Tennis. *The children play tennis.*

(Herr Braun) _____*Spielen Sie Tennis!*_____ (Herr Braun is addressed formally.)

1. Meine Mutter ist gesund. *My mother is well.*

(das Kind) _____

2. Der Mann steht auf. *The man stands up.*

   (Professor Schmidt) _____

3. Sie machen die Fenster auf. *They open the windows.*

   (Hans und Sabine) _____

4. Die Männer essen in der Küche. *The men eat in the kitchen.*

   (Karl) _____

5. Meine Eltern besuchen Onkel Heinz. *My parents visit Uncle Heinz.*

   (Tina, Max und Erik) _____

6. Ich verkaufe den alten Wagen. *I sell the old car.*

   (Frau Schneider) _____

7. Wir warten an der Tür. *We wait at the door.*

   (mein Bruder) _____

8. Die Touristen sprechen nur Deutsch. *The tourists only speak German.*

   (Thomas) _____

9. Die Gäste kommen um sieben Uhr. *The guests come at seven o'clock.*

   (Herr Benz und Frau Keller) _____

10. Sie helfen mir damit. *They help me with that.*

    (mein Freund) _____

Review 1

ÜBUNG
R1·1

Unit 1. *In the blanks provided, insert the appropriate definite article.*

1. _____ Brunnen

2. _____ Prüfung

3. _____ Liebe

4. _____ Vogel

5. _____ Land

ÜBUNG
R1·2

Unit 2. *Rewrite the sentences by changing the nouns in boldface to the ones in parentheses. Provide the correct gender.*

1 **Die Schule** ist groß. (Auto)_____

2. **Diese Schauspielerin** ist krank. (Gärtner) _____

3. **Die Tante** ist alt. (Bild) _____

4. **Der Fernsehapparat** ist neu. (Fenster)_____

5. **Das Restaurant** ist klein. (Uhr) _____

Unit 3. *Rewrite the sentences by changing the nouns in boldface to the appropriate pronouns. Then rewrite each sentence again by changing the nouns in boldface to the plural.*

1. **Die Landkarte** ist sehr alt. _____ / _____

2. **Das Mädchen** ist jung. _____ / _____

3. **Der Bruder** ist jung. _____ / _____

4. **Das Haus** ist hier. _____ / _____

5. **Die Frau** ist da. _____ / _____

Unit 4. *In the blanks provided, select the word that best completes the sentence.*

1. Er ist in _____

2. Die Frau _____ in München.

3. Seid ihr _____?

4. _____ ist die Bibliothek?

5. Das ist _____ Bäckerei.

Diplomat   Schule   Norwegen

wohnt   wo   Tochter

Dame   Kirche   zu Hause

Wer   Wo   Ihre

der   was   eine

Unit 5. *Fill in the blanks with the correct form of the word in parentheses.*

1. Ich (haben) _____ keine Zeit.

2. Seine Schwester (werden) _____ Lehrerin.

3. Hast du (kein) _____ Prüfung?

4. (Haben) _____ ihr Durst?

5. Sie ist (kein) _____ Richterin.

6. Ich (sein) _____ kein Arzt.

7. (haben) _____ du Geld?

8. Nein, das ist (nicht) _____ meine Schwester.

9. (sein) _____ ihr zu Hause?

10. Es (werden) _____ dunkel.

Unit 6. *Provide the present tense conjugation of the verbs in parentheses with the subject pronouns.*

1. (probieren) ich _____ er _____ wir _____

2. (antworten) du _____ ihr _____ Sie _____

3. (lächeln) sie (*sing.*) _____ sie (*plur.*) _____ ich _____

4. (haben) du _____ er _____ ihr _____

5. (singen) ich _____ wir _____ sie (*plur.*) _____

6. (reißen) sie (*sing.*) _____ ich _____ du _____

7. (bellen) du _____ er _____ sie (*plur.*) _____

8. (kosten) es _____ er _____ sie (*plur.*) _____

9. (paddeln) ich _____ sie _____ wir _____

10. (sein) du _____ ihr _____ sie _____

11. (warten) sie pl. _____ ich _____ er _____

12. (wandern) sie _____ du _____ sie (*plur.*) _____

13. (baden) ich _____ er _____ wir _____

14. (werden) du _____ sie _____ ihr _____

15. (glauben) er _____ wir _____ sie (*plur.*) _____

Unit 6. *Complete the sentences with the correct written form of the numbers provided in parentheses: cardinal or ordinal.*

1. Die Frau ist am (10) _____ gestorben. Zwanzig weniger (3) _____ sind

   (17) _____.

2. Heute ist der (20) _____ Juni. Achtzehn plus (5) _____ sind

   (23) _____.

Unit 7. *Change the words or phrases in boldface to the appropriate pronouns.*

1. Marianne hat **das Geld.** _____, Wo ist **die Landkarte**? _____,

   Der Lehrer ist krank. _____

2. Sabine hat **einen Computer.** _____, Liebt ihr **das Kind**? _____,

   Wo ist **der Tisch**? _____

3. Sie kauft **ein Kleid.** _____, Sie kennt **meinen Bruder.** _____,

   Wir hören **Radio.** _____

4. Sie hat **die Landkarte.** _____, Er sucht **die Kinder.** _____,

   Ich finde **einen Roman.** _____

5. Liebst du **dieses Mädchen?** _____, Peter kennt **Frau Schiller.** _____,

   Luise hat **Martin** gern. _____

Unit 7. Now change the pronouns in boldface to any appropriate noun.

6. Mein Vater hat **es**. _____ , Der Mann kauft **ihn**. _____ ,

 Was haben **sie**? _____

7. Wir finden **ihn**. _____ , Ich kenne **sie** (pl.) _____ ,

 Er sucht **sie**. _____

8. Ich höre **sie**. _____ , Sie kauft **ihn**. _____ ,

 Liebt ihr **ihn**? _____

9. Sie hat **es**. _____ , Die Frauen kaufen **sie** (pl.). _____ ,

 Er braucht **es**. _____

10. Wir haben **sie**. _____ , Findest du **ihn**? _____ , Wir haben **es**.

 _____

Unit 8. Rewrite the sentences with the subjects provided in parentheses.

1. Sie stehlen Geld. (ich) _____ , (er) _____

2. Wir nehmen es. (du) _____ , (ihr) _____

3. Ihr wisst nicht. (sie sing.) _____ , (ich) _____

4. Lesen Sie die Zeitung? (er) _____ , (ihr) _____

5. Wo schläft er? (Sie) _____ , (du) _____

6. Ich esse Wurst. (er) _____ , (du) _____

7. Ich gebe es Tina. (du) _____ , (ihr) _____

8. Wir helfen Thomas. (sie sing.) _____ , (du) _____

Unit 9. *Rewrite the sentence with the subject pronouns provided.*

1. Der Mann bekommt einen Brief.

   ich _____

   du _____

   er _____

   wir _____

   ihr _____

   Sie _____

2. Der Mann bringt ihn mit.

   ich _____

   du _____

   er _____

   wir _____

   ihr _____

   sie *(plur.)* _____

3. Der Mann versucht es.

   ich _____

   du _____

   er _____

   wir _____

   ihr _____

   Sie _____

4. Der Mann macht das Fenster zu.

   ich _____

   du _____

   sie *(sing.)* _____

   wir _____

   ihr _____

   sie *(plur.)* _____

ÜBUNG

R1·12

Unit 9. Conjugate the infinitives with the pronouns provided.

1. wiederholen

ich _____ du _____ er _____

wir _____ ihr _____ sie (*pl.*) _____

2. aufhören

ich _____ du _____ er _____

wir _____ ihr _____ sie (*pl.*) _____

ÜBUNG

R1·13

Unit 9. Provide the **du**-imperative, **ihr**-imperative, and **Sie**-imperative of the infinitives provided.

	DU	IHR	SIE
1. sein	_____	_____	_____
2. haben	_____	_____	_____
3. aufmachen	_____	_____	_____
4. werden	_____	_____	_____
5. kaufen	_____	_____	_____
6. behalten	_____	_____	_____
7. fortsetzen	_____	_____	_____
8. vorstellen	_____	_____	_____
9. entdecken	_____	_____	_____
10. ansehen	_____	_____	_____

Accusative case prepositions and interrogatives

The German accusative case as described in Chapter 7 is used to identify direct objects. In the following sentence, the bolded word is the direct object.

> Martin kauft **meinen Wagen**.   *Martin buys **my car**.*

It answers the question *What does Martin buy?* If the direct object is a person, it answers the question *Whom does Martin see?*

> Martin sieht **meinen Bruder**.   *Martin sees **my brother**.*

Remember that only masculine nouns have a declensional change in the accusative case.

	MASCULINE	FEMININE	NEUTER	PLURAL
nom	der Mann	die Frau	das Kind	die Kinder
acc	den Mann	die Frau	das Kind	die Kinder

Another function of the accusative case is to identify the object of an accusative preposition. The accusative prepositions are:

bis	*until, 'til*
durch	*through*
entlang	*along(side), down*
für	*for*
gegen	*against*
ohne	*without*
wider	*against, contrary to (poetical)*
um	*around, at (a time of the clock)*

Nouns that follow one of these prepositions will appear in the accusative case. For example:

Er bleibt **bis** nächsten Montag.	*He is staying **until** next Monday.*
Sie laufen **durch** das Haus.	*They run **through** the house.*
Sie gehen die Straße **entlang**.	*They go **down** the street.*
Das ist ein Geschenk **für** Ihren Mann.	*That is a gift **for** your husband.*
Er schlägt **gegen** die Tür.	*He bangs **on** the door.*
Er kommt **ohne** Frau Benz.	*He comes **without** Ms. Benz.*
Es ist **wider** alle Vernunft.	*It is **against** all reason.*
Sie fahren schnell **um** die Ecke.	*They drive quickly **around** the corner.*

Note that **entlang** follows the accusative object: **die Straße entlang**.

Complete each sentence with the given phrases.

FOR EXAMPLE: Ich bleibe bis _____.

(sechs Uhr) _____ *Ich bleibe bis sechs Uhr.* _____

(Montag) _____ *Ich bleibe bis Montag.* _____

Ein Vogel fliegt durch _____. *A bird flies through . . . .*

1. das Fenster _____

2. die Tür _____

3. der Garten _____

4. der Wald (*woods*) _____

Ich habe diese Blumen für _____. *I have these flowers for . . . .*

5. Ihre Mutter _____

6. Ihr Vater _____

7. mein Onkel _____

8. meine Schwestern _____

Ist er gegen _____? *Is he against . . . .*

9. dieser Rechtsanwalt _____

10. meine Idee (*idea*) _____

11. Ihre Freundin _____

12. mein Bruder _____

Kommen Sie ohne _____? *Are you coming without . . . .*

13. ein Geschenk _____

14. Ihr Großvater (*grandfather*) _____

15. ein Regenschirm (*umbrella*) _____

16. Ihre Bücher _____

Sie sorgt sich um _____. *She worries about . . . .*

17. mein Sohn (*son*) _____

18. dieses Problem _____

19. meine Eltern _____

20. der Zahnarzt _____

Pronouns also have a new form in the accusative case. Compare the nominative case and accusative case pronouns that follow.

NOMINATIVE	ACCUSATIVE
ich	mich
du	dich
er	ihn
sie (*sing.*)	sie (*sing.*)
es	es
wir	uns
ihr	euch
Sie	Sie
sie (*pl.*)	sie (*pl.*)
wer	wen
was	was

The accusative case pronouns are used when the pronoun is a direct object. For example:

Meine Schwester besucht **mich**.	*My sister visits **me**.*
Kennst du **ihn**?	*Do you know **him**?*
Die Kinder lieben **euch**.	*The children love **you**.*

ÜBUNG
10·2

In the blank provided, write the correct accusative case form of the pronoun provided in parentheses.

FOR EXAMPLE: (ich) Die Kinder lieben _____*mich.*_____

1. (Sie) Meine Familie begrüßt _____.

2. (du) Ich kenne _____ nicht.

3. (es) Die Jungen essen _____.

4. (sie [*pl.*]) Wir haben _____.

5. (er) Die Schüler legen _____ auf den Tisch. (*The students lay it on the table.*)

6. (wir) Die Touristen fotografieren _____. (*The tourists photograph us.*)

7. (ihr) Er liebt _____ nicht.

8. (ich) Meine Eltern besuchen _____ in Hamburg.

9. (wer) _____ siehst du?

10. (was) _____ schreibt der Mann?

11. (sie [*sing.*]) Die Mädchen suchen _____.

12. (er) Niemand liest _____.

13. (du) Meine Mutter ruft _____ an. (*My mother phones you.*)

14. (wir) Die Frauen begrüßen _____.

15. (es) Wer bekommt _____?

If a pronoun follows an accusative preposition, the pronoun must be in the accusative case. For example:

Ich habe ein Geschenk für **dich**.   *I have a gift for **you**.*
Sie schickt die Nachricht durch **ihn**.   *She sends the news through **him**.*

ÜBUNG
10·3

Complete each sentence with the pronouns provided in parentheses. Note that some sentences will require a nominative case pronoun and others an accusative case pronoun. If the pronoun is in the nominative case, it is the subject of the sentence, which can affect the conjugation of the verb.

FOR EXAMPLE: _____ hat kein Geld.

(ich) _____   *Ich habe kein Geld.* _____

(er) _____   *Er hat kein Geld.* _____

_____ wohnt in Heidelberg.

1. (du) _____

2. (wir) _____

3. (ihr) _____

4. (Sie) _____

5. (sie [*sing.*]) _____

Erik spielt gegen _____. *Erik plays against . . . .*

6. (ich) _____

7. (er) _____

8. (wir) _____

9. (ihr) _____

10. (sie [*pl.*]) _____

Meine Eltern sorgen sich um _____.

11. (du) _____

12. (sie [*sing.*]) _____

13. (ihr) _____

14. (Sie) _____

15. (sie [*pl.*]) _____

_____ entdeckt eine kleine Insel.

16. (ich) _____

17. (er) _____

18. (wir) _____

19. (Sie) _____

20. (wer) _____

Sie gehen ohne _____ wandern. *They go hiking without . . . .*

21. (du) _____

22. (er) _____

23. (sie [*sing.*]) _____

24. (wir) _____

25. (ihr) _____

The third-person pronouns (**er**, **sie** [*sing.*], **es**, and **sie** [*pl.*]) are the replacements for nouns. If those nouns refer to persons or other animates, a prepositional phrase as previously illustrated is used. For example:

Ich komme **ohne** meine Eltern.   *I come **without** my parents.*
Ich komme **ohne sie**.   *I come **without** them.*

But if the noun refers to an inanimate object, a different type of prepositional phrase is formed. It is called a *prepositional adverb*. A prepositional adverb is the combination of the prefix **da-** and the preposition. For example:

dadurch   *through it*
dafür   *for it*
dagegen   *against it*
darum   *around it*

Because the preposition **um** begins with a vowel, the prefix becomes **dar-**.

In the blank provided, write the prepositional phrase with the pronoun replacement for the noun in the original prepositional phrase.

FOR EXAMPLE: für den Mann _____*für ihn*_____

1. durch das Fenster _____

2. um die Kinder _____

3. für meine Eltern _____

4. für diesen Artikel _____

5. gegen die Tänzerin _____

6. um die Ecke _____

7. durch meinen Bruder _____

8. für meinen Freund und mich _____

9. gegen diese Idee _____

10. ohne Frau Keller _____

11. wider den Rechtsanwalt _____

12. um meine Freundin _____

13. durch den Wald _____

14. ohne meinen Sohn _____

15. um die Stadt _____

You have encountered the interrogatives **wer**, **wen**, **was**, **wo**, **wie**, and **wann**. Two more important interrogative words are **warum** (*why*) and **wessen** (*whose*).

Warum asks for a reason for an action. The most common response is with the conjunction **denn** (*because*).

Warum ist Tina zu Hause? | **Why** is Tina at home?
Sie ist zu Hause, **denn** sie ist krank. | *She is at home, **because** she is sick.*

Wessen asks about ownership. And the response often requires the use of a possessive pronoun. They are:

PRONOUN	POSSESSIVE
ich	mein
du	dein
er	sein
sie (*sing.*)	ihr
es	sein
wir	unser
ihr	euer
Sie	Ihr
sie (*pl.*)	ihr
wer	wessen

The possessive pronouns are **ein**-words and show gender and case like the other **ein**-words.

MASCULINE	FEMININE	NEUTER	PLURAL
dein Bruder	deine Schwester	dein Kind	deine Kinder
unser Freund	unsere Freundin	unser Haus	unsere Bücher

Let's look at some example questions with **wessen** and possible answers to those questions:

Wessen Buch ist das? | *Whose book is that?*
Das ist dein Buch. | *That is your book.*

Wessen Eltern wohnen da? | *Whose parents live there?*
Seine Eltern wohnen da. | *His parents live there.*

Wessen Vater spricht Deutsch? | *Whose father speaks German?*
Euer Vater spricht Deutsch. | *Your father speaks German.*

*Using the provided phrases, answer the questions that ask **warum**.*

FOR EXAMPLE: Warum ist er nicht hier?

Er hat keine Zeit. _____*Er ist nicht hier, denn er hat keine Zeit.*_____

1. Warum ist Sabine in Berlin?

   Sie besucht ihren Onkel. _____

   Sie arbeitet in der Hauptstadt. _____

   Sie sucht einen Freund. _____

2. Warum bleibt er in Kanada?

   Er lernt Englisch. _____

   Seine Eltern wohnen da. _____

   Seine Freundin arbeitet in Toronto. _____

3. Warum kaufst du einen VW?

   Ich brauche ein Auto. _____

   Ein BMW ist teuer. (*expensive*) _____

   Ein VW ist billig. (*cheap*) _____

*Using the pronoun provided in parentheses as your cue, answer the questions that ask **wessen**. Use the appropriate possessive pronoun form.*

FOR EXAMPLE: Wessen Haus ist das?

(ich) _____*Das ist mein Haus.*_____

Wessen Hut ist das?

1. (er) _____

2. (sie [*sing.*]) _____

3. (wir) _____

4. (ihr) _____

5. (Sie) _____

Wessen Freund sieht er?

6. (ich) _____

7. (du) _____

8. (ihr) _____

9. (Sie) _____

10. (sie [*pl.*]) _____

Wessen Fahrrad (*bicycle*) kaufen sie?

11. (du) _____

12. (er) _____

13. (sie [*sing.*]) _____

14. (wir) _____

15. (ihr) _____

Wessen Eltern wohnen in der Hauptstadt?

16. (ich) _____

17. (du) _____

18. (er) _____

19. (wir) _____

20. (sie [*pl.*]) _____

The interrogative **wie** is often combined with other words to form new interrogatives. For example:

wie alt	*how old*
wie hoch	*how high*
wie klein	*how small*
wie lange	*how long*
wie oft	*how often*
wie schnell	*how fast*
wie spät	*how late*
wie viel	*how much*

The following questions demonstrate such interrogatives:

Wie alt ist er?	*How old is he?*
Wie hoch ist das Rathaus?	*How high is city hall?*
Wie oft gehst du in die Bibiliothek?	*How often do you go to the library?*
Wie viel kostet das Hemd?	*How much does the shirt cost?*

ÜBUNG
10·7

*Write the question with **wie** that would be asked to elicit each of the answers provided.*

FOR EXAMPLE: Er ist vier Jahre alt. (*He is four years old.*)

Wie alt ist er?

1. Sie fährt jeden Tag in die Stadt. (*She drives into the city every day.*)

_____

2. Sie bleiben nur vier Tage hier. (*They are staying here for only four days.*)

_____

3. Das Buch kostet elf Euro. (*The book costs eleven euros.*)

_____

4. Sie kommt zwei Stunden zu spät. (*She is coming two hours too late.*)

_____

5. Der alte Herr hat viel Geld. (*The old gentleman has a lot of money.*)

_____

An interrogative can be formed by the combination of an accusative preposition and **wen**. It asks *whom* with the meaning of the preposition. For example:

für wen	*for whom*
gegen wen	*against whom*
ohne wen	*without whom*

If the object of the preposition is not a person but an inanimate object, a prepositional adverb is formed with the prefix **wo(r)-**. **Wor-** is used with prepositions that begin with a vowel. For example:

wofür	*for what*
wogegen	*against what*
worum	*around what*

ÜBUNG
10·8

In the blank provided, write the question that asks about the underlined prepositional phrase. In the second blank, write the correct prepositional phrase with a pronoun that can replace the underlined prepositional phrase in each sentence.

FOR EXAMPLE: Er hat ein Buch <u>für seine Schwester</u>.

Für wen hat er ein Buch?

für sie

Er sorgt sich <u>um das Problem</u>.

Worum sorgt er sich?

darum

1. Thomas war <u>gegen seine Familie</u>. (*Thomas was against his family.*)

_____

_____

2. Frau Braun fährt <u>ohne ihre Kinder</u> ab. (*Ms. Braun departs without her children.*)

_____

_____

Accusative case prepositions and interrogatives   **101**

3. Ich schreibe den Brief <u>für den Schüler</u>. (*I write the letter for the pupil.*)

_____

_____

4. Der Sportler schwimmt <u>durch den Fluss</u>. (*The athlete swims through the river.*)

_____

_____

5. Die Zwillinge danken uns <u>für die Geschenke zum Geburtstag</u>. (*The children thank us for the gifts for their birthday.*)

_____

_____

6. Die Jungen laufen <u>durch den Friedhof</u>. (*The boys run through the cemetery.*)

_____

_____

7. Der alte Mann bittet <u>um Hilfe</u>. (*The old man asks for help.*)

_____

_____

8. Ich kenne ein gutes Mittel <u>gegen die Krankheit</u>. (*I know a good remedy for the disease.*)

_____

_____

9. Erik kommt nach Hause <u>ohne seine Freundin</u>. (*Erik comes home without his girlfriend.*)

_____

_____

10. Wir schicken das Paket <u>durch die Post</u>. (*We send the package through the mail.*)

_____

_____

Regular verbs in the past tense and word order

Regular past tense

A large group of German verbs form the past tense by following the same conjugational pattern. This past tense form is called the *regular past tense*. The basic suffix for the regular past tense is **-te**. Look at the following verbs for the full conjugation.

	glauben (*believe*)	**folgen** (*follow*)	**tanzen** (*dance*)
ich	glaubte	folgte	tanzte
du	glaubtest	folgtest	tanztest
er/sie/es	glaubte	folgte	tanzte
wir	glaubten	folgten	tanzten
ihr	glaubtet	folgtet	tanztet
Sie	glaubten	folgten	tanzten
sie (*pl.*)	glaubten	folgten	tanzten

ÜBUNG
11·1

In the blank provided, write the past tense conjugation of the given verb for the subject provided.

1. ich _____ spielen

2. du _____ hören

3. wir _____ sagen

4. Sie _____ fragen

5. der Diplomat _____ reisen (*travel*)

6. sie (*sing.*) _____ machen

7. ihr _____ stellen

8. sie (*pl.*) _____ setzen

9. er _____ dienen

10. ich _____ sorgen

11. seine Eltern _____ holen (*get, fetch*)

12. du _____ suchen

13. wir _____ kaufen

14. ihr _____ pflanzen (*plant*)

15. Erik _____ flüstern (*whisper*)

Write the full conjugation of each verb with the subjects provided.

1. lernen

2. lächeln

ich _____   _____

du _____   _____

er _____   _____

wir _____   _____

ihr _____   _____

Sie _____   _____

man _____   _____

3. feiern (*celebrate*)

4. leben

ich _____   _____

du _____   _____

er _____   _____

wir _____   _____

ihr _____   _____

Sie _____   _____

wer _____   _____

5. lieben

6. wohnen

ich _____   _____

du _____   _____

er _____   _____

wir _____   _____

ihr _____   _____

Sie _____   _____

Tina _____   _____

If a verb stem ends in **-t** or **-d**, the basic regular past tense ending will be **-ete**. For example:

	arbeiten (*work*)	**baden** (*bathe*)
ich	arbeitete	badete
du	arbeitetest	badetest
er/sie/es	arbeitete	badete
wir	arbeiteten	badeten
ihr	arbeitetet	badetet
Sie	arbeiteten	badeten
sie (*pl.*)	arbeiteten	badeten

ÜBUNG
11·3

Write the full conjugation of each verb with the subjects provided.

1. enden (*end*)   **2. fürchten** (*fear*)

ich _____   _____

du   _____   _____

er   _____   _____

wir _____   _____

ihr _____   _____

Sie _____   _____

man _____   _____

3. reden (*talk*)   **4. antworten** (*answer*)

ich _____   _____

du   _____   _____

er   _____   _____

wir _____   _____

ihr _____   _____

Sie _____   _____

wer _____   _____

The separable and inseparable prefixes function in the same way in the regular past tense as they do in the present tense. For example:

	zumachen (*close*)	**erzählen** (*tell*)
ich	machte zu	erzählte
du	machtest zu	erzähltest
er/sie/es	machte zu	erzählte
wir	machten zu	erzählten
ihr	machtet zu	erzähltet
Sie	machten zu	erzählten
sie (*pl.*)	machten zu	erzählten

In the blank provided, write the past tense conjugation of the given verb for the subject provided.

1. ich _____ warten

2. du _____ besuchen

3. er _____ erwarten (*expect*)

4. wir _____ abholen (*pick up, fetch*)

5. ihr _____ vorbereiten (*prepare*)

6. Sie _____ nachfragen (*inquire*)

7. sie (*sing.*) _____ verkaufen

8. seine Eltern _____ zuhören (*listen*)

9. man _____ aufhören (*stop, cease*)

10. ein Lehrer _____ verlangen (*demand*)

11. ich _____ umpflanzen (*transplant*)

12. sie (*pl.*) _____ zurückkehren (*turn back, return*)

13. wir _____ sagen

14. du _____ einkaufen (*shop*)

15. ihr _____ ersetzen (*replace*)

Word order

In a German sentence where the subject begins the sentence, the verb follows the subject.

Mein Vater **spricht** kein Englisch.	*My father **speaks** no English.*
Das Haus **ist** sehr klein.	*The house **is** very small.*

But if something other than the subject begins the sentence, the verb will precede the subject. For example:

Wir **fahren** nach Hause.	*We **are driving** home.*
Heute **fahren** wir nach Hause.	*Today we **are driving** home.*
Mein Bruder **arbeitet** in der Stadt.	*My brother **works** in the city.*
Im Winter **arbeitet** mein Bruder in der Stadt.	*In winter my brother **works** in the city.*

Rewrite the following sentences with the phrase in parentheses as the first element of the sentence.

FOR EXAMPLE: (heute) Ich gehe zum Park. (*I am going to the park.*)

Heute gehe ich zum Park.

1. (im Sommer) Die Kinder schwimmen gern. (*The children like to swim.*)

_____

2. (in Deutschland) Das Wetter ist oft sehr schön. (*The weather is often very nice.*)

_____

3. (gestern [*yesterday*]) Unsere Eltern kauften einen neuen Wagen.

_____

4. (heute) Meine Töchter spielen Schach. (*My daughters are playing chess.*)

_____

5. (um sieben Uhr [*at seven o'clock*]) Ich stehe auf. (*I get up.*)

_____

6. (morgen [*tomorrow*]) Meine Familie reist nach Paris. (*My family is traveling to Paris.*)

_____

7. (gestern) Wir wohnten noch in München. (*We still lived in Munich.*)

_____

8. (im Mai) Sie feierten meinen Geburtstag. (*They celebrated my birthday.*)

_____

9. (im Frühling [*in the spring*]) Ich besuchte meine Tante in Amerika.

_____

10. (morgen) Du verkaufst dein Fahrrad. (*You sell your bicycle.*)

_____

Word order is not affected when using the four conjunctions **und**, **aber**, **oder**, and **denn**. For example:

Ich lerne Spanisch, **und** Maria lernt Deutsch.	*I learn Spanish, **and** Maria learns German.*
Das Haus ist alt, **aber** es ist sehr groß.	*The house is old, **but** it is very big.*

Hat er einen Bruder, **oder** hat er eine Schwester?   *Does he have a brother, **or** does he have a sister?*

Sie bleibt zu Hause, **denn** sie ist krank.   *She stays home **because** she is sick.*

ÜBUNG
11·6

*Combine each pair of sentences with the conjunction **und**.*

1. Ich spiele das Klavier. Sonja singt. (*I play the piano. Sonja sings.*)

   _____

2. Martin wohnt in der Hauptstadt. Ich wohne in Bremen. (*Martin lives in the capital. I live in Bremen.*)

   _____

3. Der Hund ist krank. Die Katze ist alt. (*The dog is sick. The cat is old.*)

   _____

*Combine each pair of sentences with the conjunction **aber**.*

4. Ich lese den Roman. Ich verstehe nichts. (*I read the novel. I understand nothing.*)

   _____

5. Mein Bruder ist stark. Er ist faul. (*My brother is strong. He is lazy.*)

   _____

6. Das Wetter ist schön. Wir bleiben zu Hause. (*The weather is good. We stay at home.*)

   _____

*Combine each pair of sentences with the conjunction **oder**.*

7. Sind sie reich? Sind sie arm? (*Are they rich? Are they poor?*)

   _____

8. Kaufte sie ein Kleid? Kaufte sie eine Bluse? (*Did she buy a dress? Did she buy a blouse?*)

   _____

*Combine each pair of sentences with the conjunction **denn**.*

9. Der Mann arbeitet nicht. Er ist müde. (*The man is not working. He is tired.*)

   _____

10. Die Touristen verstehen nichts. Sie sprechen kein Deutsch. (*The tourists do not understand anything. They do not speak German.*)

    _____

Some conjunctions require a significant change in word order. Two such conjunctions are **dass** and **weil**. In a phrase that follows these conjunctions, the verb becomes the last element in the sentence. Notice how the position of the verb changes when the example sentence is placed after one of these conjunctions.

Er wohnt in der Schweiz.	*He lives in Switzerland.*
Ich weiß, **dass** er in der Schweiz **wohnt.**	*I know **that** he lives in Switzerland.*
Die alte Frau hat kein Geld.	*The old woman has no money.*
Karl sagt, **dass** die alte Frau kein Geld **hat.**	*Karl says **that** the old woman has no money.*
Sie ist müde.	*She is tired.*
Sie legt sich hin, **weil** sie müde **ist.**	*She lies down, **because** she is tired.*
Er hat eine gute Stimme.	*He has a good voice.*
Er singt gern, **weil** er eine gute Stimme **hat.**	*He likes to sing, **because** he has a good voice.*

ÜBUNG 11·7

Complete each sentence with the given phrase.

FOR EXAMPLE: Ich weiß, dass _____.

Er ist krank.

_____ *Ich weiß, dass er krank ist.* _____

Ich weiß, dass _____.

1. Du kauftest einen neuen VW.

   _____

2. Meine Eltern wohnten viele Jahre im Ausland. (*My parents lived abroad for many years.*)

   _____

3. Frau Keller besuchte deinen Bruder.

   _____

4. Ihr Sohn schwimmt sehr gut.

   _____

5. Er spielt sehr schlecht Klavier. (*He plays the piano very badly.*)

   _____

Meine Tante wohnt in Berlin, weil _____.

6. Ihre Tochter wohnt da. (*Her daughter lives there.*)

   _____

7. Ihr Mann arbeitet in der Hauptstadt. (*Her husband works in the capital.*)

   _____

8. Sie hat da eine große Wohnung. (*She has a large apartment there.*)

   _____

9. Wohnungen in Berlin sind billig. (*Apartments in Berlin are cheap.*)

_____

10. Sie geht gern ins Theater. (*She likes going to the theater.*)

_____

ÜBUNG
11·8

Circle the letter of the word or phrase that best completes each sentence.

1. Mein Onkel _____ das Klavier.
   a. lebte
   b. kaufen
   c. spielte
   d. verkauftet

2. _____ machte die Fenster zu.
   a. Die Männer
   b. Niemand
   c. Seine Töchter
   d. Du

3. Mein Sohn wohnt in Bonn, _____ meine Tochter wohnt in Heidelberg.
   a. und
   b. wer
   c. dass
   d. wen

4. _____ fahren wir in die Schweiz.
   a. Weil
   b. Sie
   c. Heute
   d. Was

5. Im _____ schwimmen wir gern.
   a. Hauptstadt
   b. Thomas und ich
   c. Straße
   d. Sommer

6. Wir wissen, _____ Herr Schmidt Frau Benz gern hat.
   a. denn
   b. oder
   c. dass
   d. wessen

7. Was _____ der Mann?
   a. erzählte
   b. verstehst
   c. bekommen
   d. zumachen

8. Sie bleibt zu Hause, _____ sie ist sehr krank.
   a. weil
   b. dass
   c. wann
   d. denn

9. _____ feierten wir meinen Geburtstag.
   a. Gestern
   b. Aber
   c. Morgen
   d. Meine Eltern

10. Was _____ ihr?
    a. antwortetet
    b. verkauftest
    c. lernte
    d. besuchten

Indirect objects and the dative case

You have already discovered that direct objects in German take the accusative case. Indirect objects, however, take the dative case. An indirect object is usually a person or other living thing and is the object in a sentence *to whom* or *for whom* something is done. Let's look at some examples in English:

> *John gives Mary a book. (To whom does John give a book?)*
> → *Mary is the indirect object.*

> *We buy the children some ice cream. (For whom do we buy some ice cream?)*
> → **The children** *are the indirect object.*

It works the same way in German:

> Johann gibt **seiner Frau** ein Buch.   *Johann gives **his wife** a book.*
> **Wem** gibt er ein Buch?   ***To whom** does he give a book?*
> → **seiner Frau** *is the indirect object.*

> Ich kaufe **den Kindern** neue Schuhe.   *I buy **the children** new shoes.*
> **Wem** kaufe ich neue Schuhe?   ***For whom** do I buy new shoes?*
> → **den Kindern** *is the indirect object.*

Indirect objects in German are in the dative case. The dative case declension requires the following endings:

MASCULINE	FEMININE	NEUTER	PLURAL
dem Mann	der Frau	dem Kind	den Kindern
einem Lehrer	einer Lehrerin	einem Mädchen	keinen Lehrern
diesem Arzt	dieser Ärztin	diesem Kind	diesen Frauen

Notice that the dative plural noun has an **-n** ending.

Rewrite each of the following phrases in the dative case.

1. der Rechtsanwalt _____

2. die Dame _____

3. das Kind _____

4. die Leute (*people*) _____

5. keine Krankenschwester _____

6. diese Mädchen _____

7. ein Schüler _____

8. meine Brüder _____

9. unsere Freundin _____

10. eure Eltern _____

ÜBUNG

12·2

Rewrite each sentence with the phrase provided. Note each phrase will be the indirect object of the sentence.

Ich schicke _____ einen Brief.

1. mein Vater _____

2. diese Dame _____

3. unser Professor _____

4. ihre Freunde _____

5. deine Mutter _____

Wir schenkten _____ einen Computer. (*We gave . . . a computer.*)

6. unsere Töchter _____

7. seine Tante _____

8. das Mädchen _____

9. der Zahnarzt _____

10. ihr Onkel _____

Was geben Sie _____?

11. Ihre Frau _____

12. seine Kinder _____

13. diese Sportler _____

14. die Tänzerin _____

15. die Schauspieler _____

Some masculine nouns require an additional **-n** or **-en** ending in the accusative and dative cases. They are certain old German words and foreign words with the accent on the final syllable. In addition, masculine words that end in **-e** also have this ending.

nom	der Herr	der Mensch	der Diplomat	der Junge
acc	den Herrn	den Menschen	den Diplomaten	den Jungen
dat	dem Herrn	dem Menschen	dem Diplomaten	dem Jungen

Just as pronouns have an accusative form, they also have a dative declension.

NOMINATIVE	ACCUSATIVE	DATIVE
ich	mich	mir
du	dich	dir
er	ihn	ihm
sie (*sing.*)	sie (*sing.*)	ihr
es	es	ihm
wir	uns	uns
ihr	euch	euch
Sie	Sie	Ihnen
sie (*pl.*)	sie (*pl.*)	ihnen
wer	wen	wem

ÜBUNG
12·3

Rewrite each sentence with the pronoun or noun provided. Note that each pronoun or noun will be the indirect object of the sentence.

Ich gebe es _____.

1. du _____

2. er _____

3. sie (*sing.*) _____

4. der Löwe (*lion*) _____

5. mein Student _____

Niemand sendet _____ ein Geschenk. (*No one sends . . . a gift.*)

6. ich _____

7. wir _____

8. ihr _____

9. dieser Herr _____

10. der Soldat (*soldier*) _____

Diese Frau kaufte _____ eine Zeitschrift. (*This woman bought . . . a magazine.*)

11. Sie _____

12. sie (*pl.*) _____

13. dieser Schauspieler _____

14. diese Schauspielerin _____

15. ich _____

The same dative declension is required in prepositional phrases that are introduced by a dative preposition. The dative prepositions are as follows:

aus	*out, from*
außer	*except for, apart from*
bei	*by, near, at (the home)*
gegenüber	*opposite, across from*
mit	*with*
nach	*after, to a region*
seit	*since*
von	*from, of*
zu	*to, to (someone's home)*

Let's look at the dative prepositions as they are used in phrases.

aus der Flasche	*out of the bottle*
außer mir	*except for me*
bei meinen Eltern	*at my parents' house*
dem Rathaus gegenüber	*opposite the town hall*
mit Ihnen	*with you*
nach dem Konzert	*after the concert*
seit dem Krieg	*since the war*
von meinem Freund	*from my friend*
zu uns	*to our house*

If a pronoun refers to an inanimate object, it cannot be used as the object of a dative preposition. Instead, a prepositional adverb with **da-** or **dar-** is formed. **Dar-** precedes the prepositions that start with a vowel. To use prepositional adverbs in questions, use the prefixes **wo-** and **wor-**. For example:

von der Schule	davon	*from it*	wovon?
mit dem Auto	damit	*with it*	womit?
aus dem Fenster	daraus	*out of it*	woraus?

However, **gegenüber** does not form a prepositional adverb and follows pronouns. It can either precede or follow nouns. For example:

ihm gegenüber	*opposite him*
gegenüber dem Park	*opposite the park*
dem Park gegenüber	*opposite the park*

Rewrite each sentence with the pronoun or noun provided.

Wir sprechen mit _____.

1. der Polizist _____

2. ein Gärtner (*gardener*) _____

3. sie (*pl.*) _____

Doktor Schneider ist heute bei _____.

4. sie (*sing.*) _____

5. wir _____

6. sein Sohn _____

Das ist ein Geschenk von _____.

7. er _____

8. ich _____

9. ein Matrose (*sailor*) _____

Kommst du nach _____ zu mir?

10. das Konzert _____

11. die Oper (*opera*) _____

12. ihre Vorlesungen (*lectures*) _____

Die Kinder laufen zu _____.

13. der Stadtpark (*city park*) _____

14. die Schule _____

15. du _____

Rewrite each prepositional phrase after changing the noun object to a pronoun.

1. von einem Freund _____

2. mit diesem Buch _____

3. bei deiner Freundin _____

4. gegenüber einem Soldaten _____

5. aus der Schule _____

6. nach der Oper _____

7. zu der Tür _____

8. zu den Gästen _____

9. außer diesem Studenten _____

10. mit Herrn Keller _____

There is a group of verbs called *dative verbs*. The object of such verbs must be in the dative case. The English translation of sentences with dative verbs makes the object of these verbs appear to be direct objects. But in German they are not in the accusative case. Here is a list of some commonly used dative verbs:

begegnen	*meet, encounter*
danken	*thank*
dienen	*serve*
drohen	*threaten*
folgen	*follow*
gefallen	*like, please*
gehören	*belong to*
glauben	*believe*
helfen	*help*
imponieren	*impress*
raten	*advise*
schaden	*harm*
vertrauen	*trust*

In sentences they look like this.

Ich **glaube** dir nicht.	*I do not **believe** you.*
Wir **danken** den Gästen.	*We **thank** the guests.*
Das **imponierte** uns.	*That **impressed** us.*

ÜBUNG

12·6

Rewrite each sentence with the pronoun or noun provided.

Die Jungen helfen _____ damit.

1. die Frauen _____

2. ich _____

3. wir _____

4. ihre Freunde _____

5. sie (*pl.*) _____

Ich danke _____ dafür.

6. du _____

7. er _____

8. Sie _____

9. meine Freundin _____

10. der Matrose _____

Wo begegneten Sie _____?

11. die Diplomaten _____

12. sie (*sing.*) _____

13. mein Freund _____

14. sie (*pl.*) _____

15. seine Großmutter _____

ÜBUNG
12·7

Circle the letter of the word or phrase that best completes each sentence.

1. Ich _____ ihm nicht.
   a. sehe
   b. versuche
   c. vertraue
   d. erwarte

2. Thomas gibt _____ eine Blume.
   a. ihr
   b. dich
   c. ihn
   d. Sie

3. Die Kinder spielen _____.
   a. damit
   b. Ihnen
   c. außer
   d. seit

4. Die Kirche ist dem Rathaus _____.
   a. gegenüber
   b. bei
   c. davon
   d. womit

5. Er _____ uns ein neues Fahrrad.
   a. besucht
   b. imponiert
   c. erzählte
   d. kaufte

6. Mein Onkel schickte _____ einen Brief.
   a. ihn
   b. sie
   c. euer
   d. mir

7. Die Jungen laufen aus _____ Schule.
   a. diese
   b. einem
   c. der
   d. ihren

8. Warum _____ du mir nicht?
   a. findest
   b. machst
   c. sendest
   d. glaubst

9. Nach _____ Konzert fahren wir nach Hause.
   a. der
   b. diesen
   c. diese
   d. dem

10. Meine Schwester tanzt mit _____.
    a. einem Soldaten
    b. es
    c. dieser Kirche
    d. der Löwe

Irregular verbs in the past tense

Verbs that follow a consistent pattern in forming the past tense use the regular past tense ending **-te**. But many verbs do not conform to this pattern. They form their past tense in irregular ways. This also occurs in English. For example:

REGULAR PAST TENSE	IRREGULAR PAST TENSE
talk → talked	come → came
like → liked	see → saw
miss → missed	go → went

German is similar to English in that it usually forms the irregular past tense by a vowel change rather than with a past tense suffix. The vowels **e**, **o**, **u**, **i**, and **ie** in the verb stem often change to the vowel **a** to form the past tense. For example:

INFINITIVE	PRESENT TENSE	PAST TENSE
beginnen	er beginnt	begann
bitten	er bittet	bat
essen	er isst	aß
finden	er findet	fand
geben	er gibt	gab
helfen	er hilft	half
kommen	er kommt	kam
lesen	er liest	las
liegen	er liegt	lag
nehmen	er nimmt	nahm
schwimmen	er schwimmt	schwamm
sehen	er sieht	sah
singen	er singt	sang
sitzen	er sitzt	saß
sprechen	er spricht	sprach
stehen	er steht	stand
treffen	er trifft	traf
trinken	er trinkt	trank
tun	er tut	tat

Other vowel changes can also occur in the irregular past tense.

INFINITIVE	PRESENT TENSE	PAST TENSE
beißen	er beißt	biss
bleiben	er bleibt	blieb
einladen	er lädt ein	lud ein
fahren	er fährt	fuhr
fallen	er fällt	fiel
fangen	er fängt	fing

INFINITIVE	PRESENT TENSE	PAST TENSE
fliegen	er fliegt	flog
frieren	er friert	fror
gehen	er geht	ging
greifen	er greift	griff
halten	er hält	hielt
heißen	er heißt	hieß
lassen	er lässt	ließ
laufen	er läuft	lief
leihen	er leiht	lieh
lügen	er lügt	log
rufen	er ruft	rief
scheinen	er scheint	schien
schießen	er schießt	schoss
schlafen	er schläft	schlief
schlagen	er schlägt	schlug
schließen	er schließt	schloss
schreiben	er schreibt	schrieb
steigen	er steigt	stieg
tragen	er trägt	trug
wachsen	er wächst	wuchs
waschen	er wäscht	wusch
verlieren	er verliert	verlor
ziehen	er zieht	zog

Now let's look at the complete conjugation of the irregular past tense.

	geben (*give*)	**schreiben** (*write*)	**verlieren** (*lose*)
ich	gab	schrieb	verlor
du	gabst	schriebst	verlorst
er/sie/es	gab	schrieb	verlor
wir	gaben	schrieben	verloren
ihr	gabt	schriebt	verlort
Sie	gaben	schrieben	verloren
sie (*pl.*)	gaben	schrieben	verloren

Prefixes function with irregular verbs in the same way as they function with regular verbs in the present or past tense.

	abfahren (*depart*)	**beschreiben** (*describe*)
ich	fuhr ab	beschrieb
du	fuhrst ab	beschriebst
er/sie/es	fuhr ab	beschrieb
wir	fuhren ab	beschrieben
ihr	fuhrt ab	beschriebt
Sie	fuhren ab	beschrieben
sie (*pl.*)	fuhren ab	beschrieben

ÜBUNG

13·1

In the blank provided, write the past tense of the given verb with the subject provided.

1. laufen (*run*) er _____

2. kommen (*come*) du _____

3. gehen (*go*) wir _____

4. sprechen (*speak*) ich _____

5. versprechen (*promise*) sie (*sing.*) _____

6. trinken der Matrose _____

7. essen ihr _____

8. ziehen (*pull*) sie (*pl.*) _____

9. heißen die Tänzerin _____

10. singen Sie _____

11. waschen du _____

12. treffen er _____

13. lassen ich _____

14. bekommen sie (*sing.*) _____

15. annehmen (*accept*) wir _____

16. anrufen (*call, phone*) Sie _____

17. verstehen (*understand*) sein Bruder _____

18. tun (*do*) wir _____

19. helfen du _____

20. schlafen er _____

21. aussteigen (*get off, alight*) ich _____

22. anfangen (*start*) sie (*pl.*) _____

23. scheinen (*seem*) es _____

24. erfinden (*invent*) ihr _____

25. sitzen niemand _____

ÜBUNG
13·2

Write the full conjugation of each verb with the subjects provided.

	1. halten	2. fallen
ich	_____	_____
du	_____	_____
er	_____	_____
wir	_____	_____

ihr	_____	_____
Sie	_____	_____
man	_____	_____

	3. schließen (*close*)	4. begreifen (*understand, grasp*)
ich	_____	_____
du	_____	_____
er	_____	_____
wir	_____	_____
ihr	_____	_____
Sie	_____	_____
wer	_____	_____

	5. ausgeben (*spend*)	6. fliegen (*fly*)
ich	_____	_____
du	_____	_____
er	_____	_____
wir	_____	_____
ihr	_____	_____
Sie	_____	_____
Tina	_____	_____

Three important verbs that are irregular in the present tense are also irregular in the past tense. Let's look at their conjugations:

	haben	**sein**	**werden**
ich	hatte	war	wurde
du	hattest	warst	wurdest
er/sie/es	hatte	war	wurde
wir	hatten	waren	wurden
ihr	hattet	wart	wurdet
Sie	hatten	waren	wurden
sie (*pl.*)	hatten	waren	wurden

You have probably noticed that the first-person and second-person singular past tense endings are always identical. This is true of both regular and irregular verbs.

ich lachte	ich suchte	ich sprach	ich lief
er lachte	er suchte	er sprach	er lief

Write the full conjugation of each verb with the subjects provided.

	1. haben	2. sein
ich	_____	_____
du	_____	_____
er	_____	_____
wir	_____	_____
ihr	_____	_____
Sie	_____	_____
man	_____	_____

	3. werden
ich	_____
du	_____
er	_____
wir	_____
ihr	_____
Sie	_____
wer	_____

A small group of verbs have a vowel change in the past tense. But they also have a **-te** past tense suffix. Such verbs are called *mixed*. These verbs are:

INFINITIVE	PAST TENSE	
brennen	er brannte	*burn*
bringen	er brachte	*bring*
denken	er dachte	*think*
kennen	er kannte	*know, be acquainted*
nennen	er nannte	*name*
rennen	er rannte	*run*
senden	er sandte	*send*
wenden	er wandte	*turn*
wissen	er wusste	*know, have knowledge*

The same past tense endings that are used in the regular past tense are used with this group of verbs. For example:

ich	brannte
du	branntest
er/sie/es	brannte
wir	brannten

ihr	branntet
Sie	brannten
sie (*pl.*)	brannten

ÜBUNG
13·4

In the blank provided, write the past tense of the verb in parentheses with the subject provided.

1. (kennen) er _____

2. (denken) du _____

3. (wissen) ich _____

4. (bringen) sie (*pl.*) _____

5. (nennen) Sie _____

6. (rennen) sie (*sing.*) _____

7. (wenden) wir _____

8. (senden) ihr _____

9. (brennen) du _____

10. (wissen) Sie _____

ÜBUNG
13·5

Write the full conjugation of each verb with the subjects provided.

	1. kennen	2. denken
ich	_____	_____
du	_____	_____
er	_____	_____
wir	_____	_____
ihr	_____	_____
Sie	_____	_____
man	_____	_____

	3. wissen	4. bringen
ich	_____	_____
du	_____	_____

er	_____	_____
wir	_____	_____
ihr	_____	_____
Sie	_____	_____
wer	_____	_____

In the blank provided, write in the correct past tense conjugation of the verb in parentheses.

FOR EXAMPLE: Er _____ *sprach* _____ mit seinem Bruder. (sprechen)

1. Wir _____ ihn nicht. (kennen)

2. Er _____, dass sie krank war. (wissen)

3. _____ Sie keine Zeit? (haben)

4. Herr Walthers _____ reich. (sein)

5. Es _____ sehr kalt. (werden)

6. Sie _____ ihre Tochter Tina. (nennen)

7. Ich _____, dass Erik in Berlin war. (denken)

8. Sonja _____ ein Problem. (haben)

9. Mein Onkel _____ gesund. (werden)

10. _____ du zu Hause? (sein)

Rewrite each sentence in the past tense.

FOR EXAMPLE: Er ist in Berlin.

Er war in Berlin.
_____

1. Es wird um sieben Uhr dunkel.

_____

2. Er kommt ohne seine Frau.

_____

3. Die Kinder haben Durst.

_____

4. Was bringen Sie uns?

_____

5. Meine Eltern fahren zu alten Freunden.

_____

6. Ich weiß es nicht.

_____

7. Siehst du die Berge (*mountains*)?

_____

8. Das Wetter wird schlecht.

_____

9. Ich sende ihm eine Ansichtskarte (*postcard*).

_____

10. Der Junge steht um sechs Uhr auf.

_____

11. Kennt ihr diesen Herrn?

_____

12. Nennt sie ihren Namen (*name*)?

_____

13. Wo bist du?

_____

14. Ich rufe meine Freundin an.

_____

15. Lesen Sie eine Zeitschrift?

_____

Modal auxiliaries in the present and past tenses

The modal auxiliaries are a group of verbs that can act alone or together with other verbs. The modals are the auxiliary verbs, and the accompanying verbs are in infinitive form. Let's look at some examples of how modals function in English and change the meaning of a sentence.

Modal *can*	You *can* ride the bike.
Modal *may*	You *may* ride the bike.
Modal *must*	You *must* ride the bike.

The German modal auxiliaries function in the same way. They are:

dürfen	*may, be allowed to*
können	*can, be able to*
mögen	*may, might, like*
müssen	*must, have to*
sollen	*should, be supposed to*
wollen	*want*

These verbs follow a unique pattern in the present tense.

	dürfen	**können**	**mögen**
ich	darf	kann	mag
du	darfst	kannst	magst
er	darf	kann	mag
wir	dürfen	können	mögen
ihr	dürft	könnt	mögt
Sie	dürfen	können	mögen
sie (*pl.*)	dürfen	können	mögen

	müssen	**sollen**	**wollen**
ich	muss	soll	will
du	musst	sollst	willst
er	muss	soll	will
wir	müssen	sollen	wollen
ihr	müsst	sollt	wollt
Sie	müssen	sollen	wollen
sie (*pl.*)	müssen	sollen	wollen

On the lines provided, rewrite the sentence with the correct conjugation of the modal auxiliary for the subjects given.

Wir <u>wollen</u> zu Hause bleiben. (*We want to stay home.*)

1. Ich _____.

2. Du _____.

3. Er _____.

4. Sie _____.

Thomas <u>soll</u> ihr helfen. (*Thomas should help her.*)

5. Sie (*sing.*) _____.

6. Sie (*pl.*) _____.

7. Wir _____.

8. Ihr _____.

Ich <u>kann</u> den Brief nicht lesen. (*I cannot read the letter.*)

9. Du _____.

10. Wer _____?

11. Sie _____.

12. Ihr _____.

Sie <u>dürfen</u> die Bibliothek benutzen. (*You are allowed to use the library.*)

13. Ich _____.

14. Sie (*sing.*) _____.

15. Wir _____.

16. Die Studenten _____.

Er <u>muss</u> heute abend arbeiten. (*He has to work this evening.*)

17. Du _____.

18. Sie _____.

19. Ihr _____.

20. Niemand _____.

The modal auxiliary **mögen** has some special uses. It can be used alone to mean that someone likes to do something. For example:

Sie **mag** gern Eis.   *She likes ice cream.*

When used with an infinitive, **mögen** can mean *must*, but not in the sense of what someone is obliged to do but rather *what is the likely possibility*. It is most commonly used with the verb **sein**. For example:

Die Frau **mag** vierzig sein.   *The woman must be forty.*

With other verbs, its meaning is *may* or *be allowed to*.

Du **magst** gehen, wohin du willst.   *You may go wherever you want.*

ÜBUNG
14·2

*On the lines provided, rewrite the sentence with the correct conjugation of the modal auxiliary **mögen** for the subjects given.*

mögen gern Bier (*to like beer*)

1. Ich _____.

2. Du _____.

3. Er _____.

4. Wir _____.

5. Ihr _____.

6. Sie _____.

7. Sie (*pl.*) _____.

8. Die Männer _____.

mögen jünger sein (*must be younger*)

9. Ich _____.

10. Du _____.

11. Sie (*sing.*) _____.

12. Wir _____.

13. Ihr _____.

14. Sie _____.

15. Sie (*pl.*) _____.

16. Frau Keller _____.

The past tense of the modal auxiliaries resembles the regular past tense. However, if a modal has an umlaut in the infinitive, that umlaut is omitted in the past tense. For example:

	dürfen	können	mögen
ich	durfte	konnte	mochte
du	durftest	konntest	mochtest
er	durfte	konnte	mochte
wir	durften	konnten	mochten
ihr	durftet	konntet	mochtet
Sie	durften	konnten	mochten
sie (*pl.*)	durften	konnten	mochten

	müssen	sollen	wollen
ich	musste	sollte	wollte
du	musstest	solltest	wolltest
er	musste	sollte	wollte
wir	mussten	sollten	wollten
ihr	musstet	solltet	wolltet
Sie	mussten	sollten	wollten
sie (*pl.*)	mussten	sollten	wollten

ÜBUNG
14·3

Rewrite the present tense sentences in the past tense.

1. Du sollst fleißig (*diligently*) arbeiten.

_____

2. Wir müssen ihnen helfen.

_____

3. Ich will eine Reise durch Italien machen. (*I want to take a trip through Italy.*)

_____

4. Der Mann mag viel älter sein. (*The man must be much older.*)

_____

5. Der Ausländer (*foreigner*) kann es nicht verstehen.

_____

6. Sie dürfen nicht länger bleiben. (*You may not stay any longer.*)

_____

7. Wir sollen mehr Geld sparen. (*We should save more money.*)

_____

8. Du musst an deine Mutter schreiben. (*You have to write to your mother.*)

_____

9. Wollt ihr bei uns übernachten? (*Do you want to spend the night at our house?*)

_____

10. Können die Jungen kochen? (*Can the boys cook?*)

_____

The verb **mögen** has a special and very high-frequency usage in its subjunctive form. (The subjunctive is described in detail in Chapter 25.) It is the polite form used in place of *want*.

Ich **will** ein Glas Bier.	I **want** a glass of beer.
Ich **möchte** ein Glas Bier.	I **would like** a glass of beer.
Er **will** wissen, wo du wohnst.	He **wants** to know where you live.
Er **möchte** wissen, wo du wohnst.	He **would like** to know where you live.

This form of **mögen** can also be used with an accompanying infinitive. For example:

Möchten Sie eine Fahrkarte kaufen?	**Would** you **like** to buy a ticket?
Sie **möchte** etwas essen.	She **would like** something to eat.

ÜBUNG
14·4

*Rewrite each sentence by adding the correct form of **möchte**.*

FOR EXAMPLE: Er steht spät auf.

Er möchte spät aufstehen.

1. Ich besuche das Theater.

_____

2. Gehen Sie nach Hause?

_____

3. Er kauft neue Handschuhe.

_____

4. Frau Benz fragt den Polizisten.

_____

5. Niemand schreibt die Briefe.

_____

6. Trinkst du etwas?

_____

7. Wir frühstücken um neun Uhr. (*We have breakfast at nine o'clock.*)

_____

8. Fahrt ihr mit uns?

_____

9. Sie liest die neue Zeitung.

_____

10. Ich steige hier aus.

_____

Six other verbs—**lassen, sehen, hören, helfen, lernen, gehen**—function in a similar way to modal auxiliaries. They have a basic meaning and can stand alone in a sentence. But they can also be used with an accompanying infinitive. For example:

Er **lässt** seinen Wagen waschen.	*He **gets** his car washed.*
Wir **sahen** die Kinder spielen.	*We **saw** the children playing.*
Hörst du die Mädchen singen?	*Do you **hear** the girls singing?*
Ich **half** ihr den Koffer tragen.	*I **helped** her carry the suitcase.*
Er **lernte** seine Mutter verstehen.	*He **learned** to understand his mother.*
Sie **gehen** heute schwimmen.	*They **go** swimming today.*

Just like the modals, these verbs can be used in either the present tense or past tense as just illustrated.

ÜBUNG
14·5

If the sentence is in the present tense, rewrite it in the past tense. If it is in the past, rewrite it in the present.

1. Sie lässt ein neues Kleid machen. (*She has a new dress made.*)

_____

2. Er half seinem Vater kochen.

_____

3. Der Hund hört zwei Männer kommen.

_____

4. Gehst du um elf Uhr spazieren? (*Are you going for a walk at eleven?*)

_____

5. Ich sah sie im Garten arbeiten.

_____

6. Die Schüler lernen lesen und schreiben.

_____

7. Sie gingen am Montag radfahren. (*They went biking on Monday.*)

   _____

8. Wir ließen das alte Fahrrad reparieren. (*We had the old bike repaired.*)

   _____

9. Niemand hilft uns die Sätze übersetzen. (*No one helped us translate the sentences.*)

   _____

10. Hörtet ihr ihn pfeifen? (*Did you hear him whistling?*)

   _____

ÜBUNG
14·6

Add the provided subject and verb to the sentence, and make any necessary changes. Retain the tense of the original verb.

FOR EXAMPLE: Die Kinder schlafen.   er, sehen

   Er sieht die Kinder schlafen.

1. Seine Freunde flüstern vor der Tür.   Erik, hören

   _____

2. Erik bereitete das Frühstück vor. (*Erik prepared breakfast.*)   wir, helfen

   _____

3. Thomas trägt große Pakete. (*Thomas is carrying large packages.*)   ihr, sehen.

   _____

4. Sie sprachen Deutsch.   ich, hören

   _____

5. Frau Bauer macht die Küche sauber. (*Ms. Bauer cleans up the kitchen.*)   er, helfen

   _____

Circle the letter of the word or phrase that best completes each sentence.

1. Niemand _____ uns damit helfen.
   a. lässt
   b. wollten
   c. kann
   d. durftet

2. Wolltest _____ in der Hauptstadt arbeiten?
   a. mein Freund
   b. meine Freunde
   c. ihr
   d. du

3. Ich _____ die kleine Uhr reparieren.
   a. ließ
   b. wollten
   c. könnt
   d. sollt

4. Wir hörten die Kinder _____.
   a. kamen
   b. müssen
   c. arbeiteten
   d. singen

5. Der alte Hund _____ einen jungen Mann kommen.
   a. lässt
   b. will
   c. sieht
   d. konnte

6. Gestern _____ ich meinen Sohn vom Rathaus abholen.
   a. kann
   b. soll
   c. helfe
   d. musste

7. Was _____ Sie gern trinken?
   a. mögen
   b. sehen
   c. wollte
   d. hören

8. Wo _____ er das Hemd machen?
   a. ließ
   b. könnt
   c. möchten
   d. lerntet

9. Möchte _____ mich morgen besuchen?
   a. ihr
   b. ihn
   c. wir
   d. sie

10. Ich will im Juni ins Ausland _____.
    a. lassen
    b. reisen
    c. bekommen
    d. lernen

The accusative-dative prepositions

You have already had experience with the accusative prepositions (**bis**, **durch**, **für**, **gegen**, **ohne**, **wider**, **um**) and the dative prepositions (**aus**, **außer**, **bei**, **gegenüber**, **mit**, **nach**, **seit**, **von**, **zu**). Another category of prepositions can require either the accusative case or the dative case. These prepositions are:

an	*at*
auf	*on, onto*
hinter	*behind*
in	*in, into*
neben	*next to*
über	*over*
unter	*under, among*
vor	*before, in front of*
zwischen	*between*

Choosing the correct case is quite simple. If the preposition indicates a motion to a place, use the accusative. If the preposition indicates a location, use the dative. For example:

Er läuft **an** die Tür. (*acc.*)	*He runs **to** the door.*
Er steht **an** der Tür. (*dat.*)	*He stands **at** the door.*
Ich gehe **in** die Bibliothek. (*acc.*)	*I go **into** the library.*
Ich lese **in** der Bibliothek. (*dat.*)	*I read **in** the library.*
Er setzt sich **zwischen** die Kinder.	*He sits down **between** the children.*
Er sitzt **zwischen** den Kindern.	*He sits **between** the children.*

The signal to use the accusative case is most often a *verb of motion*. This kind of verb indicates that someone or something is moving from one place to another. Typical verbs of motion are:

fahren	*drive, travel*
fliegen	*fly*
gehen	*go*
kommen	*come*
laufen	*run*
legen	*lay*
reisen	*travel*
rennen	*run*
setzen	*set*
stellen	*place*

The signal to use the dative case with these prepositions is a verb that indicates a stationary position or a locale where the action is being carried out. Such verbs include:

arbeiten	*work*
bleiben	*remain, stay*
kaufen	*buy*
liegen	*lie*
schlafen	*sleep*
sitzen	*sit*
stehen	*stand*
verkaufen	*sell*
warten	*wait*

In the blank provided, complete each sentence with the correct form of words in parentheses.

FOR EXAMPLE: (die Bank) Er wartet vor _____ *der Bank.* _____

Er stellte sein Fahrrad hinter _____.

1. (das Haus) _____

2. (die Tür) _____

3. (die Bäume [*trees*]) _____

4. (die Garage [*garage*]) _____

5. (der Laden [*shop*]) _____

Der Matrose will neben _____ sitzen.

6. (dieses Mädchen) _____

7. (unsere Eltern) _____

8. (seine Freundin) _____

9. (ein Schulkamerad [*school friend*]) _____

10. (der Fernsehapparat [*television set*]) _____

Geht ihr in _____?

11. (der Keller [*cellar*]) _____

12. (die Kirche) _____

13. (das Restaurant) _____

14. (die Garage) _____

15. (dieser Laden) _____

Der alte Hund wollte auf _____ schlafen.

16. (unser Bett) _____

17. (das Sofa) _____

18. (eine Decke [*blanket*]) _____

19. (diese Kissen [*pillows*]) _____

20. (der Boden [*floor*]) _____

Wir hängen sein Bild über _____. *We hang his picture over . . .*

21. (das Klavier) _____

22. (der Tisch) _____

23. (der Schrank [*cabinet*]) _____

24. (die Stühle [*chairs*]) _____

25. (das Sofa) _____

Some verbs are not clear signals as to whether *motion* or *location* is indicated. Study the following two lists, which contain verbs that are followed by accusative-dative prepositions, but use only one of those cases.

Accusative

sich beklagen über	*complain about*
denken an	*think about*
sich erinnern an	*remember*
sich freuen auf	*look forward to*
sich freuen über	*be glad about*
glauben an	*believe in*
reden über	*talk about*
schreiben an	*write to*
schreiben über	*write about*
sprechen über	*speak about*
sich verlieben in	*fall in love with*
warten auf	*wait for*

Dative

erkennen an	*recognize by*
leiden an	*suffer from*
schützen vor	*protect from*
sterben an	*die from*
teilnehmen an	*take part in*
warnen vor	*warn against*

Some prepositions tend to form a contraction with the definite article that follows. For example:

an das	→	ans
an dem	→	am
auf das	→	aufs
bei dem	→	beim
für das	→	fürs
in das	→	ins
in dem	→	im
um das	→	ums
von dem	→	vom
zu dem	→	zum
zu der	→	zur

Although the preposition followed by a definite article is a correct form, it is more common to hear it used in its contracted form.

CORRECT		MORE COMMON
an dem Tor	*at the gate*	am Tor
in dem Garten	*in the garden*	im Garten

Rewrite the following prepositional phrases in their contracted form wherever possible.

1. auf dem Sofa _____

2. in der Schule _____

3. an dem Theater _____

4. in dem Wasser (*water*) _____

5. vor der Tür _____

6. an dem Fluss (*river*) _____

7. auf das Bett _____

8. in das Rathaus _____

9. an dem Bahnhof (*train station*) _____

10. auf den Stühlen _____

You have already used these contractions in expressions that tell *on what day* (**am Montag**), *in what month* (**im Oktober**), or *in what season* (**im Sommer**). But they are also used to tell *in what year* and *on what date*. For example:

Er ist **im** Jahre 1955 geboren.	*He was born **in** 1955.*
Im Jahre 1776 war die Revolution.	*The revolution was **in** 1776.*
Sie ist **am** achten Mai gestorben.	*She died **on** the eighth of May.*
Die Party war **am** zehnten Juni.	*The party was **on** the tenth of June.*

It is common to say *in what year* something occurred and omit the prepositional phrase **im Jahre: Er ist 1955 geboren.**

In order to say on what date something occurred, you have to know the *ordinal numbers*. You have already encountered the *cardinal numbers* (**eins, zwei, elf, zwanzig**). The ordinal numbers are the adjectival form of the cardinal numbers. From one to nineteen, the ordinal numbers add the suffix **-te**. Note the three irregular forms (in bold) in the following examples:

erste	*first*
zweite	*second*
dritte	*third*
vierte	*fourth*
fünfte	*fifth*
sechste	*sixth*

siebte	*seventh*
elfte	*eleventh*
siebzehnte	*seventeenth*
neunzehnte	*nineteenth*

Beginning with twenty, the ordinal numbers use the suffix **-ste**.

zwanzigste	*twentieth*
einundzwanzigste	*twenty-first*
dreißigste	*thirtieth*
vierunddreißigste	*thirty-fourth*
hunderste	*hundredth*
tausendste	*thousandth*

When giving a date on the calendar, the preposition **an** is used in the dative case. This requires an **-n** ending on the ordinal number.

am ersten September	**on** *the first of September*
am neunten Dezember	**on** *the ninth of December*
am einunddreißigsten Oktober	**on** *the thirty-first of October*

When dates are given numerically in German, the day precedes the month. For example:

6/3 am sechsten März	*3/6 on the sixth of March*

ÜBUNG

15·3

In the blank provided, write out the year in which something occurred or the date on which something occurred. Use the numerical information provided in parentheses.

FOR EXAMPLE: (1990) Er ist _____ *im Jahre 1990* _____ geboren.

(8/12) Er ist _____ *am achten Dezember* _____ geboren.

1. (1892) Sie ist _____ gestorben.

2. (2003) Das Kind ist _____ geboren.

3. (1945) Der Krieg endete _____.

4. (2010) Er kam nach Berlin _____.

5. (1917) Die Revolution begann _____.

6. (5/9) Seine Frau ist _____ gestorben.

7. (1/1) Sie wurde _____ sehr krank.

8. (23/7) Mein Geburtstag ist _____.

9. (25/12) Weihnachten ist _____.

10. (3/11) Ich fuhr _____ nach Hamburg ab.

Just as with other prepositions, the accusative-dative prepositions can form prepositional adverbs when the pronoun is a replacement for an inanimate object. For example:

Ich warte **auf** Herrn Keller.	*I am waiting for Mr. Keller.*
Ich warte **auf** ihn.	*I am waiting for him.*
Ich warte **auf** den Zug.	*I am waiting for the train.*
Ich warte **darauf**.	*I am waiting for it.*

The prepositional adverbs formed with the accusative-dative prepositions are:

an	daran	woran?
auf	darauf	worauf?
hinter	dahinter	wohinter?
in	darin	worin?
neben	daneben	woneben?
über	darüber	worüber?
unter	darunter	worunter?
vor	davor	wovor?
zwischen	dazwischen	N/A

However, a prepositional adverb with **da-** is not formed when there is motion into a place. Instead, the word **dahin** or **dorthin** (*to there*) is used. Location in that place is shown by **da** or **dort**. Also, a prepositional adverb with **wo-** is not formed when asking about motion to a place or location at a place. Instead ask **wohin** about motion to a place and **wo** about location at a place. For example:

in die Bibliothek	*into the library*	dahin	*to that place*	Wohin?	*Where to?*
in der Bibliothek	*in the library*	da	*there*	Wo?	*Where?*

ÜBUNG
15·4

Rewrite the underlined prepositional phrase with the pronoun replacement for the noun. In the second blank, write the form needed to ask a question.

FOR EXAMPLE: (animate) Wir warten <u>auf meinen Sohn</u>.

<u>   *auf ihn*   </u>   <u>   *auf wen*   </u>

(inanimate) Wir warten <u>auf den Bus</u>.

<u>   *darauf*   </u>   <u>   *worauf*   </u>

1. Wir fliegen <u>über den See</u> (*lake*).

2. Ich denke oft <u>an meinen Bruder</u>.

3. Martin steht <u>vor dem Fenster</u>.

4. Wir sprachen <u>über seine Töchter</u>.

5. Ich erkannte ihn an seinem Schnurrbart (*moustache*).

   _____   _____

6. Die Katze schläft in einer Schublade (*drawer*).

   _____   _____

7. Tina ist müde und schläft auf meinem Bett.

   _____   _____

8. Wir warteten auf den jungen Diplomaten.

   _____   _____

9. Die Studenten liefen in die Kirche.

   _____   _____

10. Erik steht zwischen Herrn Bauer und Frau Keller.

    _____   _____

11. Ein großes Bild hängt über dem Klavier.

    _____   _____

12. Er setzte sich neben seinen Sohn.

    _____   _____

13. Sie fahren vor einen Laden.

    _____   _____

14. Ich freue mich sehr über dieses Geschenk.

    _____   _____

15. Wir glauben an Freiheit und Frieden (*freedom and peace*).

    _____   _____

Regular verbs in the present perfect tense and more imperatives

Regular present perfect tense

The German present perfect tense is the preferred tense for expressing ideas that have taken place in the past. The simple past tense is more commonly used in narratives. The present perfect tense consists of the conjugation of an auxiliary (**haben** or **sein**) followed by a past participle.

A regular past participle is formed by adding the prefix **ge-** and the suffix -**t** to the stem of a verb. For example:

INFINITIVE	STEM	PAST PARTICIPLE
machen	mach	gemacht
suchen	such	gesucht
danken	dank	gedankt

When conjugated in the present perfect tense, these verbs look like the following:

	machen	**suchen**	**danken**
ich	habe gemacht	habe gesucht	habe gedankt
du	hast gemacht	hast gesucht	hast gedankt
er/sie/es	hat gemacht	hat gesucht	hat gedankt
wir	haben gemacht	haben gesucht	haben gedankt
ihr	habt gemacht	habt gesucht	habt gedankt
Sie	haben gemacht	haben gesucht	haben gedankt
sie (*pl.*)	haben gemacht	haben gesucht	haben gedankt

Such conjugations can be translated as the English present perfect tense or simple past tense. For example:

ich habe gemacht	*I have made/I made*
er hat gesucht	*he has sought/he sought*
wir haben gedankt	*we have thanked/we thanked*

ÜBUNG
16·1

In the blank provided, write the past participle for each verb.

1. lernen _____

2. kaufen _____

3. sagen _____

4. fragen _____

5. tanzen _____

6. decken (*cover, set the table*) _____

7. spielen _____

8. stören (*disturb*) _____

9. packen (*pack*) _____

10. putzen (*clean, polish*) _____

11. hören _____

12. brauchen _____

13. wünschen (*wish*) _____

14. wohnen _____

15. leben _____

16. lachen _____

17. weinen (*cry*) _____

18. holen (*get, fetch*) _____

19. kochen _____

20. stellen _____

21. legen _____

22. setzen _____

23. wecken (*waken*) _____

24. reisen _____

25. pflanzen _____

If the verb stem ends in **-d**, **-n**, or **-t**, an **e** is added to the suffix **-t**: **baden—gebadet, öffnen—geöffnet, kosten—gekostet**.

Write the full present perfect tense conjugation of each verb with the subjects provided.

	1. enden	2. warten
ich	_____	_____
du	_____	_____
er	_____	_____
wir	_____	_____
ihr	_____	_____
Sie	_____	_____
man	_____	_____

	3. antworten	4. lieben
ich	_____	_____
du	_____	_____
er	_____	_____
wir	_____	_____
ihr	_____	_____
Sie	_____	_____
wer	_____	_____

	5. zeigen (*show*)	6. schicken
ich	_____	_____
du	_____	_____
er	_____	_____
wir	_____	_____
ihr	_____	_____
Sie	_____	_____
Erik	_____	_____

If the infinitive of a verb ends in **-ieren**, its past participle does not require the **ge-** prefix. For example:

reparieren	→	er hat repariert
fotografieren	→	er hat fotografiert
studieren	→	er hat studiert

Here is a list of commonly used verbs that end in -**ieren**.

sich amüsieren	*amuse oneself*
demonstrieren	*demonstrate*
existieren	*exist*
funktionieren	*function*
informieren	*inform*
sich interessieren	*be interested*
korrigieren	*correct*
marschieren	*march*
operieren	*operate*
passieren	*happen*
probieren	*try, taste*
regieren	*rule*
servieren	*serve*
telefonieren	*telephone*

Write the full present perfect tense conjugation of each verb with the subjects provided.

1. demonstrieren   2. korrigieren

ich _____   _____

du _____   _____

er _____   _____

wir _____   _____

ihr _____   _____

Sie _____   _____

man _____   _____

3. probieren   4. studieren

ich _____   _____

du _____   _____

er _____   _____

wir _____   _____

ihr _____   _____

Sie _____   _____

wer _____   _____

Prefixes have an effect on how a past participle is formed. If the prefix is separable, it is placed directly in front of the participial prefix **ge-**: <u>zu</u>gemacht, <u>auf</u>gepasst, <u>ab</u>geholt. If the prefix is inseparable, it replaces the participial prefix **ge-**: <u>be</u>sucht, <u>ver</u>kauft, <u>er</u>wartet.

ÜBUNG
16·4

Write the full present perfect tense conjugation of each verb with the subjects provided.

	1. aufmachen	2. einkaufen
ich	_____	_____
du	_____	_____
er	_____	_____
wir	_____	_____
ihr	_____	_____
Sie	_____	_____
man	_____	_____

	3. bestellen	4. zerstören (*destroy*)
ich	_____	_____
du	_____	_____
er	_____	_____
wir	_____	_____
ihr	_____	_____
Sie	_____	_____
wer	_____	_____

It was stated previously that there are two auxiliaries for the German present perfect tense—**haben** and **sein**. If a verb is transitive (i.e., if it takes a direct object), its auxiliary will be **haben**. If a verb is intransitive (i.e., if it is a verb of motion or shows a radical change), its auxiliary will be **sein**.

Look at the following example sentences with the direct object in bold. Notice that in the present perfect tense the auxiliary used is **haben**.

Er hat **ein Buch** gekauft.	*He bought **a book**.*
Wir haben **die Tür** zugemacht.	*We closed **the door**.*
Ich habe **Schach** gespielt.	*I played **chess**.*

Note that a sentence may have a transitive verb without stating a direct object. For example:

Wir haben im Park gespielt.	*We played in the park.*
Sie haben im Garten gearbeitet.	*They worked in the garden.*

Among regular verbs only a few take **sein** as their auxiliary. Four such verbs are **eilen** (*hurry*), **folgen**, **marschieren**, and **reisen**. Look how this auxiliary functions in the present perfect tense, and take note that **sein** in this tense is translated as *have/has* just like **haben**.

	eilen	folgen
ich	bin geeilt (*have hurried*)	bin gefolgt (*have followed*)
du	bist geeilt	bist gefolgt
er/sie/es	ist geeilt	ist gefolgt
wir	sind geeilt	sind gefolgt
ihr	seid geeilt	seid gefolgt
Sie	sind geeilt	sind gefolgt
sie (*pl.*)	sind geeilt	sind gefolgt

You have probably noticed that the past participle is the last element in a sentence, in which the verb is in the present perfect tense.

Die Kinder haben mit dem Hund **gespielt**.
Wir sind nach Hause **geeilt**.

ÜBUNG
16·5

Write the full present perfect tense conjugation of the verb in each given phrase, using the subjects provided.

Marschieren durch die Stadt

1. Ich _____.

2. Du _____.

3. Er _____.

4. Wir _____.

5. Ihr _____.

6. Sie _____.

7. Die Soldaten _____.

Reisen in die Schweiz

8. Ich _____.

9. Du _____.

10. Er _____.

11. Wir _____.

12. Ihr _____.

13. Sie _____.

14. Der Tourist _____.

More about imperatives

Most imperatives are directed to the second person (**du**, **ihr**, and **Sie**). For example:

DU	IHR	SIE
Komm!	Kommt!	Kommen Sie!
Sei!	Seid!	Seien Sie!

But there is another form of imperative, which includes the speaker or writer in the command. In English, such an imperative is introduced by *Let's*.

> *Let's order a pizza.*
> *Let's not go to the movies tonight.*

The German version of this kind of imperative is quite simple. Merely invert the positions of the present tense verb in a sentence with the pronoun **wir**. For example:

STATEMENT:	Wir fahren in die Stadt.	*We're driving into the city.*
IMPERATIVE:	**Fahren wir** in die Stadt!	*Let's drive into the city.*

**ÜBUNG
16·6**

*Rewrite each sentence as a **wir**-imperative.*

1. Wir sprechen nur Deutsch.

   _____

2. Wir kaufen einen neuen Mercedes.

   _____

3. Wir rufen die Polizei an. (*We call the police.*)

   _____

4. Wir bleiben im Wohnzimmer. (*We stay in the living room.*)

   _____

5. Wir stellen unsere Eltern vor.

   _____

6. Wir gehen ins Restaurant.

   _____

7. Wir spielen Karten. (*We play cards.*)

   _____

8. Wir machen die Fenster zu.

   _____

9. Wir trinken ein Glas Wein.

_____

10. Wir setzen es auf den Tisch.

_____

Another form of imperative that uses a command directed to the second person requires the use of the verb **lassen** with the pronoun **uns**. The use of this verb gives the command the meaning of _let's_ and infers that the speaker or writer is included in the command. For example:

du	**Lass uns** ins Theater gehen!	_**Let's go** to the theater._
ihr	**Lasst uns** Mutter helfen!	_**Let's help** Mother._
Sie	**Lassen Sie** uns an der Ecke warten!	_**Let's wait** on the corner._

ÜBUNG
16·7

Write the appropriate **lassen**-imperative for each sentence. Use the words given as your signal to form the imperative for **du**, **ihr**, or **Sie**.

FOR EXAMPLE: Wir fahren nach Hause.

mein Sohn _____ _Lass uns nach Hause fahren!_ _____

1. Wir reisen in die Berge.

   meine Frau _____

2. Wir lesen die Zeitungen.

   Professor Keller _____

3. Wir spielen nicht im Wohnzimmer.

   die Kinder _____

4. Wir bleiben bis nächsten Dienstag.

   der Arzt _____

5. Wir steigen vor dem Bahnhof aus.

   meine Freundin _____

Genitive case, the comparative, and the superlative

Genitive case

The genitive case is the fourth and last case in the German language. One of its functions is to provide the vehicle for showing possession. In English, possession is shown in two ways: with an apostrophe *s* or by the preposition *of*.

> *the woman's new dress*
> *the color of the sky*

The German genitive case functions in place of those two types of English possession.

das neue Kleid der Frau	*the woman's new dress*
die Farbe des Himmels	*the color of the sky*

The genitive case endings for **der**-words and **ein**-words follow:

MASCULINE	FEMININE	NEUTER	PLURAL
des Mannes	der Frau	des Kindes	der Kinder
dieses Jungen	dieser Dame	dieses Hauses	dieser Leute
eines Wagens	einer Schule	eines Buches	deiner Brüder
keines Gartens	keiner Zeitung	keines Gymnasiums	keiner Schüler

The typical genitive noun ending for masculine and neuter nouns is **-s**. But many nouns that are monosyllabic or end in a sibilant sound (**s**, **ss**, **ß**, **sch**) use the ending **-es**. Also, masculine nouns that are certain old German words or foreign words with the accent on the final syllable add an **-n** or **-en** in the genitive case.

> des Stuhles
> des Einflusses (*influence*)
> des Herrn
> des Diplomaten

ÜBUNG

17·1

*In the blank provided, write the genitive case form for each noun given. Use the correct form of the **der**-word or **ein**-word.*

1. die Tasse (*cup*) _____

2. dieses Glas _____

3. meine Eltern _____

4. seine Tochter _____

5. eine Prüfung _____

6. Ihr Bleistift (*pencil*) _____

7. das Geld _____

8. ihre Gesundheit (*health*) _____

9. unser Garten _____

10. das Flugzeug (*airplane*) _____

11. dieser Zug _____

12. die Blume _____

13. diese Nacht (*night*) _____

14. dein Geburtstag _____

15. unsere Freundinnen (*girlfriends*) _____

16. der Hund _____

17. ihre Katze _____

18. das Jahr _____

19. diese Pferde (*horses*) _____

20. ein Apfel (*apple*) _____

21. kein Dichter (*poet*) _____

22. die Gäste _____

23. der Student _____

24. ein Löwe _____

25. das Schiff (*ship*) _____

ÜBUNG
17·2

In the blank provided, complete each sentence by writing the noun in parentheses in the genitive case.

FOR EXAMPLE: (mein Bruder) Die Frau ___*meines Bruders*___ ist sehr krank. (*My brother's wife is very sick.*)

1. (seine Schwester) Die Kinder _____ müssen zu Hause bleiben.

2. (die Lehrer) Viele (*many*) _____ helfen ihnen.

3. (dieser Herr) Die Jacke (*jacket*) _____ ist alt.

4. (meine Töchter) Das Schlafzimmer (*bedroom*) _____ ist sehr schön.

5. (unser Gast) Der Mantel _____ liegt auf dem Boden.

6. (der Chef [*boss*]) Hast du die Rede _____ gehört?

7. (ihr Freund) Das Haus _____ ist weit von hier.

Genitive case, the comparative, and the superlative　**153**

8. (dieses Problem) Die Lösung (*solution*) _____ ist sehr einfach (*simple*).

9. (deine Tante) Das Auto _____ ist kaputt (*broken*).

10. (Ihre Freundin) Wurde die Tochter _____ Ärztin?

In the spoken language, it is common to substitute a prepositional phrase introduced by **von** for the genitive case.

WRITTEN OR FORMAL LANGUAGE	SPOKEN LANGUAGE	
das Haus meines Bruders	das Haus von meinem Bruder	*my brother's house*
viele der Kinder	viele von den Kindern	*many of the children*

Just as certain prepositions require the accusative or dative case, certain prepositions require the genitive case, as well.

anstatt *or* statt	*instead of*
angesichts	*in the face of*
außerhalb	*outside of*
diesseits	*this side of*
jenseits	*that side of*
trotz	*despite/in spite of*
unterhalb	*below*
während	*during*
wegen	*because of*

Nouns that follow these prepositions will be in the genitive case. For example:

anstatt meines Bruders	*instead of my brother*
diesseits der Grenze	*this side of the border*
trotz des Wetters	*in spite of the weather*
während des Krieges	*during the war*
wegen eines Sturmes	*because of a storm*

ÜBUNG
17·3

Rewrite each sentence with the words provided.

Wegen _____ bleiben alle zu Hause. (*Because of . . . everyone stays home.*)

1. der Regen (*rain*) _____

2. das Gewitter (*storm*) _____

3. seine Erkältung (*his cold*) _____

4. das Wetter _____

5. die Prüfungen _____

Wir waren während _____ in Kanada. (*We were in Canada during . . .*)

6. mein Geburtstag _____

7. der Krieg _____

8. der Angriff (*attack*) _____

9. die Konferenz _____

10. die Verhandlungen (*negotiations*) _____

Anstatt _____ musste ich ihr helfen. (*Instead of . . . I had to help her.*)

11. mein Onkel _____

12. die Jungen _____

13. ein Matrose _____

14. die Familie _____

15. unsere Eltern _____

Trotz _____ wollte sie nicht Tennis spielen. (*In spite of . . . she did not want to play tennis.*)

16. unsere Freundschaft (*friendship*) _____

17. das Wetter _____

18. der Sonnenschein (*sunshine*) _____

19. mein Alter (*my age*) _____

20. meine Bitte (*request*) _____

Wir wohnten diesseits _____. (*We lived on this side of . . .*)

21. der Fluss (*river*) _____

22. die Grenze (*border*) _____

23. die Brücke (*bridge*) _____

24. die Berge (*mountains*) _____

25. die Alpen (*Alps*) _____

Refer to Appendix C for a summary of the genitive case and the other cases.

Comparative and superlative

The comparative is a comparison between two persons or things. The superlative describes the person or thing that has no equal. In English these two forms look like the following:

COMPARATIVE: *He is **taller** than James.*
SUPERLATIVE: *She is the **tallest** in her family.*

Just like English, German adds **-er** to many adjectives or adverbs to form the comparative. For example:

kleiner	*smaller*
netter	*nicer*
schöner	*prettier, nicer*
kühler	*cooler*
heißer	*hotter*
weiter	*farther*

Often an umlaut is added in the comparative. For example:

alt	→ älter	*older*
kalt	→ kälter	*colder*
jung	→ jünger	*younger*

Unlike English, there is no difference between the adjective and adverb forms of the comparative and superlative.

ADJECTIVE: Er ist **schnell/schneller/am schnellsten.**

ADVERB: Sie läuft **schnell/schneller/am schnellsten.**

ÜBUNG 17·4

In the blank provided, write the comparative form of each adjective or adverb.

1. schnell (*fast*) _____

2. langsam (*slow*) _____

3. grün (*green*) _____

4. weiß (*white*) _____

5. dick (*thick, fat*) _____

6. neu _____

7. lang (*long*) _____

8. schwer (*heavy, difficult*) _____

9. leicht (*light, easy*) _____

10. kurz (*short*) _____

11. nah (*near*) _____

12. hell (*bright*) _____

13. alt _____

14. fleißig (*diligent*) _____

15. breit (*wide, broad*) _____

The superlative is often formed as a prepositional phrase introduced by **am (an dem)**. It uses the ending -**sten**. For example:

am kleinsten	*the smallest*
am schnellsten	*the fastest*
am schwersten	*the hardest*

If the adjective or adverb ends in -**d**, -**t**, -**s**, -**ss**, -**ß**, -**sch**, or -**z**, the superlative ending becomes -**esten**.

am ältesten	*the oldest*
am blödesten	*the most stupid*
am hübschesten	*the most beautiful*

And a slight spelling shift takes place in the comparative with adjectives and adverbs that end in **-el**, **-er**, and **-en**.

POSITIVE	COMPARATIVE	SUPERLATIVE
dunkel (*dark*)	dunkler	am dunkelsten
teuer (*expensive*)	teurer	am teuersten
trocken (*dry*)	trockner	am trockensten

English uses another form of comparative and superlative with long words—particularly foreign words.

more interesting   most interesting
more talkative   most talkative

German does not follow this pattern. The same approach to comparative and superlative used with shorter words is also used with longer words.

POSITIVE	COMPARATIVE	SUPERLATIVE	
interessant	interessanter	am interessantesten	*more/most interesting*
wichtig	wichtiger	am wichtigsten	*more/most important*
glücklich	glücklicher	am glücklichsten	*more/most fortunate*

Just like English, German has a few comparative and superlative forms that are irregular.

POSITIVE		COMPARATIVE	SUPERLATIVE
bald	*soon*	eher	am ehesten
groß	*big*	größer	am größten
gut	*good*	besser	am besten
hoch	*high*	höher	am höchsten
nah	*near*	näher	am nächsten
viel	*much*	mehr	am meisten

Comparisons are made by using the word **als** (*than*). The superlative requires no such word.

Mein Freund ist älter **als** mein Bruder.   *My friend is older **than** my brother.*
Mein Freund ist am ältesten.   *My friend is the oldest.*

ÜBUNG
17·5

Read the original sentence with the positive form of the adjective or adverb. Then using the first signal in parentheses, make a comparison with the noun in the original sentence. Using the second signal in parentheses, write the sentence in the superlative.

FOR EXAMPLE: Mein Vater ist alt.

(mein Onkel, mein Großvater)

Mein Vater ist älter als mein Onkel.

Mein Großvater ist am ältesten.

1. Seine Tochter war jung.

(seine Schwester, Tante Angela)

_____

_____

2. Die Kinder laufen langsam.

   (Thomas, mein Sohn)

   _____

   _____

3. Das Gymnasium ist groß.

   (die Grundschule _primary school_, die Universität _university_)

   _____

   _____

4. Erik spricht gut.

   (seine Kusine _cousin,_ der Professor)

   _____

   _____

5. Der Doppeldecker (_biplane_) fliegt hoch.

   (der Zeppelin, diese Flugzeuge)

   _____

   _____

6. Unsere Gäste kamen spät (_late_).

   (ich, du)

   _____

   _____

7. Diese Geschichte (_story_) war langweilig (_boring_).

   (ihr Roman, sein Gedicht)

   _____

   _____

8. Diese Straßen sind breit.

   (unsere Straße, die Autobahn [_superhighway_])

   _____

   _____

9. Diese Prüfung ist schwer.

   (die Hausaufgabe [_assignment_], das Examen)

   _____

   _____

10. Frau Bauer kam früh (_early_).

    (ihr Mann, ihr)

    _____

    _____

Irregular verbs in the present perfect tense and adjectives

·18·

Irregular present perfect tense

The present perfect tense is composed of an auxiliary (**haben** or **sein**) and a past participle. Many verbs form their past participle in an irregular way. A majority have a change in the stem and an **-en** ending. Transitive verbs use **haben** as their auxiliary. Let's look at the conjugation in the present perfect tense of some irregular verbs.

	sprechen	**verstehen**	**ausgeben**
ich	habe gesprochen	habe verstanden	habe ausgegeben
du	hast gesprochen	hast verstanden	hast ausgegeben
er/sie/es	hat gesprochen	hat verstanden	hat ausgegeben
wir	haben gesprochen	haben verstanden	haben ausgegeben
ihr	habt gesprochen	habt verstanden	habt ausgegeben
Sie	haben gesprochen	haben verstanden	haben ausgegeben
sie (*pl.*)	haben gesprochen	haben verstanden	haben ausgegeben

As just illustrated, inseparable and separable prefixes function in the irregular present perfect tense as they do in the regular present perfect tense.

The following is a list of commonly used verbs that take **haben** as their auxiliary and have an irregular present perfect tense.

Stem change to -i- or -ie-

INFINITIVE	THIRD-PERSON CONJUGATION	
beißen	er hat gebissen	*he has bitten*
greifen	er hat gegriffen	*he has grabbed*
pfeifen	er hat gepfiffen	*he has whistled*
schreiben	er hat geschrieben	*he has written*
schweigen	er hat geschwiegen	*he has remained silent*
streiten	er hat gestritten	*he has argued*

Stem change to -o-

INFINITIVE	THIRD-PERSON CONJUGATION	
befehlen	er hat befohlen	*he has commanded*
brechen	er hat gebrochen	*he has broken*
frieren	er hat gefroren	*he has frozen*
heben	er hat gehoben	*he has raised*
lügen	er hat gelogen	*he has lied*
nehmen	er hat genommen	*he has taken*
schließen	er hat geschlossen	*he has closed*
stehlen	er hat gestohlen	*he has stolen*
treffen	er hat getroffen	*he has met*
verlieren	er hat verloren	*he has lost*
werfen	er hat geworfen	*he has thrown*
ziehen	er hat gezogen	*he has pulled*

INFINITIVE	THIRD-PERSON CONJUGATION (CONTINUED)	
werfen	er hat geworfen	*he has thrown*
ziehen	er hat gezogen	*he has pulled*

Stem change to -u-

INFINITIVE	THIRD-PERSON CONJUGATION	
binden	er hat gebunden	*he has tied*
finden	er hat gefunden	*he has found*
singen	er hat gesungen	*he has sung*
trinken	er hat getrunken	*he has drunk*

Some participles of high-frequency verbs do not follow a specific pattern. For example:

INFINITIVE	THIRD-PERSON CONJUGATION	
bitten	er hat gebeten	*he has requested*
essen	er hat gegessen	*he has eaten*
fressen	er hat gefressen	*he has eaten (like an animal)*
liegen	er hat gelegen	*he has lain*
rufen	er hat gerufen	*he has called*
schlafen	er hat geschlafen	*he has slept*
schlagen	er hat geschlagen	*he has hit*
sehen	er hat gesehen	*he has seen*
sitzen	er hat gesessen	*he has sat*
tun	er hat getan	*he has done*
waschen	er hat gewaschen	*he has washed*

ÜBUNG
18·1

In the blank provided, write the present perfect conjugation for the verb in parentheses with the accompanying subject.

1. (ziehen) wir _____

2. (anziehen [*put on*]) ich _____

3. (singen) du _____

4. (schlagen) Sie _____

5. (erschlagen [*kill*]) sie (*sing.*) _____

6. (erfinden [*invent*]) ihr _____

7. (versprechen) er _____

8. (beißen) ich _____

9. (waschen) du _____

10. (beschreiben [*describe*]) man _____

11. (essen) wir _____

12. (fressen) der Löwe _____

13. (schweigen) die Kinder _____

14. (brechen) niemand _____

15. (ansehen [*look at*]) ihr _____

16. (treffen) ich _____

17. (mitnehmen [*take along*]) Sie _____

18. (schließen) seine Eltern _____

19. (tun) sie (*pl.*) _____

20. (begreifen) er _____

Write each sentence using the provided subject and the present perfect tense conjugation of the verb in the given phrase.

Trinken ein Glas Milch (*To drink a glass of milk*)

1. Ich _____.

2. Du _____.

3. Er _____.

4. Wir _____.

5. Ihr _____.

6. Sie _____.

7. Der Soldat _____.

Sitzen im Wohnzimmer

8. Ich _____.

9. Du _____.

10. Er _____.

11. Wir _____.

12. Ihr _____.

13. Sie _____.

14. Die Touristen _____.

Intransitive verbs, verbs of motion, and verbs that indicate a radical change use **sein** as their auxiliary and often have irregular past participles. Some high-frequency verbs that do this are:

INFINITIVE	THIRD-PERSON CONJUGATION	
bleiben	er ist geblieben	*he has stayed*
einschlafen	er ist eingeschlafen	*he has fallen asleep*
ertrinken	er ist ertrunken	*he has drowned*
fahren	er ist gefahren	*he has driven*

fallen	er ist gefallen	*he has fallen*
fliegen	er ist geflogen	*he has flown*
gebären	er ist geboren	*he was born*
gehen	er ist gegangen	*he has gone*
geschehen	es ist geschehen	*it has happened*
kommen	er ist gekommen	*he has come*
laufen	er ist gelaufen	*he has run*
schwimmen	er ist geschwommen	*he has swum*
springen	er ist gesprungen	*he has jumped*
sterben	er ist gestorben	*he has died*
wachsen	er ist gewachsen	*he has grown*

ÜBUNG
18·3

Write each sentence using the provided subject and the present perfect tense conjugation of the verb in the given phrase.

Bleiben zu Hause

1. Ich _____.

2. Du _____.

3. Er _____.

4. Wir _____.

5. Ihr _____.

6. Sie _____.

7. Der Matrose _____.

Fliegen nach Deutschland

8. Ich _____.

9. Du _____.

10. Er _____.

11. Wir _____.

12. Ihr _____.

13. Sie _____.

14. Der Ausländer _____.

Fallen ins Wasser (*Fall in the water*)

15. Ich _____.

16. Du _____.

17. Er _____.

18. Wir _____.

19. Ihr _____.

20. Sie _____.

21. Wer _____?

Einschlafen um elf Uhr

22. Ich _____.

23. Du _____.

24. Er _____.

25. Wir _____.

26. Ihr _____.

27. Sie _____.

28. Die alte Dame _____.

The verbs **haben**, **sein**, and **werden** play a special role in tense formation and can themselves be conjugated in the present perfect tense.

	haben	**sein**	**werden**
ich	habe gehabt	bin gewesen	bin geworden
du	hast gehabt	bist gewesen	bist geworden
er/sie/es	hat gehabt	ist gewesen	ist geworden
wir	haben gehabt	sind gewesen	sind geworden
ihr	habt gehabt	seid gewesen	seid geworden
Sie	haben gehabt	sind gewesen	sind geworden
sie (*pl.*)	haben gehabt	sind gewesen	sind geworden

ÜBUNG
18·4

Write each sentence using the provided subject and the present perfect tense conjugation of the verb in the given phrase.

Haben viele Probleme

1. Ich _____.

2. Du _____.

3. Er _____.

4. Wir _____.

5. Ihr _____.

6. Sie _____.

7. Die Lehrerin _____.

Sein nicht in der Stadt

8. Ich _____.

9. Du _____.

10. Er _____.

11. Wir _____.

12. Ihr _____.

13. Sie _____.

14. Die Ausländerin _____.

Werden müde (*get tired*)

15. Ich _____.

16. Du _____.

17. Er _____.

18. Wir _____.

19. Ihr _____.

20. Sie _____.

21. Niemand _____.

The verb **wissen** changes the vowel in its stem as other irregular verbs do but uses a **-t** ending to form the past participle.

INFINITIVE	THIRD-PERSON CONJUGATION	
wissen	er hat gewusst	*he has known*

Several other verbs follow this same pattern. They are called *mixed verbs*.

INFINITIVE	THIRD-PERSON CONJUGATION	
brennen	er hat gebrannt	*he has burned*
bringen	er hat gebracht	*he has brought*
denken	er hat gedacht	*he has thought*
kennen	er hat gekannt	*he has known*
nennen	er hat genannt	*he has named*
rennen	er ist gerannt	*he has run*
senden	er hat gesandt	*he has sent*
wenden	er hat gewandt	*he has turned*

ÜBUNG
18·5

Write each sentence using the provided subject and the present perfect tense conjugation of the verb in the given phrase.

Wissen, wo der Mann wohnt

1. Ich _____.

2. Du _____.

3. Er _____.

4. Wir _____.

5. Ihr _____.

6. Sie _____.

7. Niemand _____.

Nennen das Baby Angela (*Call the baby Angela*)

8. Ich _____.

9. Du _____.

10. Er _____.

11. Wir _____.

12. Ihr _____.

13. Sie _____.

14. Die Eltern _____.

Denken an die Ausländer (*Think about the foreigners*)

15. Ich _____.

16. Du _____.

17. Er _____.

18. Wir _____.

19. Ihr _____.

20. Sie _____.

21. Wer _____?

Rennen aus dem Schlafzimmer

22. Ich _____.

23. Du _____.

24. Er _____.

25. Wir _____.

26. Ihr _____.

27. Sie _____.

28. Das Dienstmädchen (*servant girl*) _____.

You encountered the present and past tenses of the modal auxiliaries in Chapter 14. The modals also have a present perfect tense formation that is partly irregular, and each one takes **haben** as its auxiliary.

INFINITIVE	PAST PARTICIPLE
dürfen	gedurft
können	gekonnt
mögen	gemocht
müssen	gemusst

INFINITIVE	PAST PARTICIPLE (CONTINUED)
sollen	gesollt
wollen	gewollt

Write each sentence using the provided subject and the present perfect tense conjugation of the verb in the given phrase.

Mögen es nicht

1. Ich _____.

2. Du _____.

3. Er _____.

4. Wir _____.

5. Ihr _____.

6. Sie _____.

7. Wer _____?

Wollen alles (*want everything*)

8. Ich _____.

9. Du _____.

10. Er _____.

11. Wir _____.

12. Ihr _____.

13. Sie _____.

14. Die Kinder _____.

Können Englisch und Deutsch (*know English and German*)

15. Ich _____.

16. Du _____.

17. Er _____.

18. Wir _____.

19. Ihr _____.

20. Sie _____.

21. Die Studentin _____.

Adjectives

You are already familiar with the **der**-words and the **ein**-words. When adjectives accompany these words, they must have specific endings for each gender and case. For example:

Der-words

	MASCULINE	FEMININE
nom	der klein**e** Garten	die jung**e** Dame
acc	diesen klein**en** Garten	diese junge Dame
dat	jenem klein**en** Garten	jener jung**en** Dame
gen	des klein**en** Gartens	der jung**en** Dame

	NEUTER	PLURAL
nom	das alt**e** Haus	die alt**en** Häuser
acc	dieses alte Haus	diese alt**en** Häuser
dat	jenem alt**en** Haus	jenen alt**en** Häusern
gen	des alt**en** Hauses	der alt**en** Häuser

Ein-words

	MASCULINE	FEMININE
nom	ein klein**er** Garten	eine junge Schwester
acc	seinen klein**en** Garten	seine junge Schwester
dat	unserem klein**en** Garten	unserer jung**en** Schwester
gen	keines klein**en** Gartens	keiner jung**en** Schwester

	NEUTER	PLURAL
nom	ein alt**es** Haus	meine alt**en** Häuser
acc	ihr alt**es** Haus	deine alt**en** Häuser
dat	eurem alt**en** Haus	Ihren alt**en** Häusern
gen	keines alt**en** Hauses	keiner alt**en** Häuser

ÜBUNG
18·7

Write each adjective with the correct adjective ending as it would appear in the sentence.

FOR EXAMPLE: Er hat ein _____ Buch.

gut _____*gutes*_____

neu _____*neues*_____

Wir haben in einer _____ Stadt gewohnt.

1. groß _____

2. klein _____

3. amerikanisch (*American*) _____

4. alt _____

5. schmutzig (*dirty*) _____

Hast du seinen _____ Pullover gefunden?

6. neu _____

7. braun _____

8. rot _____

9. billig _____

10. billiger _____

Martin wollte mit den _____ Katzen spielen.

11. klein _____

12. weiß _____

13. jung _____

14. schwarz _____

15. älteste _____

Hier wohnt ein _____ Mann.

16. reich _____

17. arm _____

18. nett _____

19. hübsch _____

20. krank _____

Niemand hat sein _____ Hemd gekauft.

21. schmutzig _____

22. gelb _____

23. groß _____

24. billig _____

25. klein _____

Review 2

ÜBUNG
R2·1

Unit 10. *Translate the word or phrase in parentheses and write it in the blank.*

1. (*against what*) _____ sprechen die Lehrer?

2. (*without his son*) Herr Keller kam _____.

3. (*for my brother*) Ich habe ein Geschenk _____.

4. (*through*) Ein Schmetterling fliegt _____ den Garten.

5. (*me*) Tante Luise besucht _____.

ÜBUNG
R2·2

Unit 11. *In the blanks provided, write the past tense of the infinitives in parentheses.*

1. (feiern) Wir _____ bis Mitternacht.

2. (arbeiten) Wo _____ Ihre Eltern?

3. (zumachen) Ich _____ die Fenster _____.

4. (besuchen) Wer _____ dich am Montag?

5. (warten) Ein alter Herr _____ an der Tür.

169

Unit 11. Rewrite each sentence, making the word or phrase in boldface the first element in the sentence.

1. Sie reisten **gestern** nach Bremen. _____

2. Er ging **um zehn Uhr** zum Park. _____

Unit 11. Fill in the blanks with the word or phrase in parentheses.

1. Ich weiß, dass _____. (Frau Schneider hat keine Kinder.)

2. Mein Onkel schläft, denn _____. (Er ist müde.)

3. Er bleibt in Berlin, weil _____. (Er besucht seinen Sohn.)

Unit 12. Select one of the words in boldface and circle it as the best completion for the sentence.

1. Was geben Sie dem **Soldat Lehrerin Herrn**?

2. Sie kaufte **mich ihr wer** ein Eis.

3. **Außer Ohne Wessen** Frau Benz kenne ich niemand.

4. Wir **hören senden besuchen** ihnen Rosen und Nelken.

5. Sie sitzen im Cafe dem Rathaus **von aus gegenüber**.

6. Thomas spricht mit dem **Gärtner Matrose Großmutter**.

7. **Stadtpark Womit Drohen** spielen die Mädchen?

8. Es **imponierte lächelte folgen** mir sehr.

9. Ich bringe **Sie diese euch** die Zeitungen.

10. Was **kaufen schenkte wem** Sie Herrn Braun?

Unit 13. Rewrite the boldface verbs in the past tense.

1. Sie **versteht** es nicht. _____

2. Wir **haben** keine Zeit. _____

3. Sie **heißt** Marianne Keller. _____

4. **Kennst** du den Mann? _____

5. Es **wird** sehr kalt. _____

6. **Wissen** die Männer, wo Herr Schultz wohnt? _____

7. **Seid** ihr zu Hause? _____

8. Wir **essen** im neue Restaurant. _____

9. Um wieviel Uhr **kommst** du nach Hause? _____

10. Erik **verliert** zwanzig Euro. _____

Unit 14. Rewrite the modals in boldface in the past tense.

1. Sie **mag** jünger sein. _____

2. Die Frauen **können** es tun. _____

3. **Musst** du an deine Eltern schreiben? _____

4. Sie **sollen** uns helfen. _____

5. Ich **will** Schach spielen. _____

Unit 14. Rewrite the boldface modals in the present tense.

1. Die Kinder **durften** im Garten spielen. _____

2. Ihr **wolltet** eine Reise nach Bonn machen. _____

3. Die Sportler **konnten** hier übernachten. _____

4. Du **solltest** mehr Geld verdienen. _____

5. Wir **mochten** gern Bier. _____

Unit 15. Circle the word or phrase in boldface as the appropriate completion to the sentence.

1. Ich fahre **in die, in der** Stadt.

2. Er will neben **dieses, diesem** Mädchen sitzen.

3. Der alte Hund läuft unter **den Tisch, dem Tisch.**

4. Ich hänge sein Bild über **das Bett, dem Bett.**

5. Er ist **in das, im** Jahre 1999 geboren.

6. Erik liegt auf **das Sofa, den Boden, der Decke** un schläft.

7. Gudrun stellte ihr Fahrrad **hinter das Haus, vor der Schule, im Garten.**

8. Er ging **auf der, an die,** über den Tür.

9. Die Jungen reden über **dem Fußballspiel, der Garage, den Film.**

10. Ich erinnere mich **an ihn, auf sie, zwischen ihnen.**

Unit 16. Circle **haben** or **sein** to indicate which is the appropriate auxiliary for the participle.

1. geeilt	**haben**	**sein**
2. bestellt	**haben**	**sein**
3. aufgemacht	**haben**	**sein**
4. passiert	**haben**	**sein**
5. gereist	**haben**	**sein**

Unit 16. *Rewrite the verbs in the present or past tense in the present perfect tense with the appropriate auxiliary.*

1. ich lache _____

2. wir marschierten _____

3. ihr spieltet _____

4. du zerstörst _____

5. sie antworten _____

Unit 16. *Write the **du**-form, the **ihr**-form, and the **Sie**-form of the infinitives provided.*

	DU	IHR	SIE
1. bleiben	_____	_____	_____
2. anrufen	_____	_____	_____
3. sein	_____	_____	_____
4. lassen	_____	_____	_____
5. aussteigen	_____	_____	_____

Unit 17. *In the blanks provided, write the appropriate genitive form for the word or phrase in parentheses.*

1. (das Gewitter) Wegen _____ spielen sie im Keller.

2. (meine Schwester) Das Auto _____ ist sehr alt.

3. (der Junge) Anstatt _____ musste ich im Garten arbeiten.

4. (der Winter) Während _____ gehen wir Schilaufen.

5. (dieses Problem) Die Lösung _____ ist nicht einfach.

ÜBUNG

R2·14

Unit 18. Provide both the comparative and superlative of the adjectives.

1. lang _____ _____

2. gut _____ _____

3. jung _____ _____

4. groß _____ _____

5. nah _____ _____

ÜBUNG

R2·15

Unit 18. Rewrite the verb in the sentence in the present perfect tense.

1. Sie zieht die Handschuhe an. _____

2. Du singst zu laut. _____

3. Ich bin müde. _____

4. Sie wissen es nicht. _____

5. Können Sie es? _____

6. Was brennt? _____

7. Sie kommen nach Hause. _____

8. Sie rennt aus der Küche. _____

Unit 19. *In the blanks provided, write the adjectives in parentheses with the appropriate ending as they would appear in the sentence.*

1. Hier wohnt ein _____ Mann. (arm, krank) _____ _____

2. Niemand hat meinen _____ Wagen gekauft. (alt, rot) _____

   _____

3. Warum schläft der Hund mit der _____ Katze? (klein, kleiner) _____

   _____

4. Hat sie ihr _____ Kleid gefunden? (neu, weiß) _____ _____

5. An der Ecke steht eine _____ Frau. (hübsch, älter) _____

   _____

6. Die Farbe des _____ Hauses war weiß. (kleinste, schmutzig) _____

   _____

7. Erik hat seinen _____ Paß verloren. (neu, amerikanisch) _____

   _____

Past perfect, future, and future perfect tenses

The past perfect tense is identical in structure to the present perfect tense. The difference is that the auxiliary (**haben** or **sein**) is conjugated in the past tense rather than in the present tense. Compare the following verbs conjugated in the present perfect and the past perfect tenses.

	Present perfect	**Past perfect**
ich	habe gesprochen	hatte verstanden
du	hast gesprochen	hattest verstanden
er/sie/es	hat gesprochen	hatte verstanden
wir	haben gesprochen	hatten verstanden
ihr	habt gesprochen	hattet verstanden
Sie	haben gesprochen	hatten verstanden
sie (*pl.*)	haben gesprochen	hatten verstanden

	Present perfect	**Past perfect**
ich	bin gegangen	war gefahren
du	bist gegangen	warst gefahren
er/sie/es	ist gegangen	war gefahren
wir	sind gegangen	waren gefahren
ihr	seid gegangen	wart gefahren
Sie	sind gegangen	waren gefahren
sie (*pl.*)	sind gegangen	waren gefahren

Use the present perfect tense to describe an action that began in the past but has ended in the present or is ongoing in the present. Use the past perfect tense to describe an action that began and ended in the past.

ÜBUNG
19·1

In the blank provided, write the past perfect conjugation for the verb in parentheses with the accompanying subject.

1. (ziehen) wir _____

2. (bleiben) ich _____

3. (singen) du _____

4. (reisen) sie (*sing.*) _____

5. (zumachen) meine Schwester _____

6. (sterben) der Mann _____

7. (fliegen) wir _____

8. (essen) Sie _____

9. (erwarten) ihr _____

10. (spielen) ich _____

11. (anziehen) er _____

12. (passieren) es _____

13. (besuchen) du _____

14. (lachen) ihr _____

15. (schlagen) sie (*pl.*) _____

16. (gefallen) es _____

17. (fallen) er _____

18. (einschlafen) das Baby _____

19. (rennen) wir _____

20. (wissen) niemand _____

21. (kommen) Sonja _____

22. (bekommen) ihr _____

23. (zerstören) sie (*pl.*) _____

24. (vergessen [*forget*]) ich _____

25. (geschehen) es _____

Rewrite each sentence in the past perfect tense.

1. Wir sprechen mit dem Kellner (*waiter*).

   _____

2. Wer lernt Deutsch?

   _____

3. Die Frauen weinen.

   _____

4. Ich laufe zum Rathaus.

   _____

5. Steigen sie an der Bushaltestelle (*bus stop*) aus?

   _____

6. Die kleinen Kinder hören Radio.

_____

7. Du nennst ihn Bertolt.

_____

8. Was passiert am Mittwoch?

_____

9. Der Hund schläft unter dem Tisch.

_____

10. Mein Großvater baut (*build*) eine neue Garage.

_____

The German future tense consists of the present tense conjugation of the verb **werden** accompanied by an infinitive. The infinitive becomes the last element in a sentence, as it does when it accompanies a modal auxiliary. Look at the following future tense sentences:

Ich **werde** in Berlin wohnen.	*I **will** live in Berlin.*
Du **wirst** keine Zeit haben.	*You **will** not have any time.*
Er **wird** nach Bremen reisen.	*He **will** travel to Bremen.*
Sie **wird** Tennis spielen.	*She **will** play tennis.*
Es **wird** kalt werden.	*It **will** get cold.*
Wir **werden** dieses Haus kaufen.	*We **will** buy this house.*
Werdet ihr in die Stadt fahren?	***Will** you drive into the city?*
Sie **werden** ein Geschenk bekommen.	*You **will** receive a gift.*
Werden sie am Samstag arbeiten?	***Will** they work on Saturday?*

ÜBUNG
19·3

Rewrite each sentence in the future tense.

FOR EXAMPLE: Er lernt Englisch.

_____*Er wird Englisch lernen.*_____

1. Die Schüler sprechen mit dem neuen Lehrer.

_____

2. Ich habe ein großes Problem.

_____

3. Wirst du Schauspieler?

_____

4. Es ist sehr kalt.

_____

5. Meine Mutter fragt einen Polizisten.

_____

6. Herr Becker besucht seine Tochter in Bonn.

_____

7. Der Zug kommt um elf Uhr.

_____

8. Die Studentin kauft einen neuen Computer.

_____

9. Es regnet (*rain*).

_____

10. Schneit (*snow*) es?

_____

The future perfect tense is composed of the conjugation of **werden** accompanied by a past participle and its appropriate auxiliary (**haben** or **sein**). The structure can be illustrated in the following way:

       werden + past participle + **haben**

or

       werden + past participle + **sein**

Like English, German does not use this tense with regularity. When it is used, it usually infers a *probability* or an *action that will be completed some time in the future*. Let's look at some sentences in the future perfect tense:

Sie **wird** nach Hause **gefahren sein**.	She **probably has driven** home.
Er **wird** das alte Fahrrad **verkauft haben**.	He **probably has sold** the old bike.
Wenn sie zurückkommen, **werden** sie vier Jahre im Ausland **gewohnt haben**.	When they come back, they **will have lived** overseas for four years.
Wenn ich ein Haus kaufe, **werde** ich mehr als zehn Monate **gearbeitet haben**.	When I buy a house, I **will have worked** for more than ten months.

ÜBUNG
19·4

Rewrite each sentence in the future perfect tense.

FOR EXAMPLE: Er lernt Englisch.

              Er wird Englisch gelernt haben.

1. Wir fahren sechs Stunden lang (*for six hours*).

_____

2. Die Touristen reisen wohl (*probably*) nach Polen.

_____

3. Die Jungen spielen Fußball (*soccer*).

_____

4. Die Wanderer (*hikers*) haben Durst.

_____

5. Der Schüler kauft ein Würstchen (*sausage*).

_____

6. Du isst den ganzen Kuchen (*the whole cake*).

_____

7. Karl lernt wohl einen Beruf (*profession*).

_____

8. Die Party gefällt allen (*everyone*).

_____

9. Wir schlafen mehr als neun Stunden.

_____

10. Die Reisenden (*travelers*) kommen zu spät an.

_____

ÜBUNG
19·5

Rewrite each present tense sentence in the past tense, present perfect tense, past perfect tense, future tense, and the future perfect tense.

FOR EXAMPLE: Er lernt Englisch.

Er lernte Englisch.

Er hat Englisch gelernt.

Er hatte Englisch gelernt.

Er wird Englisch lernen.

Er wird Englisch gelernt haben.

1. Mein Onkel bezahlt die Rechnung (*pay the bill*).

_____

_____

_____

_____

_____

2. Die Mädchen schwimmen im Fluss.

_____

_____

_____

_____

_____

3. Wir sprechen oft mit unseren Nachbarn (*neighbors*).

_____

_____

_____

_____

_____

4. Meine Verwandten (*relatives*) reisen nach Amerika.

_____

_____

_____

_____

_____

5. Ich arbeite für Herrn Dorf.

_____

_____

_____

_____

_____

6. Mein Sohn besucht (*attends*) die Universität.

_____

_____

_____

_____

_____

7. Sie zieht sich eine schöne Bluse an.

_____

_____

_____

_____

_____

8. Viele Jugendliche (*young people*) wandern im Wald.

_____

_____

_____

_____

_____

9. Er macht alle Fenster auf.

_____

_____

_____

_____

_____

10. Die Gäste essen mehr als dreimal (*three times*) mexikanisch (*Mexican food*).

_____

_____

_____

_____

_____

Relative pronouns

When a noun in one sentence is identical to a noun in a second sentence, one of the nouns can be replaced by a *relative pronoun*. That pronoun connects the two sentences and functions like a conjunction. Look at this English example:

> *My brother likes cars. My brother bought a red sports car.*
> *My brother, **who** likes cars, bought a red sports car.*

German relative pronouns function in the same way, but German has to consider gender and case. Therefore, the pattern for German relative pronouns, which are for the most part definite articles, largely follows the declension pattern of definite articles.

	MASCULINE	FEMININE	NEUTER	PLURAL
nom	der	die	das	die
acc	den	die	das	die
dat	dem	der	dem	denen
gen	dessen	deren	dessen	deren

The German relative pronouns can be translated as *who*, *that*, or *which*. The gender and case of the noun that is replaced by a relative pronoun must be the gender and case used with the relative pronoun. For example:

Mein Bruder wohnt in Leipzig.	*My brother lives in Leipzig.*
Erik will **meinen Bruder** besuchen.	*Erik wants to visit my brother.*
Mein Bruder, **den** Erik besuchen will, wohnt in Leipzig.	*My brother, whom Erik wants to visit, lives in Leipzig.*

The first use of **mein Bruder** is the *antecedent*, and the second becomes the *relative pronoun*. Notice that the word order of the verbs in the relative clause has the conjugated verb as the last element in the relative clause (**... den Erik besuchen will.**).

The genitive relative pronoun is a substitute for a possessive pronoun.

Meine Tante ist sehr alt.	*My aunt is very old.*
Ihr Sohn kommt selten vorbei.	*Her son seldom comes by.*

The word **ihr** refers to **Tante**, and since **Tante** is feminine and **ihr** is a possessive, the feminine genitive form of the relative pronoun is used here. The fact that **Sohn** is masculine does not affect the relative pronoun; therefore, the relative pronoun used in this sentences is **deren**:

Meine Tante, **deren** Sohn selten vorbeikommt, ist sehr alt.	*My aunt, **whose** son seldom comes by, is very old.*

If a preposition is used to determine the case of the relative pronoun, that preposition must precede the relative pronoun. For example:

> der Mann, **mit dem** ich gesprochen habe
> die Schule, **zu der** die Kinder laufen

ÜBUNG 20·1

In the blank provided, write the relative pronoun that can be substituted for the given phrase. If a preposition is used, use the preposition with the relative pronoun.

FOR EXAMPLE: für den Mann _____ *für den* _____

1. das Mädchen _____

2. mit den Kindern _____

3. sein Buch _____

4. den Gästen _____

5. den Bahnhof _____

6. in der Oper _____

7. nach dem Konzert _____

8. ihre Eltern _____

9. von den Ausländern _____

10. seine Bücher _____

11. dem Fluss _____

12. in das Haus _____

13. ihr Vater _____

14. die Uhr _____

15. durch diesen Mann _____

ÜBUNG 20·2

Rewrite each numbered sentence as a relative clause for the provided sample sentence.

FOR EXAMPLE: Der Lehrer, _____, wurde wieder krank.

Mein Vater wollte mit dem Lehrer sprechen.

_____ *mit dem mein Vater sprechen wollte* _____

Das Flugzeug, _____, landete um vier Uhr. (*landed at four o'clock*)

1. Das Flugzeug ist ein Düsenjäger (*jet fighter*).

2. Ein kleiner Vogel sitzt auf dem Flugzeug.

_____

3. Niemand konnte das Flugzeug reparieren.

_____

4. Die Fluggäste steigen in das Flugzeug ein.

_____

Herr Bauer tanzt mit der Frau, _____.

5. Die Frau ist Amerikanerin.

_____

6. Ihre Kinder besuchen eine Schule in der Stadt.

_____

7. Viele Männer wollen mit der Frau tanzen.

_____

8. Ich habe gestern auf die Frau gewartet.

_____

Wir helfen den alten Leuten, _____.

9. Die alten Leute haben alles verloren.

_____

10. Ihre Töchter können ihnen nicht helfen.

_____

11. Wir haben einmal (_once_) für die alten Leute gearbeitet.

_____

12. Alle Nachbarn lieben die alten Leute.

_____

Er schläft auf einem Bett, _____.

13. Das Bett ist viel zu groß.

_____

14. Der Hund schläft auch auf dem Bett.

_____

15. Sein Großvater hatte das Bett vierzig Jahre vorher (_forty years earlier_) gekauft.

_____

The **der**-word **welcher** can replace the definite article as a relative pronoun. This can occur in all cases except the genitive.

	MASCULINE	FEMININE	NEUTER	PLURAL
nom	welcher	welche	welches	welche
acc	welchen	welche	welches	welche
dat	welchem	welcher	welchem	welchen
gen	dessen	deren	dessen	deren

This form of relative pronoun functions in the same way as the definite article. For example:

Das ist das Haus, **welches** mein Freund
  gekauft hat.

*That is the house **that** my friend
  bought.*

Ich besuche meine Verwandten, **mit welchen**
  mein Bruder jetzt wohnt.

*I am visiting my relatives, **with whom**
  my brother now lives.*

ÜBUNG
20·3

Rewrite each numbered sentence as a relative clause for the sample sentence provided. Use
a form of **welcher** as the relative pronoun.

FOR EXAMPLE: Der Lehrer, _____, wurde wieder krank.

Mein Vater wollte mit dem Lehrer sprechen.

_____ *mit welchem mein Vater sprechen wollte* _____

Das Flugzeug, _____, landete um vier Uhr. (*landed at four o'clock*)

1. Das Flugzeug ist ein Düsenjäger (*jet fighter*).

_____

2. Der Tourist hat das Flugzeug fotografiert.

_____

3. Alle reden von dem Flugzeug.

_____

Das sind die Kinder, _____.

4. Er hat einen Artikel über die Kinder geschrieben.

_____

5. Die größeren Jungen spielen gern mit den Kindern.

_____

6. Ihr Bruder hat das Geld gestohlen.

_____

7. Ich habe die Nachricht durch die Kinder bekommen.

_____

Der Zahnarzt, _____, fährt sehr schnell.

8. Der Zahnarzt hat keinen Führerschein (*driver's license*).

_____

9. Frau Keller hat den Zahnarzt gern.

_____

10. Diese Fußgänger wollen mit dem Zahnarzt sprechen.

_____

11. Der Polizist gab dem Zahnarzt einen Strafzettel (*ticket*).

_____

Seine Freundin liebt die Nelken (*carnations*), _____.

12. Thomas hat ihr die Nelken geschenkt.

_____

13. Sie will ihm für die Nelken danken.

_____

14. Ihre Schwester will von den Nelken nicht sprechen.

_____

15. Leider welken (*unfortunately wilt*) die Nelken schon.

_____

There are two more relative pronouns that function in a slightly different way. They are **wer** and **was**. **Wer** is used where there is not a specific antecedent that a relative pronoun can refer to. It is used much like the English phrase *he who*.

> *He who aids my enemy becomes my enemy.*

Let's look at some German examples:

nom	**Wer** oft lügt, dem kann man nicht glauben.	He **who** lies often cannot be believed.
acc	**Wen** meine Feinde hassen, den liebe ich.	Him **whom** my enemies hate I love.
dat	**Wem** nicht zu glauben ist, dem traut man nicht.	He **who** is not to be believed one does not trust.
gen	**Wessen** Brot wir essen, dem danken wir vielmals.	Him **whose** bread we eat we thank many times.

ÜBUNG
20·4

*Combine the example sentences by using **wer** as a relative pronoun.*

FOR EXAMPLE: Er will nicht hören. Er muss fühlen (*feel*).

> *Wer nicht hören will, der muss fühlen.*

1. Ihm gefiel der Roman nicht. Er soll ihn nicht lesen.

_____

2. Ihm traut man. Er ist ein treuer (*loyal*) Freund.

_____

3. Er ist nicht für uns. Er ist gegen uns.

_____

4. Wir laden ihn ein. Wir geben ihm den teuersten Sekt (_champagne_).

_____

5. Ich trinke seinen Wein. Ich bleibe ihm treu.

_____

6. Der Freund liebt ihn. Der Feind hasst ihn.

_____

7. Man kennt ihn nicht. Man bleibt ihm fern.

_____

8. Ich habe ihn gesehen. Ich werde ihn nie vergessen.

_____

9. Der Politiker spricht mit ihm. Er wird der neue Kandidat (_candidate_).

_____

10. Ich habe seine Freundschaft (_friendship_). Ich bleibe ihm ein guter Freund.

_____

Was acts similarly but uses certain words that signal that this form of relative pronoun is required. Such words include **alles, nichts, manches, vieles,** and **etwas.** It is also used after **das** when it is used as a demonstrative pronoun. The meaning of **was** in this structure is _that which._

Ich kaufe **alles, was** billig ist.	_I buy **everything that** is cheap._
Sie haben **etwas, was** Sie verkaufen können.	_You have **something that** you can sell._
Er sagte **das, was** nicht zu glauben war.	_He said **(that which) what** was not to be believed._

Use **was** also when the antecedent of the relative clause is an entire sentence. For example:

Martin ist Lehrer geworden, **was** seinen Vater sehr erstaunte.	_Martin became a teacher, **which** really astounded his father._
Er isst ungekochtes Fleisch, **was** uns entsetzt.	_He eats uncooked meat, **which** horrifies us._

If a preposition needs to accompany the relative pronoun **was,** a prepositional adverb is formed.

Der Professor spricht über das Internet, **wofür** ich mich sehr interessiere.	_The professor is speaking about the Internet, **in which** I am very interested. (not **für das**)_

If a neuter adjective is used as a noun and is the antecedent of a relative pronoun, **was** is used.

Die reiche Dame kaufte **das Beste, was** der Verkäufer hatte.	_The rich lady bought **the best (thing) that** the salesman had._
Was war **das Erste, was** das Kind gesagt hat?	_What was **the first (thing) that** the child said?_

Combine the example sentences by using **was** as a relative pronoun.

FOR EXAMPLE: Ich habe etwas. Etwas wird dir gefallen.

Ich habe etwas, was dir gefallen wird.

1. Der Mann sagte alles. Alles war voller Unsinn (_nonsense_).

   _____

2. Das ist das Schrecklichste (_most terrible thing_). Ich habe das Schrecklichste gesehen.

   _____

3. Es gibt (_there is_) vieles. Vieles ist sehr gefährlich (_dangerous_).

   _____

4. Sie hat das Teuerste. Das Teuerste ist nicht immer das Beste.

   _____

5. Singe etwas! Wir haben etwas noch nicht gehört.

   _____

6. Thomas hat ein Auto gestohlen. Seine Eltern haben nichts davon gewusst.

   _____

7. Unsere Tante muss heute abreisen. Wir bedauern (_regret_) das sehr.

   _____

8. Sie hat nichts verstanden. Ich habe das gesagt.

   _____

9. Wir vergessen alles. Der Politiker hat alles versprochen.

   _____

10. Unsere Nachbarn machen Krach (_noise_). Der Krach stört uns.

   _____

Modifiers, adverbs, reflexive pronouns, and conjunctions

Modifiers

We can group German modifiers into three groups: the **der-** and **ein-**words, adjectives, and intensifiers. The **der-** and **ein-**words are already familiar to you, but here we shall add a few more to their list as well as some special *determiners*.

DER-WORDS		**EIN-**WORDS	
der/die/das	*the*	ein/eine	*a*
dieser	*this*	kein	*no/not any*
jener	*that*	mein	*my*
jeder	*each, every*	dein	*your*
welcher	*which*	sein	*his, its*
mancher	*some, many a*	ihr	*her, their*
solcher	*such*	unser	*our*
		euer	*your*
		Ihr	*your*

You have already seen in Chapter 18 how adjective endings are affected by **der-**words and **ein-**words. But **solcher** requires some further explanation.

Solcher is used primarily with plural nouns. Notice that the adjective endings are identical to those for other **der-**words.

	PLURAL NOUN	PLURAL NOUN
nom	solche jungen Frauen	solche netten Leute
acc	solche jungen Frauen	solche netten Leute
dat	solchen jungen Frauen	solchen netten Leuten
gen	solcher jungen Frauen	solcher netten Leute

When used with singular nouns, **solcher** functions more like a declined adjective than a **der-**word and follows **ein**. For example:

Ein solcher Roman ist unvergesslich.	*Such a novel is unforgettable.*
Sie kaufte **eine solche** Bluse.	*She bought such a blouse.*
Ein solches Buch kann ich nicht lesen.	*I cannot read such a book.*

It can also be used in its undeclined form as a replacement for **so** (*such*).

so ein Haus	→ solch ein Haus	*such a house*
so eine Blume	→ solch eine Blume	*such a flower*

In the blanks provided, write in the missing adjective endings in each phrase.

1. mit ein_____ alt_____ Herrn

2. für dies_____ hübsch_____ Dame

3. solch_____ interessant_____ Gedichte

4. dein_____ erst_____ Geschichte

5. unser_____ best_____ Freunde

6. von jed_____ gut_____ Bürger (*citizen*)

7. ohne sein_____ neu_____ Freundin

8. zu ein_____ klein_____ Kirche

9. bei jen_____ groß_____ Restaurant

10. ein_____ solch_____ Flugzeug

11. solch_____ laut (*loud*) _____ Flugzeuge

12. durch welch_____ jung_____ Mann?

13. aus kein_____ klein_____ Fenster

14. Ihr_____ schön_____ Garten

15. nach ein_____ lang_____ Oper

There are two more **der**-words to consider. They are **alle** (*all*) and **beide** (*both*) and are used only with plural nouns.

	ALLE	BEIDE
nom	alle jungen Frauen	beide netten Leute
acc	alle jungen Frauen	beide netten Leute
dat	allen jungen Frauen	beiden netten Leuten
gen	aller jungen Frauen	beider netten Leute

There are also five other determiners, which are used only with plural nouns. They are:

einige	*some*	viele	*many*
mehrere	*several*	wenige	*few*
sämtliche	*all, all the*		

The declension with these determiners is different from those used with **der**-words and **ein**-words. For example:

	EINIGE	VIELE
nom	einige junge Frauen	viele nette Leute
acc	einige junge Frauen	viele nette Leute
dat	einigen jungen Frauen	vielen netten Leuten
gen	einiger junger Frauen	vieler netter Leute

Remember that comparative and superlative adjectives can be fully declined like other adjectives. In Chapter 17 you used them primarily in the dative case with the preposition **an: am schnellsten**, **am besten**, and so on. Let's look at their full declension.

	HIS BEST FRIEND (MASC.)	*HER NICEST DRESS* (NEUT.)
nom	sein bester Freund	ihr schönstes Kleid
acc	seinen besten Freund	ihr schönstes Kleid
dat	seinem besten Freund	ihrem schönsten Kleid
gen	seines besten Freundes	ihres schönsten Kleides

There are cases when no **der**-word, **ein**-word, or other determiner is used with an adjective and noun. Such cases have their own special declension. For example:

	COLD WATER (NEUT.)	*HOT COFFEE* (MASC.)	*FRESH MILK* (FEM.)	*NICE PEOPLE* (PL.)
nom	kaltes Wasser	heißer Kaffee	frische Milch	nette Leute
acc	kaltes Wasser	heißen Kaffee	frische Milch	nette Leute
dat	kaltem Wasser	heißem Kaffee	frischer Milch	netten Leuten
gen	kalten Wassers	heißen Kaffees	frischer Milch	netter Leute

ÜBUNG

21·2

Write the full declension for the words provided in parentheses.

1. (solch/nett/Kinder)

nom _____
acc _____
dat _____
gen _____

2. (wenig/deutsch/Männer)

_____
_____
_____
_____

3. (jeder/alt/Herr)

nom _____
acc _____
dat _____
gen _____

4. (ein/solch/Flugzeug)

_____
_____
_____
_____

5. (dein/best/Prüfung)

nom _____
acc _____
dat _____
gen _____

6. (gut/Wetter)

_____
_____
_____
_____

Adverbs

Certain modifiers merely intensify the meaning of the adjective they modify. Intensifiers are adverbs and do not decline. The most commonly used intensifiers are:

ganz	*quite*	völlig	*completely, totally*
sehr	*very*	ziemlich	*rather, pretty*
total	*totally, completely*		

And two others are used mostly in the negative:

gar	*at all*	überhaupt	*at all*

Let's look at these adverbs in sentences. Note that they can modify both adjectives and adverbs.

Das Wetter ist wieder **ganz** schlecht.	*The weather is **quite** bad again.*
Dieses Mädchen läuft **sehr** schnell.	*This girl runs **very** fast.*
Ich bin **total/völlig** erschöpft.	*I am **totally** exhausted.*
Wir haben **ziemlich** viele Gäste eingeladen.	*We invited **pretty** many guests.*
Das ist **gar** nicht wahr.	*That is not true **at all**.*
Ich habe **gar** kein Geld.	*I have no money **at all**.*
Er versteht **überhaupt** nichts.	*He does not understand anything **at all**.*
Wir hatten **überhaupt** keine Zeit.	*We had no time **at all**.*

ÜBUNG
21·3

Rewrite each sentence with the modifiers provided.

FOR EXAMPLE: Er ist krank.

sehr _____ *Er ist sehr krank.* _____

Die Kinder waren müde.

1. ganz _____

2. sehr _____

3. ziemlich _____

4. gar nicht _____

5. total _____

Sein Gedicht ist gut.

6. ziemlich _____

7. überhaupt nicht _____

8. ganz _____

9. sehr _____

10. gar nicht _____

Reflexive pronouns

The German reflexive pronouns are:

SUBJECT PRONOUN	ACCUSATIVE REFLEXIVE	DATIVE REFLEXIVE	
ich	mich	mir	*myself*
du	dich	dir	*yourself*
er	sich	sich	*himself*
sie (*sing.*)	sich	sich	*herself*
es	sich	sich	*itself*
wir	uns	uns	*ourselves*
ihr	euch	euch	*yourselves*
Sie	sich	sich	*yourself, yourselves*
sie (*pl.*)	sich	sich	*themselves*
wer	sich	sich	*himself, herself*

Reflexive pronouns are used when the direct object or indirect object of a sentence is the same person or object as the subject. Compare the following pairs of sentences:

| Er fragt uns, wo sie ist. | *He asks us where she is.* |
| Er fragt **sich**, wo sie ist. | *He asks **himself** where she is.* |

| Ich kaufe euch ein Fahrrad. | *I buy you a bicycle.* |
| Ich kaufe **mir** ein Fahrrad. | *I buy **myself** a bicycle.* |

The accusative and dative reflexive pronouns can also be used with accusative or dative prepositions and as the object of dative verbs.

| Er denkt nur an **sich**. | *He only thinks about **himself**.* |
| Warum widersprichst du **dir**? | *Why do you contradict **yourself**?* |

ÜBUNG
21·4

Rewrite each sentence by changing the underlined word to an appropriate reflexive pronoun.

FOR EXAMPLE: Wir kaufen <u>dem Mann</u> ein Glas Bier.

Wir kaufen uns ein Glas Bier.

1. Martin kaufte etwas <u>für seine Freundin</u>.

2. Ihr habt nur <u>an euren Bruder</u> gedacht.

3. Wir helfen <u>der Frau</u>, so oft wir können.

4. Ich verberge (*hide*) das Geschenk <u>hinter der Tür</u>.

5. Er setzte <u>das Paket</u> auf den kleinen Stuhl.

6. Wer wollte <u>ihm</u> ein Würstchen bestellen?

_____

7. Sie konnte <u>uns</u> nicht helfen.

_____

8. Wäschst du <u>die Kinder</u> im Badezimmer (_bathroom_)?

_____

9. Ich frage <u>ihn</u>, warum er weint.

_____

10. Warum widersprecht ihr <u>dem alten Herrn</u>?

_____

11. Mutter wird <u>Frau Dorf</u> ein paar (_a couple of_) Nelken kaufen.

_____

12. Sie finden gar keine Plätze (_seats_) <u>für sie</u>.

_____

13. Karl hat <u>mich</u> an die große Prüfung erinnert.

_____

14. Wo kann er <u>den Hund</u> waschen?

_____

15. Wir ärgern (_annoy_) <u>euch</u> nicht darüber.

_____

Conjunctions

In Chapter 11 you encountered a variety of conjunctions, among them those that require the conjugated verb to be the last element in a sentence. For example:

> Ich weiß, **dass** Herr Braun krank ist.
> Sie bleibt zu Hause, **weil** das Wetter schlecht ist.

Like **dass** and **weil**, when interrogative words combine two sentences, they function as conjunctions and place the conjugated verb at the end of a sentence.

Let's look at interrogative words that ask a question and compare them to their use as conjunctions.

Wo ist Herr Schneider?	_**Where** is Mr. Schneider?_
Wissen Sie, **wo** Herr Schneider ist?	_Do you know **where** Mr. Schneider is?_
Wie alt ist ihre Schwester?	_**How old** is her sister?_
Niemand fragte, **wie alt** ihre Schwester ist.	_No one asked **how old** her sister is._
Wen werden seine Eltern besuchen?	_**Whom** will his parents visit?_
Er liest in dem Brief, **wen** seine Eltern besuchen werden.	_He reads in the letter **whom** his parents will visit._

Rewrite each question using the introductory statement provided.

FOR EXAMPLE: Ich weiß, ...

Wo wohnt sein Onkel? _____Ich weiß, wo sein Onkel wohnt._____

Wir wussten nicht, ...

1. Warum ist sie nach Hause gegangen?

   _____

2. Was hat er im Einkaufszentrum (*shopping mall*) gekauft?

   _____

3. Mit wem hat Sabine Tennis gespielt?

   _____

4. Wie lange mussten sie im Ausland bleiben?

   _____

5. Für wen hat Erik die Blumen gekauft?

   _____

Jemand (*someone*) fragte, ...

6. Wann ist der Bus abgefahren?

   _____

7. Wessen Mercedes hat der Mann gestohlen?

   _____

8. Wohin sind die Jungen gelaufen?

   _____

9. Wofür hat sich der Wissenschaftler (*scientist*) interessiert?

   _____

10. Warum widersprichst du dir immer?

    _____

Können Sie mir sagen, ...?

11. Um wie viel Uhr kommt der Zug?

    _____

12. Wem soll ich damit helfen?

    _____

13. Was ist geschehen?

_____

14. Wie viel kosten diese Hemden?

_____

15. Wonach hat der Polizist gefragt?

_____

Double infinitive structures

·22·

Double infinitives are not used in English, but this unique structure of German verbs is very simple to understand and use. The double infinitive occurs in the perfect tenses and in the future.

As introduced in Chapter 16, in the perfect tenses there is an auxiliary (**haben** or **sein**) and a past participle.

Der Mann **hat** es **gekauft**.   Die Frau **ist** nach Hause **gegangen**.

And in the future tense, the auxiliary **werden** is accompanied by an infinitive.

Es **wird** heute **regnen**.   Die Kinder **werden** damit **spielen**.

When a modal auxiliary is combined with an infinitive in the present or past tense, the modal is conjugated, and the infinitive is the last element in the sentence.

Ich **will** es verkaufen.	*I **want** to sell it.*
Die Frau **kann** uns helfen.	*The woman **can** help us.*
Er **musste** zu Hause bleiben.	*He **had** to stay home.*
Sie **durfte** die Bibliothek benutzen.	*She was **allowed** to use the library.*

But in the perfect tenses of modal auxiliaries, the auxiliary **haben** is combined with a double infinitive—an infinitive followed by a modal in the infinitive form. For example:

Ich habe es **vekaufen wollen**.	*I have **wanted to sell** it.*
Die Frau hatte uns **helfen können**.	*The woman had **been able to help** us.*
Er hat zu Hause **bleiben müssen**.	*He has **had to stay** home.*
Sie hat die Bibliothek **benutzen dürfen**.	*She was **allowed to use** the library.*

The same thing occurs in the future tense. **Werden** is followed by a double infinitive.

Ich werde es **vekaufen wollen**.	*I will **want to sell** it.*
Die Frau wird uns **helfen können**.	*The woman will **be able to help** us.*
Er wird zu Hause **bleiben müssen**.	*He will **have to stay** home.*
Sie wird die Bibliothek **benutzen dürfen**.	*She will **be allowed to use** the library.*

Rewrite each sentence in the present perfect tense.

1. Du sollst deine Pflicht (*duty*) tun.

   _____

2. Der Mann kann nicht schwimmen.

   _____

3. Man muss sehr vorsichtig (*careful*) sein.

   _____

4. Dürfen sie mit der Katze spielen?

   _____

5. Niemand will mit mir tanzen.

   _____

6. Können Sie die Berge (*mountains*) sehen?

   _____

Rewrite each sentence in the past perfect tense.

7. Er will ins Ausland reisen.

   _____

8. Was soll er tun?

   _____

9. Die Jungen können für Sie arbeiten.

   _____

10. Ihr müsst den Hund waschen.

    _____

11. Hier darf man nicht rauchen (*smoke*).

    _____

Rewrite each sentence in the future tense.

12. Erik will ins Restaurant gehen.

    _____

13. Kannst du ihm helfen?

    _____

14. Ich soll in die Stadt fahren.

_____

15. Wir müssen ihn vom Flughafen abholen (*pick up*).

_____

The double infinitive structure occurs with several other verbs:

helfen	*help*
hören	*hear*
lassen	*get, have (something done)*
sehen	*see*

The double infinitive structure with these verbs can be used in the perfect and future tenses. For example:

Er hat mir in der Küche **arbeiten helfen**.	He **helped** me work in the kitchen.
Ich hatte die Kinder **singen hören**.	I **heard** the children **singing**.
Sie wird das Auto **reparieren lassen**.	She will **have** the car **repaired**.

Rewrite each sentence in the present perfect and future tenses.

1. Er lässt das neue Auto waschen.

_____

_____

2. Er hört seine Eltern im Keller flüstern (*whisper*).

_____

_____

3. Wir sehen den Düsenjäger über dem Wald fliegen.

_____

_____

4. Herr Dorf lässt einen neuen Anzug (*suit*) machen.

_____

_____

5. Der Junge hilft mir das alte Radio reparieren.

_____

_____

Write each phrase in the present, past, present perfect, and future tenses with the subject provided in parentheses.

FOR EXAMPLE: wollen es verkaufen (ich)

Ich will es verkaufen.

Ich wollte es verkaufen.

Ich habe es verkaufen wollen.

Ich werde es verkaufen wollen.

1. können seine Rede nicht verstehen (sie [*sing.*])

2. hören den Mann Gitarre (*guitar*) spielen (wir)

3. müssen ins Ausland reisen (du)

4. sehen die Mädchen im Fluss schwimmen (wer?)

5. dürfen nicht nach Hause gehen (der kranke Mann)

_____

_____

_____

_____

6. sollen eine neue Schule besuchen (ich)

_____

_____

_____

_____

7. können schwimmen (viele Leute)

_____

_____

_____

_____

8. wollen die Suppe probieren (*taste the soup*) (er)

_____

_____

_____

_____

9. lassen die Software installieren (*install the software*) (der Wissenschaftler)

_____

_____

_____

_____

10. helfen ihnen die Tulpen pflanzen (*plant the tulips*) (die Soldaten)

_____

_____

_____

_____

Circle the letter of the word or phrase that best completes each sentence.

1. Die Ballerina wird in Berlin tanzen _____.
   a. muss
   b. haben können
   c. wollen
   d. gemocht

2. Niemand _____ sie im Wald wandern sehen.
   a. hat
   b. wurde
   c. ist
   d. geworden

3. Sie werden heute zu Hause _____ müssen.
   a. blieben
   b. bleiben
   c. geblieben
   d. bleibt

4. Karl _____ mit Herrn Keller sprechen.
   a. mögen
   b. sollt
   c. können
   d. wollte

5. _____ du Ski laufen (*skiing*)?
   a. Müssen
   b. Hast
   c. Kannst
   d. Bist

6. Der Matrose _____ an die Nordsee (*North Sea*) fahren wollen.
   a. wird
   b. haben
   c. konnte
   d. sollen

7. Ihr _____ keinen Wein trinken.
   a. will
   b. müssen
   c. dürft
   d. habt

8. Niemand hat ihn vom Bahnhof abholen _____.
   a. gewollt
   b. können
   c. möchte
   d. musste

9. Frau Bauer _____ ein neues Kleid machen.
   a. ließ
   b. konnten
   c. wollen
   d. hörte

10. Das darf _____ nicht sagen.
    a. du
    b. alle
    c. man
    d. viele Leute

11. Was _____ du zu deinem Essen (*with your food*) trinken?
    a. magst
    b. siehst
    c. lernte
    d. wollen

12. Thomas _____ sich die Haare schneiden (*get a haircut*).
    a. können
    b. half
    c. sollt
    d. lässt

13. Warum _____ die arme Frau sterben müssen?
    a. ist
    b. hat
    c. war
    d. haben

14. Meine Verwandten _____ in die Berge fahren.
    a. sehen
    b. soll
    c. wollten
    d. hören

15. Der Professor konnte das Examen _____.
    a. kommen hören
    b. schreiben können
    c. nicht finden
    d. nicht gelesen

16. Ich werde meine Freundin in Berlin _____.
    a. besuchen wollen
    b. nicht gesehen
    c. angerufen
    d. ankommen müssen

17. Sie hat ihm den Fernsehapparat _____.
    a. gekauft haben
    b. reparieren helfen
    c. abgefahren sein
    d. lassen

18. Wir haben die Sportler Fußball _____.
    a. machen lassen
    b. wollten lernen
    c. gespielt
    d. spielen sehen

19. Habt ihr das Baby _____?
    a. gehalten haben
    b. nicht helfen
    c. fahren dürfen
    d. weinen hören

20. Ich muss noch ein paar Wochen _____.
    a. warten
    b. schon gemacht
    c. gereist sein
    d. können

Infinitive clauses

A German infinitive clause is composed of the word **zu** and an infinitive. A variety of other elements can accompany **zu** and the infinitive to form a phrase. For example:

zu sprechen	*to speak*
mit ihnen zu sprechen	*to speak with them*
ein bisschen lauter zu sprechen	*to speak a little louder*

Note that **zu** and the infinitive are the final elements of the clause.

ÜBUNG

23·1

Change each present tense sentence into an infinitive clause.

FOR EXAMPLE: Er hilft uns.

_____*uns zu helfen*_____

1. Wir lernen eine Sprache.

   _____

2. Ich gebe ihr sechs Euro.

   _____

3. Sie bringt ihm ein Glas Wasser.

   _____

4. Du wartest an der Ecke.

   _____

5. Sie haben mehr Zeit (*more time*).

   _____

6. Alle fragen nach meiner Tochter.

   _____

7. Ich arbeite in einer Fabrik (*factory*).

   _____

8. Erik sieht ihn nicht.

_____

9. Es wird schlechter.

_____

10. Ich bin heute in der Hauptstadt.

_____

Prefixes must be taken into account when working with infinitive clauses. Inseparable prefixes on infinitives are simply preceded by the word **zu.**

NO PREFIX	INSEPARABLE PREFIX
zu kommen	zu bekommen
zu stehen	zu verstehen
zu warten	zu erwarten

The word **zu** is placed between the infinitive and a separable prefix, and the verb is written as one word.

NO PREFIX	INSEPARABLE PREFIX
zu fangen	anzufangen
zu bringen	beizubringen
zu fahren	abzufahren

ÜBUNG
23·2

Change each present tense sentence into an infinitive clause.

FOR EXAMPLE: Er versteht Deutsch.

Deutsch zu verstehen
_____

1. Wir besuchen eine Schule in Bremen.

_____

2. Er vergisst die Fahrkarten.

_____

3. Sabine kommt um acht Uhr an.

_____

4. Sie ziehen sich um (_change clothes_).

_____

5. Ihr kehrt bald (_soon_) zurück.

_____

6. Ich empfehle es.

_____

7. Sie bringt einen Freund mit.

_____

8. Er verkauft einen alten Koffer (*suitcase*).

_____

9. Ich stelle die Gäste vor.

_____

10. Sie steigen in der Schillerstraße aus.

_____

If an auxiliary accompanies a verb, it functions as the infinitive in the infinitive clause. For example:

AUXILIARY **SEIN**	INFINITIVE CLAUSE	
Er ist abgefahren.	abgefahren zu sein	*to have departed*
Sie ist hier geblieben.	hier geblieben zu sein	*to have stayed here*

AUXILIARY **HABEN**	INFINITIVE CLAUSE	
Ich habe nichts gefunden.	nichts gefunden zu haben	*to have found nothing*
Sie haben das Geld gestohlen.	das Geld gestohlen zu haben.	*to have stolen the money.*

MODAL AUXILIARY	INFINITIVE CLAUSE	
Sie kann es verstehen.	es verstehen zu können	*to be able to understand it*
Du musst ihm helfen.	ihm helfen zu müssen	*to have to help him*
Ich will länger schlafen.	länger schlafen zu wollen	*to want to sleep longer*

ÜBUNG
23·3

Change each sentence into an infinitive clause.

FOR EXAMPLE: Er hat Deutsch gelernt.

_____ *Deutsch gelernt zu haben* _____

1. Wir sind zum Einkaufszentrum gefahren.

_____

2. Man soll ihnen danken.

_____

3. Es ist sehr kalt geworden.

_____

4. Du hast die Polizei angerufen.

_____

5. Ihr könnt nicht schneller laufen.

_____

6. Frau Keller hat eine Tasse Tee (*a cup of tea*) bestellt.

_____

7. Ich muss in die Schweiz reisen.

_____

8. Er hat einen Regenschirm (*umbrella*) mitgenommen.

_____

9. Sie ist langsam hereingekommen.

_____

10. Erik darf nicht alleine fahren.

_____

Infinitive clauses are most commonly used as replacements for nouns or noun phrases. For example:

Russisch ist schwierig.	*Russian is difficult.*
Russisch zu erlernen ist schwierig.	*To learn Russian is difficult.*
Er ging nach Hause ohne Tina.	*He went home without Tina.*
Er ging nach Hause, ohne seinen Regenschirm mitzunehmen.	*He went home without taking along his umbrella.*

Often sentences are introduced by **es** when that pronoun is *standing in* for an infinitive clause that ends the sentence. For example:

Es ist sehr wichtig einen Führerschein zu haben.	*It is very important to have a driver's license.*
Fiel **es** dir nicht ein deine Eltern anzurufen?	*Did it not occur to you to phone your parents?*

ÜBUNG
23·4

Change each numbered sentence into an infinitive clause that completes the main sentence.

FOR EXAMPLE: Es ist wichtig _____.

Man lernt eine zweite Sprache.

Es ist wichtig eine zweite Sprache zu lernen.

Es ist schwierig _____.

1. Ich verstehe den kranken Mann. _____

2. Wir lesen in dem dunklen Wohnzimmer. _____

3. Er rennt so schnell wie ein Pferd (*horse*). _____

4. Sie wohnen in einer kleinen Wohnung. _____

5. Sie arbeitet ohne einen Computer. _____

Ist es leicht (*easy*) _____?

6. Ich bekomme einen neuen Ausweis (*identity card*). _____

7. Sie erziehen (*raise*) elf Kinder. _____

8. Wir schicken einige Pakete nach Afghanistan. _____

9. Du trägst die schweren Koffer zum Bahnhof. _____

10. Er ist Politiker. _____

Four prepositions are frequently used with infinitive clauses: **anstatt zu**, **außer zu**, **ohne zu**, and **um zu**. The meaning of the prepositions is retained when used with infinitive phrases, except for **um**, which in English is translated as *in order to*. Let's look at some example sentences:

Sie ging nach Hause, **anstatt** uns damit **zu** helfen.	*She went home **instead of** helping us with it.*
Ich konnte nichts tun, **außer** mit ihm darüber **zu** streiten.	*I could not do anything **except** argue with him about it.*
Die Kinder verließen die Schule, **ohne** Abschied von der Lehrerin **zu** nehmen.	*The children left the school **without** saying good-bye to the teacher.*
Der Mann stiehlt das Geld, **um** Geschenke für seine Freundin **zu** kaufen.	*The man steals the money **in order** to buy his girlfriend presents.*

The phrase **um zu** can also be used following adjectives, in which case the meaning of *in order to* no longer applies. It can be simply translated as *to*.

Der Mann war zu schwach, **um** den schweren Koffer **zu** tragen.	*The man was too weak to carry the heavy suitcase.*

ÜBUNG
23·5

Change each numbered sentence into an infinitive clause with the provided preposition to complete the main sentence.

FOR EXAMPLE: Sie geht nach Hause, ohne _____.

Sie bezahlt dafür.   *Sie geht nach Hause, ohne dafür zu bezahlen.*

Sie trägt keinen Mantel.   *Sie geht nach Hause, ohne einen Mantel zu tragen.*

Erik sass einfach da, anstatt _____.

1. Er arbeitet im Garten. _____

2. Er schreibt den wichtigen Brief. _____

3. Er bereitet die Suppe vor. _____

Was konnten sie tun, außer _____?

4. Sie heben den armen Mann auf (*lift up*). _____

5. Sie bestellen noch eine Flasche Wein. _____

6. Sie strafen den unartigen (*naughty*) Jungen. _____

Sie fuhr mit dem Bus ab, ohne _____.

7. Sie hat eine Fahrkarte gekauft. _____

8. Sie nimmt von uns Abschied. _____

9. Sie weint. _____

Du bist jetzt alt genug, um _____.

10. Du wählst deine Kleider (*clothing*) aus (*choose*). _____

11. Du dienst beim Militär (*in the military*). _____

12. Du arbeitest in der Fabrik. _____

Sie sind nach Weimar gezogen, um _____.

13. Sie können mehr Geld verdienen (*earn*). _____

14. Sie suchen einen guten Job. _____

15. Sie untersuchen (*research*) Goethes Leben (*life*). _____

The passive voice

The sentences that you have been working with in this book so far have been in the *active voice*. The active voice is composed of a subject and a verb and a variety of other accompanying elements.

Er ist ein netter Mann	*He is a nice man.*
Ich kaufte einen Mantel.	*I bought a coat.*
Wir gehen zum Stadtpark.	*We go to the city park.*

The passive voice is composed of the same elements that are in an active-voice sentence that has a *transitive verb*. The transitive verb is essential, because only such verbs can have a direct object. For example, **küssen** is a transitive verb.

Martin küsste das Mädchen.	*Martin kissed the girl.*

In the example sentence, **das Mädchen** is the direct object. Let's look at the way English forms a passive-voice sentence from this example sentence. The subject becomes the object of the preposition *by*: *by Martin*. The direct object becomes the subject of the passive sentence: *the girl*. The verb *to be* is conjugated in the same tense as the original verb for the subject *the girl*: *the girl was*. The verb becomes a past participle: *kissed*. Put together, these elements create a passive sentence.

The girl was kissed by Martin.

It is a passive-voice sentence because the subject of the active sentence is now in a passive position in the new sentence and no longer functions as the subject.

Forming the German passive-voice sentence is similar. The subject of the active-voice sentence becomes the object of the preposition **von**: **von Martin**. The direct object becomes the subject of the passive sentence: **das Mädchen**. The verb **werden** is conjugated in the same tense as the original verb for the subject **das Mädchen**: **das Mädchen wurde**. The verb becomes a past participle: **geküsst**. When these elements are put together, a passive sentence is created.

Das Mädchen **wurde** von Martin **geküsst**.	*The girl was kissed by Martin.*

This sentence as well as all other passive sentences can occur in other tenses. For example:

PRESENT	Das Mädchen wird von Martin geküsst.	*The girl is kissed by Martin.*
PAST	Das Mädchen wurde von Martin geküsst.	*The girl was kissed by Martin.*
PRES PERF	Das Mädchen ist von Martin geküsst worden.	*The girl has been kissed by Martin.*
FUTURE	Das Mädchen wird von Martin geküsst werden.	*The girl will be kissed by Martin.*

Notice that the past participle for **werden** in the passive voice is **worden**. Use **geworden** only when the verb means *to become* or *to get*:

Es ist kalt geworden.   *It has become cold.*

Let's look at another example of how an active-voice sentence is changed to a passive-voice sentence.

ACTIVE	Er bestellt ein Glas Bier.	*He orders a glass of beer.*
PASSIVE	Ein Glas Bier **wird** von ihm **bestellt**.	*A glass of beer is ordered by him.*

It is necessary for the verb **werden** to be in the same tense as the original verb in the active sentence. Since **bestellt** is in the present tense, **wird** is used in the present-tense passive sentence. Let's look at this sentence in the other tenses:

PRESENT	Ein Glas Bier wird von ihm bestellt.
PAST	Ein Glas Bier wurde von ihm bestellt.
PRES PERF	Ein Glas Bier ist von ihm bestellt worden.
FUTURE	Ein Glas Bier wird von ihm bestellt werden.

ÜBUNG
24·1

Rewrite each passive sentence in the missing tenses.

1. Present <u>Die Maus wird von der Eule gefressen.</u> (*The mouse is eaten by the owl.*)

Past _____

Pres perf _____

Future _____

2. Present _____

Past   <u>Der Kranke wurde von der Ärztin geheilt.</u> (*The sick man was healed by the doctor.*)

Pres perf _____

Future _____

3. Present _____

Past _____

Pres perf <u>Der Artikel ist von ihm gelesen worden.</u> (*The article has been read by him.*)

Future _____

4. Present _____

   Past _____

   Pres perf _____

   Future Die Briefe werden von mir geschrieben werden. (*The letters will be written by me.*)

5. Present _____

   Past Die Schüler wurden vom Lehrer unterrichtet. (*The pupils were taught by the teacher.*)

   Pres perf _____

   Future _____

6. Present _____

   Past _____

   Pres perf _____

   Future Die Anzüge werden vom Schneider genäht werden. (*The suits will be sewn by the tailor.*)

7. Present Das Brot wird von Herrn Benz gekauft. (*The bread is bought by Mr. Benz.*)

   Past _____

   Pres perf _____

   Future _____

8. Present _____

   Past _____

   Pres perf Eine Tasse Kaffee ist von der Kellnerin gebracht worden. (*A cup of tea is brought by the waitress.*)

   Future _____

The prepositional phrase that is formed with **von** does not always appear in a passive sentence. In such a case, the *doer* of the action in the active-voice sentence remains anonymous. For example:

> Das Rathaus wurde im Stadtzentrum gebaut.　　*The city hall was built in the center of the city.*

The builder of the city hall is not provided in the example sentence and remains anonymous.

Also, **von** can be replaced by **durch** when the object of that preposition is the *means* by which the action of the verb was carried out or is the *cause* of that action. For example:

> Der Mann wurde **durch** einen Unfall getötet.　　*The man was killed **due to** an accident.*
> Der Brief wird **durch** die Post befördert.　　*The letter is sent **in** the mail.*

Rewrite the following active-voice sentences in the passive voice. Retain the tense of the original.

1. Der Feind (*enemy*) hat das Dorf (*village*) zerstört.

   _____

2. Ein Waldbrand bedroht (*forest fire threatens*) den Bauernhof (*farm*).

   _____

3. Ein Schuss (*shot*) tötete den alten Hund.

   _____

4. Der Bauer (*farmer*) wird viele Schweine aufziehen (*raise pigs*).

   _____

5. Der Lehrer hat die Aufsätze verbessert (*corrected the themes*).

   _____

If the object of the verb in an active sentence is in the dative case, the dative case will also be used in the passive sentence. For example:

Sie halfen meiner Mutter.	*They helped my mother.*
Meiner Mutter wurde von ihnen geholfen.	***My mother** was helped by them.*
Niemand hat ihm geglaubt.	*No one believed him.*
Ihm ist von niemandem geglaubt worden.	***He** was believed by no one.*

This passive-voice pattern is used with the dative verbs that you encountered in Chapter 12.

Rewrite the active-voice sentences in the passive voice. Retain the tense of the original verb. Note that some of the sentences have dative verbs in them.

1. Sein Gedicht imponierte dem Professor.

   _____

2. Ich habe der alten Frau geholfen.

   _____

3. Du hast dem König (*king*) gut gedient.

   _____

4. Alle werden das Lied (*song*) singen.

   _____

5. Der Dieb droht uns mit einer Pistole (*pistol*).

_____

6. Ich habe den Mann in Berlin gesehen.

_____

7. Der Soldat dankte mir für das Geschenk.

_____

8. Die Kinder werden das Eis essen.

_____

9. Das Rauchen (*smoking*) schadet der Gesundheit (*health*).

_____

10. Ein guter Freund hat ihm geraten.

_____

There can be both accusative and dative objects in an active-voice sentence. In such cases, the accusative object always becomes the subject of the passive-voice sentence. For example:

| Er gab der Frau eine Zeitung. | *He gave the woman a newspaper.* |
| **Eine Zeitung** wurde der Frau von ihm gegeben. | *A **newspaper** was given to the woman by him.* |

It is possible, however, to begin the passive-voice sentence with the dative object while still using the accusative object as the subject of the passive-voice sentence.

Der Frau wurde **eine Zeitung** von ihm gegeben.

German has another form of passive that uses **sein** as its auxiliary in place of **werden**. When **sein** is used, the meaning of the sentence is changed. With **werden**, the meaning is that an action is taking place:

| Das Haus **wird** gebaut. | *The house **is being** built.* |

With **sein**, the meaning is that the action is completed and the participle tells what the condition of the subject is. That is, the participle acts more like an adjective than a verb:

| Das Haus **ist** gebaut. | *The house **is** (already) built.* |

Let's look at a few more examples:

Das Theater **wurde** zerstört.	*The theater **was being** destroyed.*
Das Theater **war** zerstört.	*The theater **was** (already) destroyed.*
Ihr Finger **wird** verletzt.	*Her finger **is** (getting) injured.*
Ihr Finger **ist** verletzt.	*Her finger **is** (already) injured.*

Modal auxiliaries can be used in passive-voice sentences. But in such cases, the verb **werden** is used as an infinitive and follows the past participle in the sentence. For example:

Dem alten Mann **muss** geholfen werden.   *The old man **must** be helped.*
Kann das Radio nicht repariert werden?   ***Can** the radio not be repaired?*
Erik **soll** nicht eingeladen werden.   *Erik **should** not be invited.*
Dieser Aufsatz **durfte** nicht geschrieben   *This theme was not **allowed** to*
    werden.   *be written.*
Er wird fotografiert werden **wollen**.   *He **will** want to be photographed.*

ÜBUNG
24·4

Rewrite each sentence with the modal auxiliaries provided.

FOR EXAMPLE   Das Buch wird nicht gelesen.

müssen   *Das Buch muss nicht gelesen werden.*

Ein Haus wird hier gebaut.

1. müssen _____

2. können _____

3. sollen _____

Ihm wurde damit geholfen.

4. wollen _____

5. sollen _____

6. können _____

Das Problem wird auch von ihr verstanden.

7. können _____

8. müssen _____

Das Auto wird nicht repariert werden.

9. können _____

10. müssen _____

A special phrase is often used in place of a passive voice conjugation: **es/das lässt sich**. It is a replacement for the modal **können** in a passive structure and is used with an infinitive rather than a past participle. For example:

Das **lässt sich** nicht sagen.   *That **cannot be** said.*
Es **lässt sich** leicht tun.   *It **can** easily **be** done.*

This structure can be used in all the tenses.

PRESENT	Das **lässt sich** nicht tun.	*That **cannot be** done.*
PAST	Das **ließ sich** nicht tun.	*That **could not be** done.*
PRES PERF	Das hat **sich** nicht tun **lassen**.	*That **could** not be done.*
FUTURE	Das wird **sich** nicht tun **lassen**.	*That will not **be able to be** done.*

ÜBUNG
24·5

Rewrite each passive sentence in the missing tenses.

1. Present Das lässt sich nicht leicht ändern (change easily).

   Past _____

   Pres perf _____

   Future _____

2. Present _____

   Past Das Geld konnte nicht gefunden werden.

   Pres perf _____

   Future _____

3. Present _____

   Past _____

   Pres perf _____

   Future Diese Probleme werden sich schnell lösen lassen.

4. Present _____

   Past _____

   Pres perf Ihnen ist dafür gedankt worden.

   Future _____

5. Present Der Hund ist gewaschen.

   Past _____

   Pres perf _____

   Future _____

The subjunctive

Forming the subjunctive

The subjunctive conjugations have endings that are readily recognized, because they resemble so closely the endings of the German past tense. The subjunctive falls into two categories: the present subjunctive, or subjunctive I, and the past subjunctive, or subjunctive II. In this book, they will be called subjunctive I and II.

The subjunctive I conjugation is formed from the stem of a verb and the following endings: **-e, -est, -e, -en, -et, -en**. There are no differences between regular and irregular verbs or modal auxiliaries. For example:

	stellen	**besuchen**	**können**	**abfahren**
ich	stelle	besuche	könne	fahre ab
du	stellest	besuchest	könnest	fahrest ab
er	stelle	besuche	könne	fahre ab
wir	stellen	besuchen	können	fahren ab
ihr	stellet	besuchet	könnet	fahret ab
Sie	stellen	besuchen	können	fahren ab

Let's look at the three special verbs of the German language in subjunctive I.

	haben	**sein**	**werden**
ich	habe	sei	werde
du	habest	seiest	werdest
er	habe	sei	werde
wir	haben	seien	werden
ihr	habet	seiet	werdet
Sie	haben	seien	werden

ÜBUNG

25·1

Write the full subjunctive I conjugation for each of the following verbs.

1.	müssen	tragen	versuchen
ich	_____	_____	_____
du	_____	_____	_____
er	_____	_____	_____
wir	_____	_____	_____

ihr	_____	_____	_____
Sie	_____	_____	_____

2.

	ansehen	laufen	interessieren
ich	_____	_____	_____
du	_____	_____	_____
er	_____	_____	_____
wir	_____	_____	_____
ihr	_____	_____	_____
Sie	_____	_____	_____

3.

	wissen	wollen	ausgeben (*spend*)
ich	_____	_____	_____
du	_____	_____	_____
er	_____	_____	_____
wir	_____	_____	_____
ihr	_____	_____	_____
Sie	_____	_____	_____

The subjunctive II conjugation is derived from the past tense of a verb. In the subjunctive II conjugation, there is an important difference in how regular and irregular verbs are formed. Regular verbs are identical to the regular past tense. For example:

	machen	vorstellen	verkaufen
ich	machte	stellte vor	verkaufte
du	machtest	stelltest vor	verkauftest
er	machte	stellte vor	verkaufte
wir	machten	stellten vor	verkauften
ihr	machtet	stelltet vor	verkauftet
Sie	machten	stellten vor	verkauften

The subjunctive II conjugation of irregular verbs is formed from the irregular past tense of the verb. If the past tense has an umlaut vowel (**a, o, u**), an umlaut is added in the subjunctive II conjugation. The endings used in this conjugation are **-e, -est, -e, -en, -et, -en**. Let's look at some example verbs:

	sehen	bleiben	versprechen	abfahren
ich	sähe	bliebe	verspräche	führe ab
du	sähest	bliebest	versprächest	führest ab
er	sähe	bliebe	verspräche	führe ab
wir	sähen	blieben	versprächen	führen ab
ihr	sähet	bliebet	versprächet	führet ab
Sie	sähen	blieben	versprächen	führen ab

Modal auxiliaries form their past tense with a **-te** suffix, and if there is an umlaut in the infinitive, it is omitted in the past tense. However, in the subjunctive II conjugation, the umlaut is added.

	sollen	**müssen**	**können**	**mögen**
ich	sollte	müsste	könnte	möchte
du	solltest	müsstest	könntest	möchtest
er	sollte	müsste	könnte	möchte
wir	sollten	müssten	könnten	möchten
ihr	solltet	müsstet	könntet	möchtet
Sie	sollten	müssten	könnten	möchten

A small list of irregular verbs forms a new stem for the subjunctive II conjugation. They are:

INFINITIVE	SUBJUNCTIVE II	
empfehlen	empföhle	*recommend*
gelten	gölte/gälte	*be valid*
helfen	hülfe	*help*
schwimmen	schwömme	*swim*
schwören	schwüre	*swear*
stehen	stünde/stände	*stand*
sterben	stürbe	*die*
verderben	verdürbe	*spoil*
verstehen	verstünde/verstände	*understand*
werben	würbe	*recruit*
werfen	würfe	*throw*

ÜBUNG
25·2

Write the full subjunctive II conjugation for each of the following verbs.

1. | schlafen | essen | wollen |

ich _____ _____ _____

du _____ _____ _____

er _____ _____ _____

wir _____ _____ _____

ihr _____ _____ _____

Sie _____ _____ _____

2. | einladen | trinken | mitgehen |

ich _____ _____ _____

du _____ _____ _____

er _____ _____ _____

wir _____ _____ _____

| ihr | _____ | _____ | _____ |
| Sie | _____ | _____ | _____ |

3.   dürfen   verstehen   anrufen

ich	_____	_____	_____
du	_____	_____	_____
er	_____	_____	_____
wir	_____	_____	_____
ihr	_____	_____	_____
Sie	_____	_____	_____

The verbs **haben**, **sein**, and **werden** are conjugated in the following ways in subjunctive II:

	haben	**sein**	**werden**
ich	hätte	wäre	würde
du	hättest	wärest	würdest
er	hätte	wäre	würde
wir	hätten	wären	würden
ihr	hättet	wäret	würdet
Sie	hätten	wären	würden

The mixed verbs have a unique form that does not conform to regular or irregular verb patterns in the subjunctive.

	wissen	**denken**	**brennen**
ich	wüsste	dächte	brennte
du	wüsstest	dächtest	brenntest
er	wüsste	dächte	brennte
wir	wüssten	dächten	brennten
ihr	wüsstet	dächtet	brenntet
Sie	wüssten	dächten	brennten

ÜBUNG
25·3

Write the full subjunctive II conjugation for each of the following verbs.

1.   nennen   erkennen   sein

ich	_____	_____	_____
du	_____	_____	_____
er	_____	_____	_____
wir	_____	_____	_____
ihr	_____	_____	_____
Sie	_____	_____	_____

2.	haben	bringen	werden
ich	_____	_____	_____
du	_____	_____	_____
er	_____	_____	_____
wir	_____	_____	_____
ihr	_____	_____	_____
Sie	_____	_____	_____

Using the subjunctive

The subjunctive I conjugation is used most frequently in *indirect discourse*. When reporting what someone else has said, the verb in the reported statement will be in subjunctive I. For example:

Thomas sagte, dass seine Freundin krank **sei**.	*Thomas said that his girlfriend **is** sick.*
Sie berichtete, dass der Richter nach Paris fahren **werde**.	*She reported that the judge **will** travel to Paris.*
Er fragte, ob Tina es verkauft **habe**.	*He asked whether (if) Tina bought it.*
Wir fragten, ob Karl ihnen helfen **könne**.	*We asked whether Karl **can** help them.*

If the subjunctive I form is identical to the indicative, the subjunctive II conjugation is used.

Er sagte, dass sie in Frankreich **wohnten**.	*He said that they **live** in France.*
Erik fragte, ob die Kinder es verstehen **könnten**.	*Erik asked whether the children **can** understand it.*

Rewrite the incomplete sentence as indirect discourse using the given phrase.

FOR EXAMPLE: Er sagte, dass _____.

Sie wohnt in Hamburg.   *Er sagte, dass sie in Hamburg wohne.*

Der Reporter berichtete, dass _____.

1. Der Kanzler (*chancellor*) wird bald gesund.

   _____

2. Niemand versteht die Rede.

   _____

3. Die Touristen reisen nach Italien.

   _____

4. Die alte Frau ist gestorben.

   _____

5. Herr Dorf wird in Polen wohnen.

Sie haben ihn gefragt, ob _____.

6. Ist seine Frau wieder in der Schweiz?

_____

7. Können die Kinder Fußball spielen?

_____

8. Hat er genug Geld?

_____

9. Wissen sie, wo sie ist?

_____

10. Muss der Junge bestraft werden?

_____

If a sentence is in the past, present perfect, or past perfect tense, it is structured like the present perfect tense in subjunctive I. For example:

Er sang gut.	Sie sagte, dass er gut **gesungen habe.**
Er hat gut gesungen.	Sie sagte, dass er gut **gesungen habe.**
Er hatte gut gesungen.	Sie sagte, dass er gut **gesungen habe.**
Er ging mit.	Sie fragte, ob er **mitgegangen sei.**
Er ist mitgegangen.	Sie fragte, ob er **mitgegangen sei.**
Er war mitgegangen.	Sie fragte, ob er **mitgegangen sei.**

If a modal auxiliary is in the past tense, the present perfect structure is not used and the modal is conjugated in subjunctive II.

Er konnte gut singen.	Sie sagte, dass er gut singen **könnte.**	*She said that he could sing well.*

It is possible to omit **dass** in indirect discourse, which changes the word order. For example:

Er sagte, er **habe** gut gesungen.	*He said he sang well.*
Sie berichtete, der Mann **verstehe** das Problem nicht.	*She reported the man does not understand the problem.*

ÜBUNG

25·5

Rewrite the incomplete sentence as indirect discourse using the given phrase.

Der Richter hat gesagt, dass _____.

1. Der Junge spielte mit dem Hund.

_____

2. Wir haben die Uhr verloren.

_____

3. Sie waren mit dem Bus gefahren.

_____

4. Erik stahl das Auto.

_____

5. Der Dieb war zwei Stunden im Keller.

_____

Sonja berichtete, dass _____.

6. Sie hatten eine neue Speise (*food*) gekocht.

_____

7. Karl kam zu spät.

_____

8. Ihre Tochter hat gut getanzt.

_____

9. Mein Vater gab ihr zehn Euro.

_____

10. Martin dachte oft an uns.

_____

In conversational German it is common to use a subjunctive II conjugation in indirect discourse.

FORMAL	CONVERSATIONAL
Sie sagte, er **habe** keine Zeit.	Sie sagte, er **hätte** keine Zeit.

The subjunctive II conjugation is also used when stating a *wish* that is introduced by **wenn** (*if*). For example:

Wenn mein Vater nur hier **wäre**!	*If only my father **were** here.*
Wenn wir doch bei unseren Eltern **wären**!	*If we **were** only with our parents.*
Wenn sie nur mehr Zeit **hätte**!	*If only she **had** more time.*

Wenn can be omitted; then the sentence would begin with the verb:

Wäre mein Vater nur hier!	*If only my father **were** here.*
Könntest du doch ihnen helfen!	*If you **could** only help them.*
Hätte er doch seine Frau nie verlassen!	*If only he **had** not left his wife.*

*Rewrite each sentence as a wish statement with **wenn** in subjunctive II.*

FOR EXAMPLE: Er hat mehr Geld.

Wenn er mehr Geld hätte!

1. Ich bin in meiner Heimat (*home/homeland*).

_____

2. Er hat mehr Mut (*courage*).

_____

3. Wir haben mehr Glück (*luck*) gehabt.

_____

4. Er ist nicht in die Stadt gefahren.

_____

5. Du hast besser gearbeitet.

_____

The subjunctive II conjugation is used in clauses that are introduced by **als ob** or **als wenn** (*as if*). For example:

Er sprach, **als ob** er alles verstehen **könnte**.   *He spoke **as if** he could understand everything.*

Sie tat so, **als wenn** sie viel schöner **wäre**.   *She acted **as if** she were much prettier.*

Complete each sentence with the phrases provided.

Der Mann schrie (*screamed*), als ob _____.

1. Er ist verletzt.

_____

2. Er hasst (*hates*) uns.

_____

3. Wir sind taub (*deaf*).

_____

Ihr Gesicht sah aus (*her face looked*), als ob _____.

4. Sie ist sehr krank gewesen.

_____

5. Sie kann ihm überhaupt nicht glauben.

_____

6. Sie hat ein Ungeheuer (*monster*) gesehen.

_____

Die Frau tat so, als ob _____.

7. Sie liebt ihn.

_____

8. Sie hat den Mann nie kennen gelernt (*never became acquainted with*).

_____

9. Ich bin ihr Diener (*servant*).

_____

10. Sie kann perfekt Deutsch sprechen.

_____

The conjunction **wenn** is used in another form that requires a subjunctive II conjugation. This occurs in a *conditional* sentence. Conditional sentences set a condition with a proposed result. In English, they look as follows:

CONDITION	RESULT
If John were here,	*he would surely help me.*
If I were rich,	*I would buy a new sports car.*

German structures conditional sentences in the same way. Where the English word *would* is used in the *result* clause, German uses the subjunctive II verb **würde**. For example:

Wenn er hier wäre, **würde** er mir helfen.	*If he were here, he **would** help me.*
Wenn ich reich wäre, **würde** ich ein großes Haus kaufen.	*If I were rich, I **would** buy a big house.*
Wenn sie mehr Zeit hätte, **würde** sie eine Suppe vorbereiten.	*If she had more time, she **would** prepare a soup.*

It is possible to place the conditional clause at the end of the sentence.

Er **würde** mir helfen, wenn er hier wäre.

To indicate conditions and results in the past, the present perfect structure is used. In such cases, the verb **würde** can be omitted.

Wenn er hier gewesen wäre, hätte er mir geholfen.	*If he had been here, he would have helped me.*
Wenn sie mehr Zeit gehabt hätte, hätte sie eine Suppe vorbereitet.	*If she had had more time, she would have prepared a soup.*

The verb **würde** can also be omitted if there is a modal auxiliary in the sentence.

Wenn ich sie sähe, könnte ich sie begrüßen. *If I saw them, I could say hello to them.*
Wenn er eine Fahrkarte hätte, müsste er nach *If he had a ticket, he would have to*
Bonn reisen. *travel to Bonn.*

To indicate conditions and results in the past, the present perfect structure is used in these sentences.

Wenn er eine Fahrkarte gehabt hätte, hätte *If he had had a ticket, he would have*
er nach Bonn reisen müssen. *had to travel to Bonn.*

ÜBUNG
25·8

*Combine each pair of sentences by introducing the first sentence as a **wenn**-clause and making the second clause the result.*

FOR EXAMPLE: Er hat mehr Zeit. Er besucht seinen Onkel.
Wenn er mehr Zeit hätte, würde er seinen Onkel besuchen.

1. Tina gewinnt im Lotto. Sie kauft sich einen Pelzmantel (*fur coat*).

_____

2. Der Mann schläft lange. Er kann nicht arbeiten.

_____

3. Sie fand das verlorene Geld. Sie musste es dem Polizisten geben.

_____

4. Das Wetter ist schlecht gewesen. Ich bin nicht auf das Land gefahren.

_____

5. Der Student war nicht aufmerksam (*attentive*). Er machte einen großen Fehler (*mistake*).

_____

6. Es ist nicht so weit. Ich gehe dorthin zu Fuß.

_____

7. Das Mädchen hat ein Gymnasium besucht. Sie konnte an einer Universität studieren.

_____

8. Die Frau arbeitet besser. Sie verdient (*earns*) mehr.

_____

9. Sie hat uns angerufen. Ich habe sie vom Bahnhof abgeholt.

_____

10. Du bist wieder gesund. Du musst wieder einen Job finden.

_____

Final Review

Use the following review exercises to check your competence with the content of this book. If you are not satisfied with the results of an exercise, review the appropriate unit and do the review again.

ÜBUNG

R3·1

Circle the letter of the answer that best completes the sentence.

1. What is the vowel sound of the combination of letters **eu?**
   A. ah
   B. oo
   C. oi
   D. oh

2. Das ist _____ Bild von meiner Mutter.
   A. keine
   B. ein
   C. der
   D. keiner

3. Das ist Herr Keller. _____ ist sehr alt.
   A. Sie
   B. Er
   C. Dies
   D. Es

4. Guten Tag. Ich _____ Thomas. Thomas Schuhmann.
   A. bist
   B. sein
   C. heiße
   D. heißt

5. Es _____ wieder regnerisch.
   A. am schlechtesten
   B. habt
   C. wird
   D. nicht

6. Heißt _____ Thomas?
   A. Sie
   B. du
   C. wir
   D. Thomas und Gudrun

7. Mein Vater kauft _____ neuen Regenmantel.
   A. einen
   B. kein
   C. mich
   D. die Kinder

8. Meine Mutter _____ einen neuen Roman.
   A. liest
   B. fandet
   C. haltet
   D. sterbt

9. Ich stelle meine Gäste _____.
   A. vor
   B. meine Familie
   C. Tante Marianne
   D. Ihnen

10. Kinder, _____ nur Deutsch!
    A. sprecht
    B. singt
    C. schriebt
    D. wider

Circle the letter of the answer that best completes each sentence.

1. Gestern _____ Sonja im Blumengarten.
   A. machte … zu
   B. wohntet
   C. hatte
   D. arbeitete

2. Wir müssen _____ danken.
   A. unsere Eltern
   B. Sie
   C. den Arzt
   D. ihnen

3. Er _____ zu viel Geld aus.
   A. findet
   B. machtet
   C. gab
   D. wusste

4. Er _____ ein neues Hemd machen.
   A. lässt
   B. solltet
   C. kaufte
   D. wollt

5. Warum müssen wir _____ warten?
   A. an sie
   B. dafür
   C. auf ihn
   D. von euch

6. Wer ist mit euch _____?
   A. finden
   B. gereist
   C. kommen
   D. badete

7. _____ Sie an dieser Universität studiert?
   A. Wird
   B. Werden
   C. Haben
   D. Gehabt

8. _____ ihr durch die Straßen marschiert?
   A. Wohin
   B. Wo
   C. Seid
   B. Ist

9. Der Pullover _____ liegt auf dem Boden.
   A. meiner Freundin
   B. an dem Gast
   C. an die Soldaten
   D. meinen Freund

10. Sie wohnen diesseits des _____.
   A. Flusses
   B. See
   C. eine See
   D. die westliche Grenze

ÜBUNG

R3·3

Circle the letter of the answer that best completes each sentence.

1. Dieser Roman ist viel interessanter _____ der Andere.
   A. von
   B. davon
   C. neuer
   D. als

2. Ich kam früh, aber meine Frau kam _____.
   A. späte
   B. längeren
   C. am frühesten
   D. früher als

3. Ich habe ein Glas Bier _____.
   A. müssen
   B. versprechen
   C. getrunken
   D. gesollt

4. Wie weit sind Sie _____?
   A. gelassen
   B. gefahren
   C. bekommen
   D. besuchen

5. Mein Sohn ist so müde _____.
   A. geworden
   B. hatte
   C. war
   D. gewollt

6. Tina hat ein _____ Kleid gekauft.
   A. teuer
   B. billiger
   C. kleines
   D. schönes

7. Seid ihr an der Bushaltestelle _____?
   A. vergessen
   B. ausgestiegen
   C. gelernt
   D. geworden

8. Der Zug _____ endlich gekommen.
   A. war
   B. hat
   C. hatte
   D. sind

9. _____ du den ganzen Kuchen gegessen?
   A. haben
   B. wirst
   C. kannst
   D. hattest

10. Ich werde es gelesen _____.
    A. sein
    B. reisen
    C. haben
    D. Machen

Circle the letter of the answer that best completes each sentence.

1. Sie hatten ihn Werner _____.
   A. sagen
   B. gefragt
   C. passieren
   D. genannt

2. Das ist der Junge, _____.
   A. welche in Schillerstraße wohnt
   B. das das Geld gefunden hat
   C. welcher schläft im Wohnzimmer
   D. den wir suchen

3. Martin tanzte mit dem Mädchen, _____.
   A. von dem er ein Geschenk bekam
   B. das wohnt in Heidelberg
   C. für den er gearbeitet hat
   D. der ich danken möchte

4. Sie liebt die roten Rosen, _____.
   A. welche Heinz für sie gekauft hat
   B. welchen ich gekauft habe
   C. an welches ich mich erinnere
   D. mit welcher ich gekommen bin

5. Tina findet etwas, _____.
   A. das in der Schublade war
   B. welche alt und schmutzig ist
   C. wessen Bruder in Amerika wohnt
   D. was aus Eichenholz und Silber ist

6. Ein _____ Flugzeug fliegt sehr schnell.
   A. so
   B. welches
   C. solches
   D. deutsche

7. Viele _____ Studentinnen mussten im Studentenheim wohnen.
   A. neuen
   B. kluger
   C. ausländische
   D. französisch

8. Herr Fischer fragte, _____.
   A. sind Sie aus Kanada
   B. wie alt meine Schwester ist
   C. wohin gehen wir heute Abend
   D. kannst du mir damit helfen

9. Ich habe mein Fahrrad nicht _____.
   A. kaufen wollen
   B. verkaufen werden
   C. verkaufen will
   D. gekauft haben

10. Der Lehrer hat die Kinder lachen _____.
   A. gesollt
   B. machen will
   C. hören
   D. sehen werden

Circle the letter of the answer that best completes each sentence.

1. Niemand hat die Mädchen im Wald ___.
   A. gegangen
   B. getrunken
   C. haben können
   D. wandern sehen

2. Es ist wichtig ___.
   A. immer fleißig zu arbeiten
   B. bekommen einen neuen Ausweis
   C. zu sein
   D. man muss ruhig sein

3. Sie gingen nach Hause, ___.
   A. bitten um Hilfe
   B. laufen zum Stadtpark
   C. den Wagen reparieren lassen
   D. ohne dafür zu bezahlen

4. Seine Familie ist nach Oslo gezogen, ___ norwegisch zu lernen.
   A. in
   B. um
   C. darüber
   D. vom

5. Die alte Frau ___ von Doktor Benz geheilt.
   A. wurde
   B. sollte
   C. kann
   D. wart

6. _____ wird auch von Erik geholfen.
   A. Mein Sohn
   B. Diesen Herrn
   C. Unserer Mutter
   D. Er

7. Das _____ sich nicht leicht reparieren.
   A. konnte
   B. könnte
   C. lässt
   D. ließen

8. Er sagte, dass der Diplomat _____.

A. nach Moskau zieht

B. eine Reise nach Amerika machen werde

C. auch Englisch lernen muss

D. genug Euro gehabt hätten

9. Sie spricht, _____ sie mich liebte.
   A. als ob
   B. wessen
   C. seitdem
   D. noch nicht

10. Wenn wir mehr Geld gehabt hätten, _____.
    A. würden wir nach Bonn reisen
    B. wäre Karl auch eingeladen worden
    C. könne er bei uns wohnen
    D. seien wir sehr traurig gewesen

APPENDIX A

The principal parts of irregular verbs

Only the second-person and third-person singular are shown in the present tense. In the past tense, the third-person singular is provided. However, because of the number of irregularities in the conjugation, the full present tense conjugation of **sein** and **tun** is shown.

INDICATIVE				SUBJUNCTIVE
INFINITIVE	PRESENT	PAST	PAST PARTICIPLE	SUBJUNCTIVE II
backen	bäckst backte	buk *or* backte	gebacken	bäckt *or* büke
befehlen	befiehlst befiehlt	befahl	befohlen	beföhle
befleißen	befleißt befleißt	befliss	beflissen	beflisse
beginnen	beginnst beginnt	begann	begonnen	begönne
beißen	beißt beißt	biss	gebissen	bisse
bergen	birgst birgt	barg	geborgen	bärge
bersten	birst birst	barst	geborsten	bärste
betrügen	betrügst betrügt	betrog	betrogen	betröge
bewegen	bewegst bewegt	bewog	bewogen	bewöge
biegen	biegst biegt	bog	gebogen	böge
bieten	bietest bietet	bot	geboten	böte
binden	bindest bindet	band	gebunden	bände
bitten	bittest bittet	bat	gebeten	bäte
blasen	bläst bläst	blies	geblasen	bliese
bleiben	bleibst bleibt	blieb	geblieben	bliebe
bleichen	bleichst bleicht	blich	geblichen	bliche

INFINITIVE	PRESENT	PAST	PAST PARTICIPLE	SUBJUNCTIVE II
braten	brätst brät	briet	gebraten	briete
brechen	brichst bricht	brach	gebrochen	bräche
brennen	brennst brennt	brannte	gebrannt	brennte
bringen	bringst bringt	brachte	gebracht	brächte
denken	denkst denkt	dachte	gedacht	dächte
dingen	dingst dingt	dingte *or* dang	gedungen *or* gedingt	dingte *or* dänge
dreschen	drischst drischt	drosch	gedroschen	drösche
dringen	dringst dringt	drang	gedrungen	dränge
dürfen	darfst darf	durfte	gedürft	dürfte
empfangen	empfängst empfängt	empfing	empfangen	empfinge
empfehlen	empfiehlst empfiehlt	empfahl	empfohlen	empföhle *or* empfähle
empfinden	empfindest empfindet	empfand	empfunden	empfände
erbleichen	erbleichst erbleicht	erbleichte *or* erblich	erbleicht *or* erblichen	erbleichte *or* erbliche
erlöschen	erlischst erlischt	erlosch	erloschen	erlösche
erschrecken	erschrickst erschrickt	erschrak	erschrocken	erschräke
erwägen	erwägst erwägt	erwog	erwogen	erwöge
essen	isst isst	aß	gegessen	äße
fahren	fährst fährt	fuhr	gefahren	führe
fallen	fällst fällt	fiel	gefallen	fiele
fangen	fängst fängt	fing	gefangen	finge
fechten	fichtst ficht	focht	gefochten	föchte
finden	findest findet	fand	gefunden	fände
flechten	flichtst flicht	flocht	geflochten	flöchte
fliegen	fliegst fliegt	flog	geflogen	flöge
fliehen	fliehst flieht	floh	geflohen	flöhe
fließen	fließt fließt	floss	geflossen	flösse

INFINITIVE	PRESENT	PAST	PAST PARTICIPLE	SUBJUNCTIVE II
fressen	frisst frisst	fraß	gefressen	fräße
frieren	frierst friert	fror	gefroren	fröre
gären	gärst gärt	gor	gegoren	göre
gebären	gebierst gebiert	gebar	geboren	gebäre
geben	gibst gibt	gab	gegeben	gäbe
gedeihen	gedeihst gedeiht	gedieh	gediehen	gediehe
gehen	gehst geht	ging	gegangen	ginge
gelten	giltst gilt	galt gölte	gegolten	gälte *or*
genesen	genest genest	genas	genesen	genäse
genießen	genießt genießt	genoss	genossen	genösse
geraten	gerätst gerät	geriet	geraten	geriete
gewinnen	gewinnst gewinnt	gewann	gewonnen gewönne	gewänne *or*
gießen	gießt gießt	goss	gegossen	gösse
gleichen	gleichst gleicht	glich	geglichen	gliche
gleiten	gleitest gleitet	glitt	geglitten	glitte
glimmen	glimmst glimmt	glomm *or* glimmte	geglommen *or* geglimmt	glömme *or* glimmte
graben	gräbst gräbt	grub	gegraben	grübe
greifen	greifst greift	griff	gegriffen	griffe
haben	hast hat	hatte	gehabt	hätte
halten	hältst hält	hielt	gehalten	hielte
hängen	hängst hängt	hing	gehangen	hinge
hauen	haust haut	hieb	gehauen	hiebe
heben	hebst hebt	hob	gehoben	höbe
heißen	heißt heißt	hieß	geheißen	hieße
helfen	hilfst hilft	half	geholfen	hülfe or hälfe
kennen	kennst kennt	kannte	gekannt	kennte

The principal parts of irregular verbs **241**

INFINITIVE	PRESENT	PAST	PAST PARTICIPLE	SUBJUNCTIVE II
klimmen	klimmst klimmt	klomm *or* klimmte	geklommen *or* geklimmt	klömme *or* klimmte
klingen	klingst klingt	klang	geklungen	klänge
kneifen	kneifst kneift	kniff	gekniffen	kniffe
kommen	kommst kommt	kam	gekommen	käme
können	kannst kann	konnte	gekonnt	könnte
kriechen	kriechst kriecht	kroch	gekrochen	kröche
laden	lädst lädt *or* ladet	lud *or* ladete	geladen *or* geladet	lüde *or* ladete
lassen	lässt lässt	ließ	gelassen	ließe
laufen	läufst läuft	lief	gelaufen	liefe
leiden	leidest leidet	litt	gelitten	litte
leihen	leihst leiht	lieh	geliehen	liehe
lesen	liest liest	las	gelesen	läse
liegen	liegst liegt	lag	gelegen	läge
lügen	lügst lügt	log	gelogen	löge
mahlen	mahlst mahlt	mahlte	gemahlen	mahlte
meiden	meidest meidet	mied	gemieden	miede
melken	melkst melkt	melkte	gemelkt *or* gemolken (*adjective*)	mölke
messen	misst misst	maß	gemessen	mässe
mögen	magst mag	mochte	gemocht	möchte
müssen	musst muss	musste	gemusst	müsste
nehmen	nimmst nimmt	nahm	genommen	nähme
nennen	nennst nennt	nannte	genannt	nennte
pfeifen	pfeifst pfeift	pfiff	gepfiffen	pfiffe
pflegen	pflegst pflegt	pflegte *or* pflog	gepflegt *or* gepflogen	pflegte *or* pflöge
preisen	preist preist	pries	gepriesen	priese
quellen	quillst quillt	quoll	gequollen	quölle

INFINITIVE	PRESENT	PAST	PAST PARTICIPLE	SUBJUNCTIVE II
raten	rätst rät	riet	geraten	riete
reiben	reibst reibt	rieb	gerieben	riebe
reißen	reißt reißt	riss	gerissen	risse
reiten	reitest reitet	ritt	geritten	ritte
rennen	rennst rennt	rannte	gerannt	rennte
riechen	riechst riecht	roch	gerochen	röche
ringen	ringst ringt	rang	gerungen	ränge
rinnen	rinnst rinnt	rann	geronnen	ränne *or* rönne
rufen	rufst ruft	rief	gerufen	riefe
salzen	salzt salzt	salzte	gesalzt or gesalzen (*figurative*)	salzte
saufen	säufst säuft	soff	gesoffen	söffe
saugen	saugst saugt	sog	gesogen	söge
schaffen	schaffst schafft	schuf	geschaffen	schüfe
schallen	schallst schallt	schallte schölle	geschallt	schallte *or*
scheiden	scheidest scheidet	schied	geschieden	schiede
scheinen	scheinst scheint	schien	geschienen	schiene
schelten	schiltst schilt	schalt	gescholten	schölte
scheren	schierst schiert	schor *or* scherte	geschoren *or* geschert	schöre *or* scherte
schieben	schiebst schiebt	schob	geschoben	schöbe
schießen	schießt schießt	schoss	geschossen	schösse
schinden	schindest schindet	geschunden	schünde
schlafen	schläfst schläft	schlief	geschlafen	schliefe
schlagen	schlägst schlägt	schlug	geschlagen	schlüge
schleichen	schleichst schleicht	schlich	geschlichen	schliche
schleifen	schleifst schleift	schliff	geschliffen	schliffe

INFINITIVE	PRESENT	PAST	PAST PARTICIPLE	SUBJUNCTIVE II
schleißen	schleißt schleißt	schliss	geschlissen	schlisse
schliefen	schliefst schlieft	schloff	geschloffen	schlöffe
schließen	schließt schließt	schloss	geschlossen	schlösse
schlingen	schlingst schlingt	schlang	geschlungen	schlänge
schmeißen	schmeißt schmeißt	schmiss	geschmissen	schmisse
schmelzen	schmilzt schmilzt	schmolz	geschmolzen	schmölze
schneiden	schneidest schneidet	schnitt	geschnitten	schnitte
schrecken	schrickst schrickt	schrak	geschrocken	schräke
schreiben	schreibst schreibt	schrieb	geschrieben	schriebe
schreien	schreist schreit	schrie	geschrieen *or* geschrien	schriee
schreiten	schreitest schreitet	schritt	geschritten	schritte
schweigen	schweigst schweigt	schwieg	geschwiegen	schwiege
schwellen	schwillst schwillt	schwoll	geschwollen	schwölle
schwimmen	schwimmst schwimmt	schwamm	geschwommen	schwömme *or* schwämme
schwinden	schwindest schwindet	schwand	geschwunden	schwände
schwingen	schwingst schwingt	schwang	geschwungen	schwänge
schwören	schwörst schwört	schwor	geschworen	schwüre *or* schwöre
sehen	siehst sieht	sah	gesehen	sähe
sein	bin bist ist sind seid sind	war	gewesen	wäre
senden	sendest sendet	sandte *or* sendete	gesandt *or* gesendet	sendete
sieden	siedest siedet	sott *or* siedete	gesotten	sötte *or* siedete
singen	singst singt	sang	gesungen	sänge
sinken	sinkst sinkt	sank	gesunken	sänke
sinnen	sinnst sinnt	sann	gesonnen	sänne *or* sönne
sitzen	sitzt sitzt	saß	gesessen	säße

INFINITIVE	PRESENT	PAST	PAST PARTICIPLE	SUBJUNCTIVE II
sollen	sollst soll	sollte	gesollt	sollte
spalten	spaltest spaltet	spaltete gespaltet	gespalten *or*	spaltete
speien	speist speit	spie	gespieen *or* gespien	spiee
spinnen	spinnst spinnt	spann	gesponnen	spönne
spleißen	spleißt spleißt	spliss	gesplissen	splisse
sprechen	sprichst spricht	sprach	gesprochen	spräche
sprießen	sprießt sprießt	spross	gesprossen	sprösse
springen	springst springt	sprang	gesprungen	spränge
stechen	stichst sticht	stach	gestochen	stäche
stecken	steckst steckt	steckte *or* stak	gesteckt	steckte *or* stäke
stehen	stehst steht	stand stände	gestanden	stünde *or*
stehlen	stiehlst stiehlt	stahl	gestohlen	stöhle or stähle
steigen	steigst steigt	stieg	gestiegen	stiege
sterben	stirbst stirbt	starb	gestorben	stürbe
stieben	stiebst stiebt	stob *or* stiebte	gestoben *or* gestiebt	stöbe *or* stiebte
stinken	stinkst stinkt	stank	gestunken	stänke
stoßen	stößt stößt	stieß	gestoßen	stieße
streichen	streichst streicht	strich	gestrichen	striche
streiten	streitest streitet	stritt	gestritten	stritte
tragen	trägst trägt	trug	getragen	trüge
treffen	triffst trifft	traf	getroffen	träfe
treiben	treibst treibt	trieb	getrieben	triebe
treten	trittst tritt	trat	getreten	träte
triefen	triefst trieft	troff	getrieft	tröffe
trinken	trinkst trinkt	trank	getrunken	tränke

INFINITIVE	PRESENT	PAST	PAST PARTICIPLE	SUBJUNCTIVE II
tun	tue tust tut tun tut tun	tat	getan	täte
verderben	verdirbst verdirbt	verdarb	verdorben	verdürbe
verdrießen	verdrießt verdrießt	verdross	verdrossen	verdrösse
vergessen	vergisst vergisst	vergaß	vergessen	vergäße
verhehlen	verhehlst verhehlt	verhelte	verhehlt	verhehlte
verlieren	verlierst verliert	verlor	verloren	verlöre
verwirren	verwirrst verwirrt	verwirrte	verwirrt *or* verworren (*adjective*)	verwirrte
wachsen	wächst wächst	wuchs	gewachsen	wüchse
wägen	wägst wägt	wog *or* wägte	gewogen	wöge *or* wägte
waschen	wäschst wäscht	wusch	gewaschen	wüsche
weichen	weichst weicht	wich	gewichen	wiche
weisen	weist weist	wies	gewiesen	wiese
wenden	wendest wendet	wandte *or* wendete	gewandt *or* gewendet	wendete
werben	wirbst wirbt	warb	geworben	würbe
werden	wirst wird	wurde	geworden	würde
werfen	wirfst wirft	warf	geworfen	würfe
wiegen	wiegst wiegt	wog	gewogen	wöge
winden	windest windet	wand	gewunden	wände
wissen	weißt weiß	wusste	gewusst	wüsste
wollen	willst will	wollte	gewollt	wollte
zeihen	zeihst zeiht	zieh	geziehen	ziehe
ziehen	ziehst zieht	zog	gezogen	zöge
zwingen	zwingst zwingt	zwang	gezwungen	zwänge

APPENDIX B

Prepositions and their required cases

Dative

aus	*out of*	**aus** der Flasche *out of the bottle*
	from	**aus** Deutschland *from Germany*
	made of	**aus** Holz *made of wood*
außer	*except for*	alle **außer** mir *everyone except for me*
	out of	**außer** Atem *out of breath*
bei	*at (someone's home)*	**bei** meinen Eltern *at my parents' house*
	near	irgendwo **bei** Hamburg *somewhere near Hamburg*
	at (a business)	**beim** Schneider *at the tailor's*
bis zu	*up to, as many as*	die Stadt hat **bis zu** 10.000 Einwohnern *the city has up to 10,000 inhabitants*
gegenüber	*opposite*	**gegenüber** der Schule *opposite the school*
	with	ihm **gegenüber** freundlich sein *be kind with someone*
mit	*with*	**mit** dem Herrn *with the gentleman*
	by (vehicle)	**mit** dem Zug *by train*

nach	*after*	**nach** der Schule *after school*
	to (a region)	**nach** Frankreich *to France*
	according to	**nach** meiner Ansicht *in my view*
seit	*since*	**seit** April *since April*
	for	**seit** Jahren *for years*
von	*from, of*	westlich **von** Berlin *west from Berlin*
	by	ein Drama **von** Goethe *a drama by Goethe*
zu	*to (someone's home)*	**zu** mir kommen *come to my house*
	with (food)	**zu** dem Käse gab es Bier *there was beer with the cheese*
	at (holiday time)	**zu** Weihnachten *at Christmas*

Accusative

bis	*till, until*	**bis** Freitag *till Friday*
	to, as far as	**bis** Bremen *to (as far as) Bremen*
durch	*through*	**durch** das Fenster *through the window*
	by	**durch** die Post *by mail*
für	*for*	ein Geschenk **für** dich *a present for you*
	as	**für** tot erklären *to declare as dead*
gegen	*against*	**gegen** mich *against me*
	toward	**gegen** Morgen *toward morning*
ohne	*without*	**ohne** seine Frau *without his wife*

um	*around*	**um** die Ecke	*around the corner*
	at (time)	**um** sechs Uhr	*at six o'clock*
	after, by	Stunde **um** Stunde	*hour after hour*
wider	*against*	**wider** alle Vernunft	*against all reason*

Dative/Accusative

an	*at*	**am** Fenster	*at the window*
	on (a day)	**am** Sonntag	*on Sunday*
auf	*on*	**auf** dem Boden	*on the floor*
	(here's) to	**auf** Ihre Gesundheit	*to your health*
hinter	*behind*	**hinter** der Tür	*behind the door*
	beyond	die nächste Station **hinter** Bonn	*the next station beyond Bonn*
in	*in (location)*	**in** Deutschland	*in Germany*
	in (period of time)	**in** drei Tagen	*in three days*
neben	*next to, beside*	**neben** dem Haus	*next to the house*
über	*over, above*	**über** dem Tisch	*over the table*
	about, of	**über** ihn reden	*talk about him*
	over (an expanse)	**über** die Straße gehen	*cross the street*
unter	*under*	**unter** einem Baum	*under a tree*
	among	**unter** anderem	*among other things*

vor	before, in front of	**vor** dem Haus
		in front of the house
	from, because of	**vor** Hunger umkommen
		die from hunger
	ago	**vor** zehn Jahren
		ten years ago
zwischen	between	**zwischen** seinen Eltern
		between his parents

Genitive

(an)statt	instead of	**statt** ihrer Schwester
		instead of her sister
angesichts	in the face of	**angesichts** der Gefahr
		in face of the danger
außerhalb	outside of	**außerhalb** der Dienstzeit
		outside of office hours
diesseits	this side of	**diesseits** der Grenze
		this side of the border
jenseits	that side of	**jenseits** der Grenze
		that side of the border
trotz	despite, in spite of	**trotz** des Gewitters
		in spite of the rainstorm
unterhalb	below	**unterhalb** der Brücke
		below the bridge
während	during	**während** des Krieges
		during the war
wegen	because of	**wegen** des schlechten Wetters
		because of the bad weather

APPENDIX C
Summary of declensions

Declension with **der**-words

	MASCULINE	FEMININE
nom	der alte Mann	diese gute Frau
acc	den alten Mann	diese gute Frau
dat	dem alten Mann	dieser guten Frau
gen	des alten Mannes	dieser guten Frau

	NEUTER	PLURAL
nom	jenes neue Haus	die alten Leute
acc	jenes neue Haus	die alten Leute
dat	jenem neuen Haus	den alten Leuten
gen	jenes neuen Hauses	der alten Leute

Declension with **ein**-words

	MASCULINE	FEMININE
nom	ein großer Garten	meine kleine Katze
acc	einen großen Garten	meine kleine Katze
dat	einem großen Garten	meiner kleinen Katze
gen	eines großen Gartens	meiner kleinen Katze

	NEUTER	PLURAL
nom	Ihr altes Auto	keine neuen Bücher
acc	Ihr altes Auto	keine neuen Bücher
dat	Ihrem alten Auto	keine neuen Büchern
gen	Ihres alten Autos	keiner neuen Bücher

Masculine nouns requiring an **-(e)n** ending

nom	der Herr	dieser Löwe	kein Mensch
acc	den Herrn	diesen Löwen	keinen Menschen
dat	dem Herrn	diesem Löwen	keinem Menschen
gen	des Herrn	dieses Löwen	keines Menschen

Neuter noun **Herz** requiring an **-en** ending

nom	das Herz
acc	das Herz
dat	dem Herzen
gen	des Herzens

Feminine and neuter nouns ending in -a in the singular and plural

nom	die Kamera	das Drama
acc	die Kamera	das Drama
dat	der Kamera	dem Drama
gen	der Kamera	des Dramas
nom	die Kameras	die Dramen
acc	die Kameras	die Dramen
dat	den Kameras	den Dramen
gen	der Kameras	die Dramen

Unpreceded adjectives (no **ein-word**/no **der-word**)

	MASCULINE	FEMININE
nom	warmer Kaffee	kalte Milch
acc	warmen Kaffee	kalte Milch
dat	warmem Kaffee	kalter Milch
gen	warmen Kaffees	kalter Milch

	NEUTER	PLURAL
nom	frisches Brot	kleine Kinder
acc	frisches Brot	kleine Kinder
dat	frischem Brot	kleinen Kindern
gen	frischen Brotes	kleiner Kinder

Relative pronouns (**der/die/das** and **welcher**)

	MASCULINE	FEMININE	NEUTER	PLURAL
nom	der	die	das	die
acc	den	die	das	die
dat	dem	der	dem	denen
gen	dessen	deren	dessen	deren
nom	welcher	welche	welches	welche
acc	welchen	welche	welches	welche
dat	welchem	welcher	welchem	welchen
gen	dessen	deren	dessen	deren

Adjectives and participles used as nouns

	MASCULINE	FEMININE
nom	der Alte	diese Beauftragte
acc	den Alten	diese Beauftragte
dat	dem Alten	dieser Beauftragten
gen	des Alten	dieser Beauftragten

	NEUTER	PLURAL
nom	das Interessanteste	keine Angeklagten
acc	das Interessanteste	keine Angeklagten
dat	dem Interessantesten	keinen Angeklagten
gen	des Interessantesten	keiner Angeklagten

Answer Key

1 Pronunciation and gender

1·1 1. g 2. o 3. f 4. n 5. e 6. m 7. l 8. d 9. k 10. j 11. c 12. i 13. b 14. h 15. a

1·2 1. der 2. die 3. die 4. der 5. die 6. der 7. der 8. die 9. die 10. der

1·3 1. das 2. die 3. die 4. der 5. das 6. das 7. die 8. die 9. die 10. der 11. der 12. das 13. die 14. der 15. der 16. die 17. die 18. die 19. die 20. die

2 Definite and indefinite articles

2·1 1. Das Kind ist da. 2. Die Blume ist da. 3. Das Haus ist da. 4. Der Garten ist da. 5. Der Wagen ist da. 6. Der Stuhl ist da. 7. Das Auto ist da. 8. Der Bruder ist da. 9. Die Schwester ist da. 10. Die Sängerin ist da. 11. Das Gymnasium ist klein. 12. Die Katze ist klein. 13. Der Sportler ist klein. 14. Das Mädchen ist klein. 15. Der Boden ist klein. 16. Die Landkarte ist klein. 17. Die Universität ist klein. 18. Der Pullover ist klein. 19. Die Schule ist klein. 20. Das Kind ist klein. 21. Das Auto ist hier. 22. Die Gärtnerin ist hier. 23. Die Frau ist hier. 24. Die Professorin ist hier. 25. Der Junge ist hier.

2·2 1. dieser Mann 2. diese Frau 3. dieses Kind 4. diese Blume 5. dieser Garten 6. diese Gärtnerin 7. diese Lehrerin 8. dieses Studium 9. dieses Bett 10. dieser Professor 11. dieser Diplomat 12. diese Bluse 13. dieser Boden 14. dieses Fenster 15. diese Schauspielerin 16. dieses Haus 17. diese Universität 18. dieses Königtum 19. dieser Gärtner 20. dieser Lehrer 21. diese Schule 22. dieses Mädchen 23. dieser Sänger 24. diese Sängerin 25. diese Landkarte

2·3 1. eine Lehrerin 2. ein Junge 3. ein Fenster 4. ein Bett 5. eine Universität 6. eine Tante 7. ein Mädchen 8. ein Arzt 9. ein Buch 10. ein Fernsehapparat 11. eine Tochter 12. ein Restaurant 13. ein Boden 14. eine Mutter 15. ein Bild

2·4 1. keine Tochter 2. kein Tisch 3. kein Fenster 4. kein Restaurant 5. kein Gärtner 6. keine Großmutter 7. kein Arzt 8. keine Ärztin 9. kein Rathaus 10. keine Butter 11. kein Junge 12. kein Schlafzimmer 13. kein Bild 14. keine Schwester 15. keine Tante 16. kein Bruder 17. keine Zeit 18. kein Fernsehapparat 19. keine Uhr 20. kein Fenster 21. kein Mantel 22. keine Frau 23. kein Geld 24. keine Mutter 25. keine Universität

2·5

1. Eine Frau ist da.
   Keine Frau ist da.
2. Ein Restaurant ist klein.
   Kein Restaurant ist klein.
3. Eine Schule ist groß.
   Keine Schule ist groß.
4. Eine Mutter ist hier.
   Keine Mutter ist hier.
5. Ein Film ist alt.
   Kein Film ist alt.
6. Ein Bild ist klein.
   Kein Bild ist klein.
7. Eine Großmutter ist alt.
   Keine Großmutter ist alt.
8. Ein Tisch ist neu.
   Kein Tisch ist neu.
9. Ein Restaurant ist groß.
   Kein Restaurant ist groß.
10. Eine Landkarte ist hier.
    Keine Landkarte ist hier.
11. Eine Tante ist alt.
    Keine Tante ist alt.
12. Ein Vater ist jung.
    Kein Vater ist jung.
13. Ein Rathaus ist neu.
    Kein Rathaus ist neu.
14. Eine Tochter ist jung.
    Keine Tochter ist jung.
15. Eine Uhr ist da.
    Keine Uhr ist da.

2·6

1. Ist der Film neu?　2. Ist dieses Kind klein?　3. Ist kein Lehrer da?　4. Ist ein Restaurant da?　5. Ist die Tochter jung?　6. Ist dieser Arzt alt?　7. Ist eine Schule neu?　8. Ist kein Bild hier?　9. Ist eine Uhr da?　10. Ist die Großmutter alt?　11. Ist dieser Professor jung?　12. Ist ein Bett hier?　13. Ist keine Butter da?　14. Ist der Boden neu?　15. Ist dieses Auto alt?

2·7

1. die eine diese keine Tochter　2. die eine diese keine Ärztin　3. der ein dieser kein Bruder　4. das ein dieses kein Bild　5. die eine diese keine Uhr　6. das ein dieses kein Fenster　7. das ein dieses kein Haus　8. der ein dieser kein Wagen　9. das ein dieses kein Gymnasium　10. das ein dieses kein Rathaus　11. das ein dieses kein Schlafzimmer　12. die eine diese keine Tante　13. die eine diese keine Großmutter　14. der ein dieser kein Mantel　15. der ein dieser kein Film　16. die eine diese keine Schauspielerin　17. der ein dieser kein Diplomat　18. das ein dieses kein Restaurant　19. die eine diese keine Schule　20. die eine diese keine Bluse　21. die eine diese keine Mutter　22. der ein dieser kein Vater　23. das ein dieses kein Buch　24. das ein dieses kein Kind　25. der ein dieser kein Garten　26. die eine diese keine Gärtnerin　27. der ein dieser kein Arzt　28. das ein dieses kein Bett　29. der ein dieser kein Junge　30. das ein dieses kein Mädchen

3　Pronouns, plurals, and the verb **sein**

3·1

1. es　2. er　3. sie　4. er　5. sie　6. es　7. es　8. sie　9. er　10. es　11. er　12. sie　13. es　14. er　15. es　16. es　17. sie　18. er　19. sie　20. es　21. er　22. er　23. sie　24. es　25. er

3·2

1. Sie sind jung.　2. Sie sind da.　3. Sie sind klein.　4. Sie sind groß.　5. Sie sind neu.　6. Sie sind hier.　7. Sie sind alt.　8. Sie sind da.　9. Sie sind jung.　10. Sie sind neu.

3·3   1. es   2. sie (*sing.*)   3. er   4. sie (*pl.*)   5. sie (*pl.*)   6. es   7. sie (*pl.*)   8. sie (*pl.*)   9. er   10. es   11. es   12. sie (*pl.*)   13. es   14. sie (*sing.*)   15. er   16. es   17. sie (*pl.*)   18. er   19. sie (*pl.*)   20. sie (*pl.*)

3·4   1. der Mantel   2. die Töchter   3. ein Auto   4. die Onkel   5. eine Kamera   6. ein Arzt   7. die Würste   8. die Schulen   9. das Mädchen   10. eine Lampe

3·5   1. Sie   2. Sie   3. du   4. ihr   5. ihr   6. du   7. Sie   8. du   9. Sie   10. du

3·6   1. ist   2. bin   3. ihr   4. ist   5. ich   6. du   7. sind   8. sind   9. sind   10. ist   11. bist   12. seid

3·7   1. Ist das Haus groß?   2. Sind die Häuser klein?   3. Ist er jung?   4. Sind sie alt?   5. Bist du klein?   6. Sind wir Töchter?   7. Sind die Kinder hier?   8. Seid ihr Brüder?   9. Ist sie Lehrerin?   10. Sind die Stühle alt?   11. Bin ich alt?   12. Ist dieser Mann Professor?   13. Ist sie neu?   14. Ist es groß?   15. Herr Braun! Sind Sie Arzt?

4   Titles, locations, and interrogatives

4·1   1. Guten Tag. Ich heiße Schäfer, Martin Schäfer.
   Guten Tag, Herr Schäfer.
   2. Guten Tag. Ich heiße Bauer, Boris Bauer.
   Guten Tag, Herr Bauer.
   3. Guten Tag. Ich heiße Schneider, Angelika Schneider.
   Guten Tag, Frau Schneider.
   4. Guten Tag. Ich heiße Schulze, Maria Schulze.
   Guten Tag, Frau Schulze.
   5. Guten Tag. Ich heiße Neumann, Erik Neumann.
   Guten Tag, Herr Neumann.
   6. Guten Tag. Ich heiße Kraus, Sonja Kraus.
   Guten Tag, Frau Kraus.
   7. Guten Tag. Ich heiße Gasse, Heinrich Gasse.
   Guten Tag, Herr Gasse.
   8. Guten Tag. Ich heiße Becker, Marianne Becker.
   Guten Tag, Frau Becker.
   9. Guten Tag. Ich heiße Schnell, Thomas Schnell.
   Guten Tag, Herr Schnell.
   10. Guten Tag. Ich heiße Kiefer, Gabriele Kiefer.
   Guten Tag, Frau Kiefer.

4·2   1. Frau Bauer ist in Italien.
   Frau Bauer wohnt in Italien.
   2. Die Kinder sind in Russland.
   Die Kinder wohnen in Russland.
   3. Der Diplomat ist in Nordamerika.
   Der Diplomat wohnt in Nordamerika.
   4. Ein Richter ist in Rom.
   Ein Richter wohnt in Rom.
   5. Frau Professor Schneider ist in München.
   Frau Professor Schneider wohnt in München.
   6. Der Direktor ist in Europa.
   Der Direktor wohnt in Europa.
   7. Meine Frau ist in Frankreich.
   Meine Frau wohnt in Frankreich.

8. Mein Mann ist in Afrika.
   Mein Mann wohnt in Afrika.
9. Ihr Bruder ist in Warschau.
   Ihr Bruder wohnt in Warschau.
10. Ihre Töchter sind in Spanien.
    Ihre Töchter wohnen in Spanien.

4·3 1. ist zu Hause 2. bin zu Hause 3. sind zu Hause 4. sind zu Hause 5. bist zu Hause 6. ist zu Hause 7. sind zu Hause 8. ist zu Hause 9. seid zu Hause 10. sind zu Hause

4·4
1. Wo ist Ihre Mutter?
   Ihre (Meine) Mutter ist im Keller.
2. Wo ist mein Bruder?
   Mein (Ihr) Bruder ist in der Garage.
3. Wo sind Martin und Angela?
   Martin und Angela sind in der Stadt.
4. Wo seid ihr?
   Ihr seid (Wir sind) in der Kirche.
5. Wo ist Thomas?
   Thomas ist im Café.
6. Wo sind wir?
   Wir sind (Ihr seid) im Wohnzimmer.
7. Wo bin ich?
   Du bist (Sie sind) im Esszimmer.
8. Wo ist Herr Doktor Bauer?
   Herr Doktor Bauer ist im Hotel.
9. Wo ist mein Onkel?
   Mein Onkel (Ihr Onkel) ist im Garten.

4·5
1. Wie heißt der Mann?
   Der Mann heißt Herr Schulze.
2. Wie heißt die Frau?
   Die Frau heißt Frau Schneider.
3. Wie heißt der Mann?
   Der Mann heißt Thomas.
4. Wie heißt die Frau?
   Die Frau heißt Anna Schäfer.
5. Wie heißt der Mann?
   Der Mann heißt Martin Neufeld.
6. Wie heißt der Mann?
   Der Mann heißt Erik Schmidt.
7. Wie heißt der Mann (die Frau)?
   Der Mann (Die Frau) heißt Professor Benz.
8. Wie heißt die Frau?
   Die Frau heißt Doktor Tina Kiefer.
9. Wie heißt der Mann?
   Der Mann heißt Wilhelm Kassel.
10. Wie heißt die Frau?
    Die Frau heißt Angela.

4·6
1. Was ist das?
   Das ist eine Kirche.
2. Was ist das?
   Das ist ein Mantel.
3. Wer ist das?
   Das ist der Polizist.
4. Wer ist das?
   Das ist die Richterin.

5. Was ist das?
   Das ist eine Bibliothek.
6. Wer ist das?
   Das ist Frau Schneider.
7. Was ist das? Was sind das?
   Das sind die Zeitungen.
8. Wer ist das?
   Das ist Herr Bauer.
9. Wer ist das? Wer sind das?
   Das sind Karl und Martin.
10. Was ist das?
    Das ist die Garage.

4·7
1. Das Konzert ist am Montag.
   Das Konzert ist im Januar.
2. Das Examen ist am Dienstag.
   Das Examen ist im März.
3. Die Reise ist am Mittwoch.
   Die Reise ist im Mai.
4. Die Oper ist am Donnerstag.
   Die Oper ist im Juli.
5. Ihr (Mein) Geburtstag ist am Freitag.
   Ihr (Mein) Geburtstag ist im September.

5 The verbs **haben** and **werden** and negation

5·1
1.	bin	2.	sind
	bist		habe
	ist		hast
	ist		hat
	ist		hat
	ist		hat
	sind		haben
	seid		habt
	ist		haben
	sind		haben

3. werde
   wirst
   wird
   wird
   wird
   werden
   werdet
   werden
   werden
   wird

5·2
1. Wird Ihr Bruder Zahnarzt?   2. Ist sie Tänzerin?   3. Habe ich Durst?   4. Ist dieser Artikel interessant?   5. Ist es heiß?   6. Wird Frau Bauer Krankschwester?   7. Haben die Kinder Hunger?   8. Wird es dunkel?   9. Haben Sie keine Fahrkarten?   10. Hat Erik Maria gern?   11. Wird mein Onkel Rechtsanwalt?   12. Ist Sonja krank?   13. Ist dieser Roman langweilig?   14. Wird es am Montag kalt?   15. Ist es kalt im Dezember?   16. Ist das Gedicht kurz?   17. Haben die Mädchen Karl gern?   18. Sind wir zu Hause?   19. Heißt der Herr Martin Schäfer?   20. Wird Frau Keller gesund?

5·3
1. habe   2. Sind   3. ist, wird   4. hat   5. Hast   6. ist   7. bist, wirst   8. hat   9. ist, wird   10. haben   11. Haben   12. seid   13. ist, wird   14. Ist   15. Hast

5·4 1. Er hat keine Schuhe. 2. Du hast keine Zeitung. 3. Frau Bauer ist keine Krankenschwester. 4. Herr Schneider ist kein Politiker. 5. Ich habe keine Zeit. 6. Das ist kein Kleid. 7. Er ist kein Polizist. 8. Kein Tourist ist in Berlin. 9. Wir haben am Mittwoch keine Prüfung. 10. Hast du kein Geld? 11. Das ist keine Bibliothek. 12. Maria ist keine Tänzerin. 13. Die Männer werden keine Politiker. 14. Er hat kein Glas Bier. 15. Das ist keine Kirche.

5·5 1. Die Touristen sind nicht in Deutschland. 2. Mein Geburtstag ist nicht im Oktober. 3. Das ist nicht Herr Dorfmann. 4. Meine Schwester wohnt nicht in der Stadt. 5. Wir haben nicht am Freitag das Examen. 6. Ist Frau Benz nicht zu Hause? 7. Es wird nicht warm. 8. Das sind nicht meine Bücher. 9. Sonja hat die Bluse nicht. 10. Das ist nicht der Lehrer. 11. Sie haben die Fahrkarten nicht. 12. Ist das nicht Herr Bauer? 13. Hast du die Zeitungen nicht? 14. Die Dame heißt nicht Frau Becker. 15. Sind das nicht meine Schuhe?

5·6 1. nicht 2. nicht 3. kein 4. keine 5. nicht 6. kein 7. nicht 8. nicht 9. nicht 10. nicht 11. nicht 12. nicht 13. keine 14. nicht 15. nicht 16. nicht 17. nicht 18. nicht 19. nicht 20. kein

5·7 1. Ja, sie hat meine Bücher.
Nein, sie hat meine Bücher nicht.
2. Ja, er ist Zahnarzt.
Nein, er ist kein Zahnarzt.
3. Ja, es wird regnerisch.
Nein, es wird nicht regnerisch.
4. Ja, die Jungen werden Sportler.
Nein, die Jungen werden keine Sportler.
5. Ja, ich bin Deutscher.
Nein, ich bin kein Deutscher.
6. Ja, wir sind zu Hause.
Nein, wir sind nicht zu Hause.
7. Ja, die Tänzerin ist in Paris.
Nein, die Tänzerin ist nicht in Paris.
8. Ja, du bist krank./Ja, Sie sind krank.
Nein, du bist nicht krank./Nein, Sie sind nicht krank.
9. Ja, ich habe das Kleid.
Nein, ich habe das Kleid nicht.
10. Ja, es wird kühl.
Nein, es wird nicht kühl.
11. Ja, wir haben Zeit.
Nein, wir haben keine Zeit.
12. Ja, Erik wird Student.
Nein, Erik wird nicht Student.
13. Ja, der Onkel ist alt.
Nein, der Onkel ist nicht alt.
14. Ja, ihr seid in München./Ja, Sie sind in München./Ja, wir sind in München.
Nein, ihr seid nicht in München./Nein, Sie sind nicht in München./Nein, wir sind nicht in München.
15. Ja, ich habe Martin gern.
Nein, ich habe Martin nicht gern.

6   The present tense and numbers

6·1 1. mache   gehe   frage
machst   gehst   fragst
macht   geht   fragt

2. sagen   hören   zeigen
sagt   hört   zeigen
sagen   hören   zeigen

3. lache   setze   schwimme
lacht   setzt   schwimmt
lachen   setzen   schwimmen

4. deckst   probierst   schickst
decken   probieren   schicken
deckt   probiert   schickt

5. denke   hoffe   liebe
denkst   hoffst   liebst
denkt   hofft   liebt
denken   hoffen   lieben
denkt   hofft   liebt
denken   hoffen   lieben
denken   hoffen   lieben

6·2

1. wette   2. sende
wettest   sendest
wettet   sendet
wetten   senden
wettet   sendet
wetten   senden
wetten   senden

3. meide   4. antworte
meidest   antwortest
meidet   antwortet
meiden   antworten
meidet   antwortet
meiden   antworten
meiden   antworten

5. huste
hustest
hustet
husten
hustet
husten
husten

6·3

1. setze   2. heiße
setzt   heißt
setzt   heißt
setzen   heißen
setzt   heißt
setzen   heißen
setzen   heißen

3. tanze   4. sitze
tanzt   sitzt
tanzt   sitzt
tanzen   sitzen
tanzt   sitzt
tanzen   sitzen
tanzen   sitzen

5. schmerze	6. reise
schmerzt	reist
schmerzt	reist
schmerzen	reisen
schmerzt	reist
schmerzen	reisen
schmerzen	reisen

7. beiße	8. niese
beißt	niest
beißt	niest
beißen	niesen
beißt	niest
beißen	niesen
beißen	niesen

6·4 1. sage 2. macht 3. schmeicheln 4. hörst 5. schmelzt 6. gehen 7. fragt 8. seid 9. schließt 10. wohnen 11. glaube 12. pflanzt 13. bellt 14. wandere 15. wird 16. raucht 17. wartet 18. feiert 19. badest 20. lächelt 21. hat 22. wünschst 23. findet 24. kostet 25. singe

6·5 1. Sechs plus/und eins sind sieben. 2. Fünf mal drei sind fünfzehn. 3. Neun minus/weniger sieben sind zwei. 4. Zwanzig plus/und drei sind dreiundzwanzig. 5. Zwölf (geteilt) durch drei sind vier. 6. Hundert minus fünfzig sind fünfzig. 7. Achtundachtzig plus zwei sind neunzig. 8. Zweihundert durch vierzig sind fünf. 9. Neunzehn minus acht sind elf. 10. Sechzig plus zwölf sind zweiundsiebzig.

6·6 1. zweite 2. elften 3. dritten 4. ersten 5. zwölfte 6. einunddreißigsten 7. einundzwanzigste 8. zehnte 9. sechzehnten 10. siebten

7 Direct objects and the accusative case

7·1 1. den Lehrer 2. den Roman 3. einen Artikel 4. einen Zahnarzt 5. diesen Politiker 6. diesen Mann 7. meinen Geburtstag 8. meinen Onkel 9. Ihren Wagen 10. keinen Sportler

7·2 1. den Schauspieler 2. meine Schuhe 3. Ihre Tante 4. einen Stuhl 5. das Mädchen 6. ein Gymnasium 7. keine Schwester 8. dieses Wetter 9. keine Zeit 10. eine Landkarte 11. einen Mantel 12. ein Kind 13. Ihre Prüfung 14. das Examen 15. meinen Garten 16. keine Universität 17. den Boden 18. die Schule 19. meinen Pullover 20. Ihre Schwester 21. diesen Garten 22. meine Bücher 23. das Glas 24. dieses Fenster 25. eine Schauspielerin

7·3 1. keine Zeit 2. Frau Schneider 3. Radio 4. die Kinder 5. ein Kleid und einen Pullover 6. dieses Mädchen 7. Maria 8. einen Wagen 9. Deutsch 10. Geld 11. keinen Mantel 12. den Roman 13. ein Problem 14. meinen Bruder 15. diese Schauspielerin

7·4 1. Kennst du mich?
Kennst du ihn?
Kennst du sie?
Kennst du uns?
2. Ja, ich habe ihn.
Ja, ich habe sie.
Ja, ich habe es.
Ja, ich habe sie.
3. Doktor Bauer hat dich gern.
Doktor Bauer hat ihn gern.
Doktor Bauer hat uns gern.
Doktor Bauer hat euch gern.

4. Meine Großmutter liebt mich.
   Meine Großmutter liebt dich.
   Meine Großmutter liebt sie.
   Meine Großmutter liebt sie.
5. Die Männer suchen dich.
   Die Männer suchen uns.
   Die Männer suchen euch.
   Die Männer suchen Sie.

7·5   1. Was brauchen die Frauen?   2. Wen kennt meine Schwester nicht?   3. Was liebe ich?   4. Wen suchen wir?   5. Was kauft Herr Benz?   6. Was finden Werner und Karl?   7. Was habt ihr?   8. Was braucht mein Bruder?   9. Wen sucht Martin?   10. Wen hören Sie?   11. Wen frage ich?   12. Was decken die Kinder?   13. Wen liebt Erik?   14. Was hat Sabine?   15. Was kaufen die Jungen?

7·6   1. Er   2. ihn   3. es   4. sie   5. sie   6. sie   7. sie   8. ihn   9. ihn   10. es   11. ihn   12. er   13. es   14. es   15. es

8   Irregular verbs in the present tense

8·1   1. fährst   2. hat   3. fallen   4. rät   5. ratet   6. backe   7. brätst   8. hält   9. lässt   10. fangen   11. wäschst   12. stößt   13. seid   14. wächst   15. schlafen   16. trägst   17. schlägt   18. fängt   19. fällt   20. rätst   21. schläft   22. werdet   23. hältst   24. wasche   25. trägt

8·2

1. wachse	2. trage
wächst	trägst
wächst	trägt
wachsen	tragen
wachst	tragt
wachsen	tragen
wächst	trägt

3. falle	4. schlage
fällst	schlägst
fällt	schlägt
fallen	schlagen
fallt	schlagt
fallen	schlagen
fällt	schlägt

5. brate	6. stoße
brätst	stößt
brät	stößt
braten	stoßen
bratet	stoßt
braten	stoßen
brät	stößt

7. lasse	8. schlafe
lässt	schläfst
lässt	schläft
lassen	schlafen
lasst	schlaft
lassen	schlafen
lässt	schläfst

8·3   1. brichst   2. vergisst   3. sprecht   4. tritt   5. steche   6. messen   7. schmilzt
8. wirfst   9. erschrecken   10. gibt   11. hilft   12. sterben   13. essen   14. frisst   15. nimmt
16. triffst   17. bergen   18. gilt   19. melke   20. trittst   21. isst   22. werft   23. geben
24. stirbt   25. brechen

8·4

1. esse	2. helfe
isst	hilfst
isst	hilft
essen	helfen
esst	helft
essen	helfen
isst	hilft

3. verderbe	4. nehme
verdirbst	nimmst
verdirbt	nimmt
verderben	nehmen
verderbt	nehmt
verderben	nehmen
verdirbt	nimmt

5. spreche	6. sterbe
sprichst	stirbst
spricht	stirbt
sprechen	sterben
sprecht	sterbt
sprechen	sterben
spricht	stirbt

7. gebe	8. treffe
gibst	triffst
gibt	trifft
geben	treffen
gebt	trefft
geben	treffen
gibt	trifft

8·5

1. sehe	2. stehle
siehst	stiehlst
sieht	stiehlt
sehen	stehlen
seht	stehlt
sehen	stehlen
sieht	stiehlt

3. empfehle	4. lese
empfiehlst	liest
empfiehlt	liest
empfehlen	lesen
empfehlt	lest
empfehlen	lesen
empfiehlt	liest

8·6   1. bricht   2. fahren   3. seid   4. stiehlt   5. fällst   6. fängt   7. sehe   8. geschieht
9. nimmt   10. lassen   11. stößt   12. wird   13. weiß   14. hilft   15. empfehlen   16. liest
17. schläft   18. weiß   19. messt   20. läuft   21. stehlen   22. trittst   23. ratet   24. weiß
25. spricht   26. rät   27. geschieht   28. lässt   29. hast   30. wissen

8·7 1. Spricht man Englisch? 2. Läufst du nach Hause? 3. Nimmt er die Fahrkarten? 4. Gebt ihr kein Geld? 5. Fährt er nach Hause? 6. Wer sieht die Bibliothek? 7. Essen sie kein Brot? 8. Empfehle ich den Roman? 9. Fängst du den Ball? 10. Weiß er nichts? 11. Treten Sie mir auf den Fuß? 12. Hilft Thomas Sonja und Sabine? 13. Liest du die Zeitung? 14. Bricht sie sich den Arm? 15. Trägt meine Schwester einen Pullover?

9 Separable and inseparable prefixes and imperatives

9·1 1. erfährst 2. entlässt 3. empfängt 4. bekomme 5. empfehlt 6. verkaufen 7. besuchst 8. gefällt 9. erstaunt 10. gebrauchen 11. verstehen 12. gelingt 13. zerstören 14. begrüße 15. erschlägt 16. entläuft 17. beschreibt 18. empfinden 19. bekommt 20. gefallen 21. erträgt 22. versuche 23. gewinnst 24. enlassen 25. behältst

9·2 1. Ich bekomme einen Brief. 2. Du bekommst einen Brief. 3. Er bekommt einen Brief. 4. Wir bekommen einen Brief. 5. Ihr bekommt einen Brief. 6. Sie bekommen einen Brief. 7. Man bekommt einen Brief. 8. Ich empfange sie mit Blumen. 9. Du empfängst sie mit Blumen. 10. Er empfängt sie mit Blumen. 11. Wir empfangen sie mit Blumen. 12. Ihr empfangt sie mit Blumen. 13. Sie empfangen sie mit Blumen. 14. Niemand empfängt sie mit Blumen. 15. Ich entdecke eine kleine Insel. 16. Du entdeckst eine kleine Insel. 17. Er entdeckt eine kleine Insel. 18. Wir entdecken eine kleine Insel. 19. Ihr entdeckt eine kleine Insel. 20. Sie entdecken eine kleine Insel. 21. Der Professor entdeckt eine kleine Insel. 22. Ich verstehe kein Wort. 23. Du verstehst kein Wort. 24. Er versteht kein Wort. 25. Wir verstehen kein Wort. 26. Ihr versteht kein Wort. 27. Sie verstehen kein Wort. 28. Die Touristen verstehen kein Wort. 29. Ich zerreiße die Zeitschriften. 30. Du zerreißt die Zeitschriften. 31. Er zerreißt die Zeitschriften. 32. Wir zerreißen die Zeitschriften. 33. Ihr zerreißt die Zeitschriften. 34. Sie zerreißen die Zeitschriften. 35. Man zerreißt die Zeitschriften.

9·3 1. kommt an 2. bringen um 3. nimmt mit 4. gehen zurück 5. bereitet vor 6. ziehe um 7. fängt an 8. lauft weg 9. machen zu 10. kommen um 11. nimmt weg 12. bringe bei 13. hören auf 14. stellen vor 15. macht auf 16. läuft weg 17. bringen mit 18. setzen fort 19. bietest an 20. räumt auf

9·4 1. Ich fahre um neun Uhr ab. 2. Du fährst um neun Uhr ab. 3. Er fährt um neun Uhr ab. 4. Wir fahren um neun Uhr ab. 5. Ihr fahrt um neun Uhr ab. 6. Sie fahren um neun Uhr ab. 7. Man fährt um neun Uhr ab. 8. Ich mache die Fenster und die Türen zu. 9. Du machst die Fenster und die Türen zu. 10. Er macht die Fenster und die Türen zu. 11. Wir machen die Fenster und die Türen zu. 12. Ihr macht die Fenster und die Türen zu. 13. Sie machen die Fenster und die Türen zu. 14. Niemand macht die Fenster und die Türen zu. 15. Ich bringe ihnen Deutsch bei. 16. Du bringst ihnen Deutsch bei. 17. Er bringt ihnen Deutsch bei. 18. Wir bringen ihnen Deutsch bei. 19. Ihr bringt ihnen Deutsch bei. 20. Sie bringen ihnen Deutsch bei. 21. Man bringt ihnen Deutsch bei. 22. Ich höre damit auf. 23. Du hörst damit auf. 24. Er hört damit auf. 25. Wir hören damit auf. 26. Ihr hört damit auf. 27. Sie hören damit auf. 28. Martin hört damit auf. 29. Ich gebe zwanzig Euro aus. 30. Du gibst zwanzig Euro aus. 31. Er gibt zwanzig Euro aus. 32. Wir geben zwanzig Euro aus. 33. Ihr gebt zwanzig Euro aus. 34. Sie geben zwanzig Euro aus. 35. Wer gibt zwanzig Euro aus?

9·5 1. Ich komme vor Langeweile um. 2. Du kommst vor Langeweile um. 3. Er kommt vor Langeweile um. 4. Wir kommen vor Langeweile um. 5. Ihr kommt vor Langeweile um. 6. Sie kommen vor Langeweile um. 7. Man kommt vor Langeweile um. 8. Ich unterbreche die Rede. 9. Du unterbrichst die Rede. 10. Er unterbricht die Rede. 11. Wir unterbrechen die Rede. 12. Ihr unterbrecht die Rede. 13. Sie unterbrechen die Rede. 14. Niemand unterbricht die Rede.

9·6 1. Trink(e)! Trinkt! Trinken Sie! 2. Kauf(e)! Kauft! Kaufen Sie! 3. Nimm! Nehmt! Nehmen Sie! 4. Paddele! Paddelt! Paddeln Sie! 5. Schlaf(e)! Schlaft! Schlafen Sie! 6. Geh(e)! Geht! Gehen Sie! 7. Sprich! Sprecht! Sprechen Sie! 8. Hör(e)! Hört! Hören Sie! 9. Stiehl! Stehlt! Stehlen Sie! 10. Schwimm(e)! Schwimmt! Schwimmen Sie!

9·7   1. Fahr(e) ab! Fahrt ab! Fahren Sie ab!   2. Gewinn(e)! Gewinnt! Gewinnen Sie!   3. Bekomm(e)! Bekommt! Bekommen Sie!   4. Bring(e) mit! Bringt mit! Bringen Sie mit!   5. Mach(e) zu! Macht zu! Machen Sie zu!   6. Versuch(e)! Versucht! Versuchen Sie!   7. Erschlag(e)! Erschlagt! Erschlagen Sie!   8. Sieh an! Seht an! Sehen Sie an!   9. Hör(e) auf! Hört auf! Hören Sie auf!   10. Komm(e) an! Kommt an! Kommen Sie an!

9·8   1. Sei gesund!   2. Stehen Sie auf!   3. Macht die Fenster auf!   4. Iss in der Küche!   5. Besucht Onkel Heinz!   6. Verkaufen Sie den alten Wagen.   7. Warte an der Tür!   8. Sprich nur Deutsch!   9. Kommen Sie um sieben Uhr!   10. Hilf mir damit!

R1 Review 1

R1·1   1. der Brunnen   2. die Prüfung   3. die Liebe   4. der Vogel   5. das Land

R1·2   1. Das Auto ist groß.   2. Dieser Gärtner ist krank.   3. Das Bild ist alt.   4. Das Fenster ist neu.   5. Die Uhr ist klein.

R1·3   1. Sie ist sehr alt. Die Landkarten sind sehr alt.   2. Es ist jung. Die Mädchen sind jung.   3. Er ist jung. Die Brüder sind jung.   4. Es ist hier. Die Häuser sind hier.   5. Sie ist da. Die Frauen sind da.

R1·4   1. Norwegen   2. wohnt   3. zu Hause   4. Wo   5. eine

R1·5   1. habe   2. wird   3. keine   4. Habt   5. keine   6. bin   7. Hast   8. nicht   9. Seid   10. wird

R1·6   1. probiere, probiert, probieren   2. antwortest, antwortet, antworten   3. lächelt, lächeln, lächele   4. hast, hat, habt   5. singe, singen, singen   6. reißt, reiße, reißt   7. bellst, bellt, bellen   8. kostet, kostet, kosten   9. paddele, paddelt, paddeln   10. bist, seid, ist   11. warten, warte, wartet   12. wandert, wanderst, wandern   13. bade, badet, baden   14. wirst, wird, werdet   15. glaubt, glauben, glauben

R1·7   1. zehnten, drei, siebzehn   2. zwanzigste, fünf, siebzehn

R1·8   1. es, sie, er   2. ihn, es, er   3. es, ihn, es   4. sie, sie, ihn   5. es, sie, ihn

R1·9   *Sample answers.* 1. ein Problem, einen Wagen, die Männer   2. den Roman, die Mädchen, die Frau   3. die Musik, einen Mantel, den Arzt   4. das Buch, die Pullover, ein Glas   5. eine Prüfung, einen Roman, ein Problem

R1·10   1. stehle, stiehlt   2. nimmst, nehmt   3. wisst, weiß   4. liest, lest   5. schlafen, schläfst   6. isst, isst   7. gibst, gebt   8. hilft, hilfst

R1·11   1. Ich bekomme, Du bekommst, Er bekommt, Wir bekommen, Sie bekommen   2. Ich bringe ... mit, Du bringst ... mit, Er bringt ... mit, Wir bringen... mit, Ihr bringt ... mit, Sie bringen ... mit   3. Ich versuche es, Du versuchst es, Er versucht es, Wir versuchen es, Ihr versucht es, Sie versuchen es   4. Ich mache ... zu, Du machst ... zu, Er macht ... zu, Wir machen ... zu, Ihr macht ... zu, Sie machen ... zu

R1·12   1. ich wiederhole, du wiederholst, er wiederholt, wir wiederholen, ihr wiederholt, sie wiederholen   2. ich höre auf, du hörst auf, er hört auf, wir hören auf, ihr hört auf, sie hören auf

R1·13   1. sei, seid, seien Sie   2. habe, habt, haben Sie   3. mache ... auf, macht ... auf, machen Sie auf   4. werde, werdet, werden Sie   5. kauf, kauft, kaufen Sie   6. behalte, behaltet, behalten Sie   7. setze ... fort, setzt ... fort, setzen Sie fort   8. stelle ... vor, stellt ... vor, stellen Sie vor   9. entdecke , entdeckt, entdecken Sie   10. sieh ... an, seht ... an, sehen Sie an

10 Accusative case prepositions and interrogatives

10·1 1. Ein Vogel fliegt durch das Fenster. 2. Ein Vogel fliegt durch die Tür. 3. Ein Vogel fliegt durch den Garten. 4. Ein Vogel fliegt durch den Wald. 5. Ich habe diese Blumen für Ihre Mutter. 6. Ich habe diese Blumen für Ihren Vater. 7. Ich habe diese Blumen für meinen Onkel. 8. Ich habe diese Blumen für meine Schwestern. 9. Ist er gegen diesen Rechtsanwalt? 10. Ist er gegen meine Idee? 11. Ist er gegen Ihre Freundin? 12. Ist er gegen meinen Bruder? 13. Kommen Sie ohne ein Geschenk? 14. Kommen Sie ohne Ihren Großvater? 15. Kommen Sie ohne Ihren Regenschirm? 16. Kommen Sie ohne Ihre Bücher? 17. Sie sorgt sich um meinen Sohn. 18. Sie sorgt sich um dieses Problem. 19. Sie sorgt sich um meine Eltern. 20. Sie sorgt sich um den Zahnarzt.

10·2 1. Meine Familie begrüßt Sie. 2. Ich kenne dich nicht. 3. Die Jungen essen es. 4. Wir haben sie. 5. Die Schüler legen ihn auf den Tisch. 6. Die Touristen fotografieren uns. 7. Er liebt euch nicht. 8. Meine Eltern besuchen mich in Hamburg. 9. Wen siehst du? 10. Was schreibt der Mann? 11. Die Mädchen suchen sie. 12. Niemand liest ihn. 13. Meine Mutter ruft dich an. 14. Die Frauen begrüßen uns. 15. Wer bekommt es?

10·3 1. Du wohnst in Heidelberg. 2. Wir wohnen in Heidelberg. 3. Ihr wohnt in Heidelberg. 4. Sie wohnen in Heidelberg. 5. Sie wohnt in Heidelberg. 6. Erik spielt gegen mich. 7. Erik spielt gegen ihn. 8. Erik spielt gegen uns. 9. Erik spielt gegen euch. 10. Erik spielt gegen sie. 11. Meine Eltern sorgen sich um dich. 12. Meine Eltern sorgen sich um sie. 13. Meine Eltern sorgen sich um euch. 14. Meine Eltern sorgen sich um Sie. 15. Meine Eltern sorgen sich um sie. 16. Ich entdecke eine kleine Insel. 17. Er entdeckt eine kleine Insel. 18. Wir entdecken eine kleine Insel. 19. Sie entdecken eine kleine Insel. 20. Wer entdeckt eine kleine Insel? 21. Sie gehen ohne dich wandern. 22. Sie gehen ohne ihn wandern. 23. Sie gehen ohne sie wandern. 24. Sie gehen ohne uns wandern. 25. Sie gehen ohne euch wandern.

10·4 1. dadurch 2. um sie 3. für sie 4. dafür 5. gegen sie 6. darum 7. durch ihn 8. für uns 9. dagegen 10. ohne sie 11. wider ihn 12. um sie 13. dadurch 14. ohne ihn 15. darum

10·5 1. Sabine ist in Berlin, denn sie besucht ihren Onkel.
Sabine ist in Berlin, denn sie arbeitet in der Hauptstadt.
Sabine ist in Berlin, denn sie sucht einen Freund.
2. Er bleibt in Kanada, denn er lernt Englisch.
Er bleibt in Kanada, denn seine Eltern wohnen da.
Er bleibt in Kanada, denn seine Freundin arbeitet in Toronto.
3. Ich kaufe einen VW, denn ich brauche ein Auto.
Ich kaufe einen VW, denn ein BMW ist teuer.
Ich kaufe einen VW, denn ein VW ist billig.

10·6 1. Das ist sein Hut. 2. Das ist ihr Hut. 3. Das ist unser Hut. 4. Das ist euer Hut. 5. Das ist Ihr Hut. 6. Er sieht meinen Freund. 7. Er sieht deinen Freund. 8. Er sieht euren Freund. 9. Er sieht Ihren Freund. 10. Er sieht ihren Freund. 11. Sie kaufen dein Fahrrad. 12. Sie kaufen sein Fahrrad. 13. Sie kaufen ihr Fahrrad. 14. Sie kaufen unser Fahrrad. 15. Sie kaufen euer Fahrrad. 16. Meine Eltern wohnen in der Hauptstadt. 17. Deine Eltern wohnen in der Hauptstadt. 18. Seine Eltern wohnen in der Hauptstadt. 19. Unsere Eltern wohnen in der Hauptstadt. 20. Ihre Eltern wohnen in der Hauptstadt.

10·7 1. Wie oft fährt sie in die Stadt? 2. Wie lange bleiben sie hier? 3. Wie viel kostet das Buch? 4. Wie spät kommt sie? 5. Wie viel Geld hat der alte Herr?

10·8 1. Gegen wen war Thomas? gegen sie 2. Ohne wen fährt Frau Braun ab? ohne sie 3. Für wen schreibe ich den Brief? für ihn 4. Wodurch schwimmt der Sportler? dadurch 5. Wofür danken uns die Zwillinge? dafür 6. Wodurch laufen die Jungen? dadurch 7. Worum bittet der alte Mann? darum 8. Wogegen kenne ich ein gutes Mittel? dagegen 9. Ohne wen kommt Erik nach Hause? ohne sie 10. Wodurch schicken wir das Paket? dadurch

11 Regular verbs in the past tense and word order

11·1   1. spielte   2. hörtest   3. sagten   4. fragten   5. reiste   6. machte   7. stelltet   8. setzten
9. diente   10. sorgte   11. holten   12. suchtest   13. kauften   14. pflanztet   15. flüsterte

11·2
1. lernte	2. lächelte
lerntest	lächeltest
lernte	lächelte
lernten	lächelten
lerntet	lächeltet
lernten	lächelten
lernte	lächelte

3. feierte	4. lebte
feiertest	lebtest
feierte	lebte
feierten	lebten
feiertet	lebtet
feierten	lebten
feierte	lebte

5. liebte	6. wohnte
liebtest	wohntest
liebte	wohnte
liebten	wohnten
liebtet	wohntet
liebten	wohnten
liebte	wohnte

11·3
1. endete	2. fürchtete
endetest	fürchtetest
endete	fürchtete
endeten	fürchteten
endetet	fürchtetet
endeten	fürchteten
endete	fürchtete

3. redete	4. antwortete
redetest	antwortetest
redete	antwortete
redeten	antworteten
redetet	antwortetet
redeten	antworteten
redete	antwortete

11·4   1. wartete   2. besuchtest   3. erwartete   4. holten ab   5. bereitetet vor   6. fragten nach
7. verkaufte   8. hörten zu   9. hörte auf   10. verlangte   11. pflanzte um   12. kehrten zurück
13. sagten   14. kauftest ein   15. ersetztet

11·5   1. Im Sommer schwimmen die Kinder gern.   2. In Deutschland ist das Wetter oft sehr schön.
3. Gestern kauften unsere Eltern einen neuen Wagen.   4. Heute spielen meine Töchter Schach.   5. Um
sieben Uhr stehe ich auf.   6. Morgen reist meine Familie nach Paris.   7. Gestern wohnten wir noch in
München.   8. Im Mai feierten sie meinen Geburtstag.   9. Im Frühling besuchte ich meine Tante in
Amerika.   10. Morgen verkaufst du dein Fahrrad.

11·6 1. Ich spiele das Klavier, und Sonja singt.   2. Martin wohnt in der Hauptstadt, und ich wohne in Bremen.   3. Der Hund ist krank, und die Katze ist alt.   4. Ich lese den Roman, aber ich verstehe nichts.   5. Mein Bruder ist stark, aber er ist faul.   6. Das Wetter ist schön, aber wir bleiben zu Hause.   7. Sind sie reich, oder sind sie arm?   8. Kaufte sie ein Kleid, oder kaufte sie eine Bluse?   9. Der Mann arbeitet nicht, denn er ist müde.   10. Die Touristen verstehen nichts, denn sie sprechen kein Deutsch.

11·7 1. du einen neuen VW kauftest   2. meine Eltern viele Jahre im Ausland wohnten   3. Frau Keller deinen Bruder besuchte   4. Ihr Sohn sehr gut schwimmt   5. er sehr schlecht Klavier spielt   6. ihre Tochter da wohnt   7. ihr Mann in der Hauptstadt arbeitet   8. sie eine große Wohnung da hat   9. Wohnungen in Berlin billig sind   10. sie gern ins Theater geht

11·8 1. c 2. b 3. a 4. c 5. d 6. c 7. a 8. d 9. a 10. a

12 Indirect objects and the dative case

12·1 1. dem Rechtsanwalt   2. der Dame   3. dem Kind   4. den Leuten   5. keiner Krankenschwester   6. diesen Mädchen   7. einem Schüler   8. meinen Brüdern   9. unserer Freundin   10. euren Eltern

12·2 1. Ich schicke meinem Vater einen brief.   2. Ich schicke dieser Dame einen Brief.   3. Ich schicke unserem Professor einen Brief.   4. Ich schicke ihren Freunden einen Brief.   5. Ich schicke deiner Mutter einen Brief.   6. Wir schenkten unseren Töchtern einen Computer.   7. Wir schenkten seiner Tante einen Computer.   8. Wir schenkten dem Mädchen einen Computer.   9. Wir schenkten dem Zahnarzt einen Computer.   10. Wir schenkten ihrem Onkel einen Computer.   11. Was geben Sie Ihrer Frau?   12. Was geben Sie seinen Kindern?   13. Was geben Sie diesen Sportlern?   14. Was geben Sie der Tänzerin?   15. Was geben Sie den Schauspielern?

12·3 1. Ich gebe es dir.   2. Ich gebe es ihm.   3. Ich gebe es ihr.   4. Ich gebe es dem Löwen.   5. Ich gebe es meinem Studenten.   6. Niemand sendet mir ein Geschenk.   7. Niemand sendet uns ein Geschenk.   8. Niemand sendet euch ein Geschenk.   9. Niemand sendet diesem Herrn ein Geschenk.   10. Niemand sendet dem Soldaten ein Geschenk.   11. Die Frau kaufte Ihnen eine Zeitschrift. 12. Die Frau kaufte ihnen eine Zeitschrift.   13. Die Frau kaufte diesem Schauspieler eine Zeitschrift. 14. Die Frau kaufte dieser Schauspielerin eine Zeitschrift.   15. Die Frau kaufte mir eine Zeitschrift.

12·4 1. dem Polizisten   2. einem Gärtner   3. ihnen   4. ihr   5. uns   6. seinem Sohn   7. ihm   8. mir   9. einem Matrosen   10. dem Konzert   11. der Oper   12. ihren Vorlesungen   13. dem Stadtpark   14. der Schule   15. dir

12·5 1. von ihm   2. damit   3. bei ihr   4. ihm gegenüber   5. daraus   6. danach   7. dazu   8. zu ihnen   9. außer ihm   10. mit ihm

12·6 1. Die Jungen helfen den Frauen damit.   2. Die Jungen helfen mir damit.   3. Die Jungen helfen uns damit.   4. Die Jungen helfen ihren Freunden damit.   5. Die Jungen helfen ihnen damit.   6. Ich danke dir dafür.   7. Ich danke ihm dafür.   8. Ich danke Ihnen dafür.   9. Ich danke meiner Freundin dafür.   10. Ich danke dem Matrosen dafür.   11. Wo begegneten den Diplomaten?   12. Wo begegneten ihr?   13. Wo begegneten meinem Freund?   14. Wo begegneten ihnen?   15. Wo begegneten seiner Großmutter?

12·7 1. c 2. a 3. a 4. a 5. d 6. d 7. c 8. d 9. d 10. a

13 Irregular verbs in the past tense

13·1 1. lief 2. kamst 3. gingen 4. sprach 5. versprach 6. trank 7. aßt 8. zogen 9. hieß 10. sangen 11. wuschst 12. traf 13. ließ 14. bekam 15. nahmen an 16. riefen an 17. verstand 18. taten 19. halfst 20. schlief 21. stieg aus 22. fingen an 23. schien 24. erfandet 25. saß

13·2

1. hielt
   hieltest
   hielt
   hielten
   hieltet
   hielten
   hielten

2. fiel
   fielst
   fiel
   fielen
   fielt
   fielen
   fielen

3. schloss
   schlosst
   schloss
   schlossen
   schlosst
   schlossen
   schloss

4. begriff
   begriffst
   begriff
   begriffen
   begrifft
   begriffen
   begriff

5. gab aus
   gabst aus
   gab aus
   gaben aus
   gabt aus
   gaben aus
   gab aus

6. flog
   flogst
   flog
   flogen
   flogt
   flogen
   flog

13·3

1. hatte
   hattest
   hatte
   hatten
   hattet
   hatten
   hatte

2. war
   warst
   war
   waren
   wart
   waren
   war

3. wurde
   wurdest
   wurde
   wurden
   wurdet
   wurden
   wurde

13·4   1. kannte   2. dachtest   3. wusste   4. brachten   5. nannten   6. rannte   7. wandten
8. sandtet   9. branntest   10. wussten

13·5

1. kannte
   kanntest
   kannte
   kannten
   kanntet
   kannten
   kannte

2. dachte
   dachtest
   dachte
   dachten
   dachtet
   dachten
   dachte

3. wusste
   wusstest
   wusste
   wussten
   wusstet
   wussten
   wusste

4. brachte
   brachtest
   brachte
   brachten
   brachtet
   brachten
   brachte

13·6   1. kannten   2. wusste   3. Hatten   4. war   5. wurde   6. nannte/nannten   7. dachte
       8. hatte   9. wurde   10. Warst

13·7   1. Es wurde um sieben Uhr dunkel.   2. Er kam ohne seine Frau.   3. Die Kinder hatten Durst.
       4. Was brachten Sie uns?   5. Meine Eltern fuhren zu alten Freunden.   6. Ich wusste es nicht.
       7. Sahst du die Berge?   8. Das Wetter wurde schlecht.   9. Ich sandte ihm eine Ansichtskarte.
       10. Der Junge stand um sechs Uhr auf.   11. Kanntet ihr diesen Herrn?   12. Nannte sie ihren Namen?
       13. Wo warst du?   14. Ich rief meine Freundin an.   15. Lasen Sie eine Zeitschrift?

14   Modal auxiliaries in the present and past tenses

14·1   1. Ich will zu Hause bleiben.   2. Du willst zu Hause bleiben.   3. Er will zu Hause bleiben.   4. Sie
       wollen zu Hause bleiben.   5. Sie soll ihr helfen.   6. Sie sollen ihr helfen.   7. Wir sollen ihr helfen.
       8. Ihr sollt ihr helfen.   9. Du kannst den Brief nicht lesen.   10. Wer kann den Brief nicht lesen?
       11. Sie können den Brief nicht lesen.   12. Ihr könnt den Brief nicht lesen.   13. Ich darf die Bibliothek
       benutzen.   14. Sie darf die Bibliothek benutzen.   15. Wir dürfen die Bibliothek benutzen.   16. Die
       Studenten dürfen die Bibliothek benutzen.   17. Du musst heute abend arbeiten.   18. Sie müssen heute
       abend arbeiten.   19. Ihr müsst heute abend arbeiten.   20. Niemand muss heute abend arbeiten.

14·2   1. Ich mag gern Bier.   2. Du magst gern Bier.   3. Er mag gern Bier.   4. Wir mögen gern Bier.
       5. Ihr mögt gern Bier.   6. Sie mögen gern Bier.   7. Sie mögen gern Bier.   8. Die Männer mögen gern
       Bier.   9. Ich mag jünger sein.   10. Du magst jünger sein.   11. Sie mag jünger sein.   12. Wir mögen
       jünger sein.   13. Ihr mögt jünger sein.   14. Sie mögen jünger sein.   15. Sie mögen jünger sein.
       16. Frau Keller mag jünger sein.

14·3   1. Du solltest fleißig arbeiten.   2. Wir mussten ihnen helfen.   3. Ich wollte eine Reise durch Italien
       machen.   4. Der Mann mochte viel älter sein.   5. Der Ausländer konnte es nicht verstehen.   6. Sie
       durften nicht länger bleiben.   7. Wir sollten mehr Geld sparen.   8. Du musstest an deine Mutter
       schreiben.   9. Wolltet ihr bei uns übernachten?   10. Konnten die Jungen kochen?

14·4   1. Ich möchte das Theater besuchen.   2. Möchten Sie nach Hause gehen?   3. Er möchte neue
       Handschuhe kaufen.   4. Frau Benz möchte den Polizisten fragen.   5. Niemand möchte die Briefe
       schreiben.   6. Möchtest du etwas trinken?   7. Wir möchten um neun Uhr frühstücken.   8. Möchtet
       ihr mit uns fahren?   9. Sie möchte die neue Zeitung lesen.   10. Ich möchte hier aussteigen.

14·5   1. Sie ließ ein neues Kleid machen.   2. Er hilft seinem Vater kochen.   3. Der Hund hörte zwei Männer
       kommen.   4. Gingst du um elf Uhr spazieren?   5. Ich sehe sie im Garten arbeiten.   6. Die Schüler
       lernten lesen und schreiben.   7. Sie gehen am Montag radfahren.   8. Wir lassen das alte Fahrrad
       reparieren.   9. Niemand half uns die Sätze übersetzen.   10. Hört ihr ihn pfeifen?

14·6   1. Erik hört seine Freunde vor der Tür flüstern.   2. Wir halfen Erik das Frühstück vorbereiten.   3. Ihr
       seht Thomas große Pakete tragen.   4. Ich hörte Sie Deutsch sprechen.   5. Er hilft Frau Bauer die Küche
       saubermachen.

14·7   1. c   2. d   3. a   4. d   5. c   6. d   7. a   8. a   9. d   10. b

15   The accusative-dative prepositions

15·1   1. das Haus   2. die Tür   3. die Bäume   4. die Garage   5. den Laden   6. diesem Mädchen
       7. unseren Eltern   8. seiner Freundin   9. einem Schulkameraden   10. dem Fernsehapparat
       11. den Keller   12. die Kirche   13. das Restaurant   14. die Garage   15. diesen Laden
       16. unserem Bett   17. dem Sofa   18. einer Decke   19. diesen Kissen   20. dem Boden   21. das
       Klavier   22. den Tisch   23. den Schrank   24. die Stühle   25. das Sofa

15·2   1. auf dem Sofa   2. in der Schule   3. am Theater   4. im Wasser   5. vor der Tür   6. am Fluss
       7. aufs Bett   8. ins Rathaus   9. am Bahnhof   10. auf den Stühlen

1. im Jahre 1892   2. im Jahre 2003   3. im Jahre 1945   4. im Jahre 2010   5. im Jahre 1917   6. am fünften September   7. am ersten Januar   8. am dreiundzwanzigsten Juli   9. am fünfundzwanzigsten Dezember   10. am dritten November

15·4   1. darüber worüber   2. an ihn an wen   3. davor wovor   4. über sie über wen   5. daran woran   6. darin worin/wo   7. darauf worauf   8. auf ihn auf wen   9. dahin wohin   10. zwischen ihnen zwischen wem   11. darüber worüber   12. neben ihn neben wen   13. davor wovor   14. darüber worüber   15. daran woran

16 Regular verbs in the present perfect tense and more imperatives

16·1   1. gelernt   2. gekauft   3. gesagt   4. gefragt   5. getanzt   6. gedeckt   7. gespielt   8. gestört   9. gepackt   10. geputzt   11. gehört   12. gebraucht   13. gewünscht   14. gewohnt   15. gelebt   16. gelacht   17. geweint   18. geholt   19. gekocht   20. gestellt   21. gelegt   22. gesetzt   23. geweckt   24. gereist   25. gepflanzt

16·2
1. habe geendet
hast geendet
hat geendet
haben geendet
habt geendet
haben geendet
hat geendet

2. habe gewartet
hast gewartet
hat gewartet
haben gewartet
habt gewartet
haben gewartet
hat gewartet

3. habe geantwortet
hast geantwortet
hat geantwortet
haben geantwortet
habt geantwortet
haben geantwortet
hat geantwortet

4. habe geliebt
hast geliebt
hat geliebt
haben geliebt
habt geliebt
haben geliebt
hat geliebt

5. habe gezeigt
hast gezeigt
hat gezeigt
haben gezeigt
habt gezeigt
haben gezeigt
hat gezeigt

6. habe geschickt
hast geschickt
hat geschickt
haben geschickt
habt geschickt
haben geschickt
hat geschickt

16·3
1. habe demonstriert
hast demonstriert
hat demonstriert
haben demonstriert
habt demonstriert
haben demonstriert
hat demonstriert

2. habe korrigiert
hast korrigiert
hat korrigiert
haben korrigiert
habt korrigiert
haben korrigiert
hat korrigiert

3. habe probiert
hast probiert
hat probiert
haben probiert
habt probiert
haben probiert
hat probiert

4. habe studiert
hast studiert
hat studiert
haben studiert
habt studiert
haben studiert
hat studiert

16·4

1. habe aufgemacht	2. habe eingekauft
hast aufgemacht	hast eingekauft
hat aufgemacht	hat eingekauft
haben aufgemacht	haben eingekauft
habt aufgemacht	habt eingekauft
haben aufgemacht	haben eingekauft
hat aufgemacht	hat eingekauft

3. habe bestellt	4. habe zerstört
hast bestellt	hast zerstört
hat bestellt	hat zerstört
haben bestellt	haben zerstört
habt bestellt	habt zerstört
haben bestellt	haben zerstört
hat bestellt	hat zerstört

16·5 1. Ich bin durch die Stadt marschiert. 2. Du bist durch die Stadt marschiert. 3. Er ist durch die Stadt marschiert. 4. Wir sind durch die Stadt marschiert. 5. Ihr seid durch die Stadt marschiert. 6. Sie sind durch die Stadt marschiert. 7. Die Soldaten sind durch die Stadt marschiert. 8. Ich bin in die Schweiz gereist. 9. Du bist in die Schweiz gereist. 10. Er ist in die Schweiz gereist. 11. Wir sind in die Schweiz gereist. 12. Ihr seid in die Schweiz gereist. 13. Sie sind in die Schweiz gereist. 14. Der Tourist ist in die Schweiz gereist.

16·6 1. Sprechen wir nur Deutsch! 2. Kaufen wir einen neuen Mercedes! 3. Rufen wir die Polizei an! 4. Bleiben wir im Wohnzimmer! 5. Stellen wir unsere Eltern vor! 6. Gehen wir ins Restaurant! 7. Spielen wir Karten! 8. Machen wir die Fenster zu! 9. Trinken wir ein Glas Wein! 10. Setzen wir es auf den Tisch!

16·7 1. Lass uns in die Berge reisen! 2. Lassen Sie uns die Zeitungen lesen! 3. Lasst uns nicht im Wohnzimmer spielen! 4. Lassen Sie uns bis nächsten Dienstag bleiben! 5. Lass uns vor dem Bahnhof aussteigen!

17 Genitive case and comparative and superlative

17·1 1. der Tasse 2. dieses Glases 3. meiner Eltern 4. seiner Tochter 5. einer Prüfung 6. Ihres Bleistifts 7. des Geldes 8. ihrer Gesundheit 9. unseres Gartens 10. des Flugzeugs 11. dieses Zuges 12. der Blume 13. dieser Nacht 14. deines Geburtstags 15. unserer Freundinnen 16. des Hundes 17. ihrer Katze 18. des Jahres 19. dieser Pferde 20. eines Apfels 21. keines Dichters 22. der Gäste 23. des Studenten 24. eines Löwen 25. des Schiffes

17·2 1. seiner Schwester 2. der Lehrer 3. dieses Herrn 4. meiner Töchter 5. unseres Gastes 6. des Chefs 7. ihres Freundes 8. dieses Problems 9. deiner Tante 10. Ihrer Freundin

17·3 1. Wegen des Regens bleiben alle zu Hause. 2. Wegen des Gewitters bleiben alle zu Hause. 3. Wegen seiner Erkältung bleiben alle zu Hause. 4. Wegen des Wetters bleiben alle zu Hause. 5. Wegen der Prüfungen bleiben alle zu Hause. 6. Wir waren während meines Geburtstags in Kanada. 7. Wir waren während des Krieges in Kanada. 8. Wir waren während des Angriffs in Kanada. 9. Wir waren während der Konferenz in Kanada. 10. Wir waren während der Verhandlungen in Kanada. 11. Anstatt meines Onkels musste ich ihr helfen. 12. Anstatt der Jungen musste ich ihr helfen. 13. Anstatt eines Matrosen musste ich ihr helfen. 14. Anstatt der Familie musste ich ihr helfen. 15. Anstatt unserer Eltern musste ich ihr helfen. 16. Trotz unserer Freundschaft wollte sie nicht Tennis spielen. 17. Trotz des Wetters wollte sie nicht Tennis spielen. 18. Trotz des Sonnenscheins wollte sie nicht Tennis spielen. 19. Trotz meines Alters wollte sie nicht Tennis spielen. 20. Trotz meiner Bitte wollte sie nicht Tennis spielen. 21. Wir wohnten diesseits des Flusses. 22. Wir wohnten diesseits der Grenze. 23. Wir wohnten diesseits der Brücke. 24. Wir wohnten diesseits der Berge. 25. Wir wohnten diesseits der Alpen.

17·4   1. schneller   2. langsamer   3. grüner   4. weißer   5. dicker   6. neuer   7. länger
8. schwerer   9. leichter   10. kürzer   11. näher   12. heller   13. älter   14. fleißiger
15. breiter

17·5   1. Seine Tochter war jünger als seine Schwester.
Tante Angela war am jüngsten.
2. Die Kinder laufen langsamer als Thomas.
Mein Sohn läuft am langsamsten.
3. Das Gymnasium ist größer als die Grundschule.
Die Universität ist am größten.
4. Erik spricht besser als seine Kusine.
Der Professor spricht am besten.
5. Der Doppendecker fliegt höher als der Zeppelin.
Diese Flugzeuge fliegen am höchsten.
6. Unsere Gäste kamen später als ich.
Du kamst am spätesten.
7. Diese Geschichte war langweiliger als ihr Roman.
Sein Gedicht war am langweiligsten.
8. Diese Straßen sind breiter als unsere Straße.
Die Autobahn ist am breitesten.
9. Diese Prüfung ist schwerer als die Hausaufgabe.
Das Examen ist am schwersten.
10. Frau Bauer kam früher als ihr Mann.
Ihr kamt am frühesten.

18 Irregular verbs in the present perfect tense and adjectives

18·1   1. haben gezogen   2. habe angezogen   3. hast gesungen   4. haben geschlagen   5. hat erschlagen
6. habt erfunden   7. hat versprochen   8. habe gebissen   9. hast gewaschen   10. hat beschrieben
11. haben gegessen   12. hat gefressen   13. haben geschwiegen   14. hat gebrochen   15. habt
angesehen   16. habe getroffen   17. haben mitgenommen   18. haben geschlossen   19. haben getan
20. hat begriffen

18·2   1. Ich habe ein Glas Milch getrunken.   2. Du hast ein Glas Milch getrunken.   3. Er hat ein Glas Milch
getrunken.   4. Wir haben ein Glas Milch getrunken.   5. Ihr habt ein Glas Milch getrunken.   6. Sie
haben ein Glas Milch getrunken.   7. Der Soldat hat ein Glas Milch getrunken.   8. Ich habe im
Wohnzimmer gesessen.   9. Du hast im Wohnzimmer gesessen.   10. Er hat im Wohnzimmer gesessen.
11. Wir haben im Wohnzimmer gesessen.   12. Ihr habt im Wohnzimmer gesessen.   13. Sie haben im
Wohnzimmer gesessen.   14. Die Touristen haben im Wohnzimmer gesessen.

18·3   1. Ich bin zu Hause geblieben.   2. Du bist zu Hause geblieben.   3. Er ist zu Hause geblieben.   4. Wir
sind zu Hause geblieben.   5. Ihr seid zu Hause geblieben.   6. Sie sind zu Hause geblieben.   7. Der
Matrose ist zu Hause geblieben.   8. Ich bin nach Deutschland geflogen.   9. Du bist nach Deutschland
geflogen.   10. Er ist nach Deutschland geflogen.   11. Wir sind nach Deutschland geflogen.   12. Ihr
seid nach Deutschland geflogen.   13. Sie sind nach Deutschland geflogen.   14. Der Ausländer ist nach
Deutschland geflogen.   15. Ich bin ins Wasser gefallen.   16. Du bist ins Wasser gefallen.   17. Er ist
ins Wasser gefallen.   18. Wir sind ins Wasser gefallen.   19. Ihr seid ins Wasser gefallen.   20. Sie sind
ins Wasser gefallen.   21. Wer ist ins Wasser gefallen?   22. Ich bin um elf Uhr eingeschlafen.   23. Du
bist um elf Uhr eingeschlafen.   24. Er ist um elf Uhr eingeschlafen.   25. Wir sind um elf Uhr
eingeschlafen.   26. Ihr seid um elf Uhr eingeschlafen.   27. Sie sind um elf Uhr eingeschlafen.
28. Die alte Dame ist um elf Uhr eingeschlafen.

18·4   1. Ich habe viele Probleme gehabt.   2. Du hast viele Probleme gehabt.   3. Er hat viele Probleme gehabt.   4. Wir haben viele Probleme gehabt.   5. Ihr habt viele Probleme gehabt.   6. Sie haben viele Probleme gehabt.   7. Die Lehrerin hat viele Probleme gehabt.   8. Ich bin nicht in der Stadt gewesen.   9. Du bist nicht in der Stadt gewesen.   10. Er ist nicht in der Stadt gewesen.   11. Wir sind nicht in der Stadt gewesen.   12. Ihr seid nicht in der Stadt gewesen.   13. Sie sind nicht in der Stadt gewesen.   14. Die Ausländerin ist nicht in der Stadt gewesen.   15. Ich bin müde geworden.   16. Du bist müde geworden.   17. Er ist müde geworden.   18. Wir sind müde geworden.   19. Ihr seid müde geworden.   20. Sie sind müde geworden.   21. Niemand ist müde geworden.

18·5   1. Ich habe gewusst, wo der Mann wohnt.   2. Du hast gewusst, wo der Mann wohnt.   3. Er hat gewusst, wo der Mann wohnt.   4. Wir haben gewusst, wo der Mann wohnt.   5. Ihr habt gewusst, wo der Mann wohnt.   6. Sie haben gewusst, wo der Mann wohnt.   7. Niemand hat gewusst, wo der Mann wohnt.   8. Ich habe das Baby Angela genannt.   9. Du hast das Baby Angela genannt.   10. Er hat das Baby Angela genannt.   11. Wir haben das Baby Angela genannt.   12. Ihr habt das Baby Angela genannt.   13. Sie haben das Baby Angela genannt.   14. Die Eltern haben das Baby Angela genannt.   15. Ich habe an die Ausländer gedacht.   16. Du hast an die Ausländer gedacht.   17. Er hat an die Ausländer gedacht.   18. Wir haben an die Ausländer gedacht.   19. Ihr habt an die Ausländer gedacht.   20. Sie haben an die Ausländer gedacht.   21. Wer hat an die Ausländer gedacht?   22. Ich bin aus dem Schlafzimmer gerannt.   23. Du bist aus dem Schlafzimmer gerannt.   24. Er ist aus dem Schlafzimmer gerannt.   25. Wir sind aus dem Schlafzimmer gerannt.   26. Ihr seid aus dem Schlafzimmer gerannt.   27. Sie sind aus dem Schlafzimmer gerannt.   28. Das Dienstmädchen ist aus dem Schlafzimmer gerannt.

18·6   1. Ich habe es nicht gemocht.   2. Du hast es nicht gemocht.   3. Er hat es nicht gemocht.   4. Wir haben es nicht gemocht.   5. Ihr habt es nicht gemocht.   6. Sie haben es nicht gemocht.   7. Wer hat es nicht gemocht?   8. Ich habe alles gewollt.   9. Du hast alles gewollt.   10. Er hat alles gewollt.   11. Wir haben alles gewollt.   12. Ihr habt alles gewollt.   13. Sie haben alles gewollt.   14. Die Kinder haben alles gewollt.   15. Ich habe Englisch und Deutsch gekonnt.   16. Du hast Englisch und Deutsch gekonnt.   17. Er hat Englisch und Deutsch gekonnt.   18. Wir haben Englisch und Deutsch gekonnt.   19. Ihr habt Englisch und Deutsch gekonnt.   20. Sie haben Englisch und Deutsch gekonnt.   21. Die Studentin hat Englisch und Deutsch gekonnt.

18·7   1. großen   2. kleinen   3. amerikanischen   4. alten   5. schmutzigen   6. neuen   7. braunen   8. roten   9. billigen   10. billigeren   11. kleinen   12. weißen   13. jungen   14. schwarzen   15. ältesten   16. reicher   17. armer   18. netter   19. hübscher   20. kranker   21. schmutziges   22. gelbes   23. großes   24. billiges   25. kleines

R2   Review 2

R2·1   1. wogegen   2. ohne seinen Sohn   3. für meinen Bruder   4. durch   5. mich

R2·2   1. feierten   2. arbeiteten   3. machte die Fenster zu   4. besuchte   5. Wartete

R2·3   1. Gestern reisten sie nach Bremen.   2. Um zehn Uhr ging er zum Park.

R2·4   1. Ich weiß, dass Frau Schneider keine Kinder hat.   2. Mein Onkel schläft, denn er ist müde.   3. Er bleibt in Berlin, weil er seinen Sohn besucht.

R2·5   1. Herrn   2. ihr   3. Außer   4. senden   5. gegenüber   6. Gärtner   7. Womit   8. imponierte   9. euch   10. kaufen

R2·6   1. verstand   2. hatten   3. hieß   4. kanntest   5. wurde   6. Wussten   7. Wart   8. aßen   9. kamst   10. verlor

R2·7   1. mochte   2. konnten   3. musstest   4. sollten   5. wollte

R2·8   1. dürfen   2. wollt   3. können   4. Sollst   5. mögen

R2·9   1. in die   2. diesem   3. den Tisch   4. das Bett   5. im   6. der Decke   7. das Hause   8. an die
9. den Film   10. an ihn

R2·10   1. sein   2. haben   3. haben   4. sein   5. Sein

R2·11   1. habe gelacht   2. sind marschiert   3. habt gespielt   4. hast zerstört   5. haben geantwortet

R2·12   1. bleibe, bleibt, beleiben Sie   2. rufe an, ruft an, rufen Sie an   3. sei, seid, seien Sie   4. lass, lasst,
lassen Sie 5. steige aus, steigt aus, steigen Sie aus

R2·13   1. des Gewitters   2. meiner Schwester   3. des Jungen   4. des Winters   5. dieses Problems

R2·14   1. länger, am längsten   2. besser, am besten   3. jünger, am jüngsten   4. größer, am größten
5. näher, am nächsten

R2·15   1. hat angezogen   2. hast gesungen   3. bin gewesen   4. haben gewusst   5. haben gekonnt
6. hat gebrannt   7. sind gekommen   8. ist gerannt

R2·16   1. armer, kranker 2. alten, roten 3. kleinen, kleineren 4. neues, weißes 5. hübsche, ältere 6. kleinsten,
schmutzigen 7. neuen, amerikanischen

19 Past perfect, future, and future perfect tenses

19·1   1. hatten gezogen   2. war geblieben   3. hattest gesungen   4. war gereist   5. hatte zugemacht
6. war gestorben   7. waren geflogen   8. hatten gegessen   9. hattet erwartet   10. hatte gespielt
11. hatte angezogen   12. war passiert   13. hattest besucht   14. hattet gelacht   15. hatten
geschlagen   16. hattet gefallen   17. war gefallen   18. war eingeschlafen   19. waren gerannt
20. hatte gewusst   21. war gekommen   22. hattet bekommen   23. hatten zerstört   24. hatte
vergessen   25. war geschehen

19·2   1. Wir hatten mit dem Kellner gesprochen.   2. Wer hatte Deutsch gelernt?   3. Die Frauen hatten
geweint.   4. Ich war zum Rathaus gelaufen.   5. Waren sie an der Bushaltestelle ausgestiegen?   6. Die
kleinen Kinder hatten Radio gehört.   7. Du hattest ihn Bertolt genannt.   8. Was war am Mittwoch
passiert? 9. Der Hund hatte unter dem Tisch geschlafen.   10. Mein Großvater hatte eine neue Garage
gebaut.

19·3   1. Die Schüler werden mit dem neuen Lehrer sprechen.   2. Ich werde ein großes Problem haben.
3. Wirst du Schauspieler werden?   4. Es wird sehr kalt sein.   5. Meine Mutter wird einen Polizisten
fragen.   6. Herr Becker wird seine Tochter in Bonn besuchen.   7. Der Zug wird um elf Uhr kommen.
8. Die Studentin wird einen neuen Computer kaufen.   9. Es wird regnen.   10. Wird es schneien?

19·4   1. Wir werden sechs Stunden lang gefahren sein.   2. Die Touristen werden wohl nach Polen gereist sein.
3. Die Jungen werden Fußball gespielt haben.   4. Die Wanderer werden Durst gehabt haben.   5. Der
Schüler wird ein Würstchen gekauft haben.   6. Du wirst den ganzen Kuchen gegessen haben.   7. Karl
wird wohl einen Beruf gelernt haben.   8. Die Party wird allen gefallen haben.   9. Wir werden mehr als
neun Stunden geschlafen haben.   10. Die Reisenden werden zu spät angekommen sein.

19·5   1. Mein Onkel bezahlte die Rechnung.
Mein Onkel hat die Rechnung bezahlt.
Mein Onkel hatte die Rechnung bezahlt.
Mein Onkel wird die Rechnung bezahlen.
Mein Onkel wird die Rechnung bezahlt haben.

2. Die Mädchen schwammen im Fluss.
   Die Mädchen sind im Fluss geschwommen.
   Die Mädchen waren im Fluss geschwommen.
   Die Mädchen werden im Fluss schwimmen.
   Die Mädchen werden im Fluss geschwommen sein.
3. Wir sprachen oft mit unseren Nachbarn.
   Wir haben oft mit unseren Nachbarn gesprochen.
   Wir hatten oft mit unseren Nachbarn gesprochen.
   Wir werden oft mit unseren Nachbarn sprechen.
   Wir werden oft mit unseren Nachbarn gesprochen haben.
4. Meine Verwandten reisten nach Amerika.
   Meine Verwandten sind nach Amerika gereist.
   Meine Verwandten waren nach Amerika gereist.
   Meine Verwandten werden nach Amerika reisen.
   Meine Verwandten werden nach Amerika gereist sein.
5. Ich arbeitete für Herrn Dorf.
   Ich habe für Herrn Dorf gearbeitet.
   Ich hatte für Herrn Dorf gearbeitet.
   Ich werde für Herrn Dorf arbeiten.
   Ich werde für Herrn Dorf gearbeitet haben.
6. Mein Sohn besuchte die Universität.
   Mein Sohn hat die Universität besucht.
   Mein Sohn hatte die Universität besucht.
   Mein Sohn wird die Universität besuchen.
   Mein Sohn wird die Universität besucht haben.
7. Sie zog sich eine schöne Bluse an.
   Sie hat sich eine schöne Bluse angezogen.
   Sie hatte sich eine schöne Bluse angezogen.
   Sie wird sich eine schöne Bluse anziehen.
   Sie wird sich eine schöne Bluse angezogen haben.
8. Viele Jugendliche wanderten im Wald.
   Viele Jugendliche sind im Wald gewandert.
   Viele Jugendliche waren im Wald gewandert.
   Viele Jugendliche werden im Wald wandern.
   Viele Jugendliche werden im Wald gewandert sein.
9. Er machte alle Fenster auf.
   Er hat alle Fenster aufgemacht.
   Er hatte alle Fenster aufgemacht.
   Er wird alle Fenster aufmachen.
   Er wird alle Fenster aufgemacht haben.
10. Die Gäste aßen mehr als dreimal mexikanisch.
    Die Gäste haben mehr als dreimal mexikanisch gegessen.
    Die Gäste hatten mehr als dreimal mexikanisch gegessen.
    Die Gäste werden mehr als dreimal mexikanisch essen.
    Die Gäste werden mehr als dreimal mexikanisch gegessen haben.

20 Relative pronouns

20·1   1. das   2. mit denen   3. dessen Buch   4. denen   5. den   6. in der   7. nach dem   8. deren Eltern   9. von denen   10. dessen Bücher   11. dem   12. in das   13. deren Vater   14. die   15. durch den

20·2   1. das ein Düsenjäger ist   2. auf dem ein kleiner Vogel sitzt   3. das niemand reparieren konnte   4. in das die Fluggäste einsteigen   5. die Amerikanerin ist   6. deren Kinder eine Schule in der Stadt besuchen   7. mit der viele Männer tanzen wollen   8. auf die ich gestern gewartet habe   9. die alles verloren haben   10. deren Töchter ihnen nicht helfen können   11. für die wir einmal gearbeitet haben   12. die alle Nachbarn lieben   13. das viel zu groß ist   14. auf dem der Hund auch schläft   15. das sein Großvater vierzig Jahre vorher gekauft hatte

20·3   1. welches ein Düsenjäger ist   2. welches der Tourist fotografiert hat   3. von welchem alle reden
4. über welche er einen Artikel geschrieben hat   5. mit welchen die größeren Jungen gern spielen
6. deren Bruder das Geld gestohlen hat   7. durch welche ich die Nachricht bekommen habe   8. welcher
keinen Führerschein hat   9. welchen Frau Keller gern hat   10. mit welchem diese Fußgänger sprechen
wollen   11. welchem der Polizist einen Strafzettel gab   12. welche Thomas ihr geschenkt hat   13. für
welche sie ihm danken will   14. von welchen ihre Schwester nicht sprechen will   15. welche leider
schon welken

20·4   1. Wem der Roman nicht gefiel, der soll ihn nicht lesen.   2. Wem man traut, der ist ein treuer Freund.
3. Wer nicht für uns ist, der ist gegen uns.   4. Wen wir einladen, dem geben wir den teuersten Sekt.
5. Wessen Wein ich trinke, dem bleibe ich treu.   6. Wen der Freund liebt, den hasst der Feind.   7. Wen
man nicht kennt, dem bleibt man fern.   8. Wen ich gesehen habe, den werde ich nie vergessen.   9. Mit
wem der Politiker spricht, der wird der neue Kandidat.   10. Wessen Freundschaft ich habe, dem bleibe ich
ein guter Freund.

20·5   1. Der Mann sagte alles, was voller Unsinn war.   2. Das ist das Schrecklichste, was ich gesehen habe.
3. Es gibt vieles, was sehr gefährlich ist.   4. Sie hat das Teuerste, was nicht immer das Beste ist.
5. Singe etwas, was wir noch nicht gehört haben!   6. Thomas hat ein Auto gestohlen, wovon seine Eltern
nichts gewusst haben.   7. Unsere Tante muss heute abreisen, was wir sehr bedauern.   8. Sie hat nichts
verstanden, was ich gesagt habe.   9. Wir vergessen alles, was der Politiker versprochen hat.   10. Unsere
Nachbarn machen Krach, was uns stört.

21   Modifiers, adverbs, reflexive pronouns, and conjugations

21·1   1. einem, alten   2. diese, hübsche   3. solche, interessanten   4. deine, erste   5. unsere, besten
6. jedem, guten   7. seine, neue   8. einer, kleinen   9. jenem, großen   10. ein, solches   11. solche,
lauten   12. welchen, jungen   13. keinem, kleinen   14. Ihr, schöner   15. einer, langen

21·2
1. solche netten Kinder	2. wenige deutsche Männer
solche netten Kinder	wenige deutsche Männer
solchen netten Kindern	wenigen deutschen Männern
solcher netten Kinder	weniger deutscher Männer

3. jeder alte Herr	4. ein solches Flugzeug
jeden alten Herrn	ein solches Flugzeug
jedem alten Herrn	einem solchen Flugzeug
jedes alten Herrn	eines solchen Flugzeugs

5. deine beste Prüfung	6. gutes Wetter
deine beste Prüfung	gutes Wetter
deiner besten Prüfung	gutem Wetter
deiner besten Prüfung	guten Wetters

21·3   1. Die Kinder waren ganz müde.   2. Die Kinder waren sehr müde.   3. Die Kinder waren ziemlich
müde.   4. Die Kinder waren gar nicht müde.   5. Die Kinder waren total müde.   6. Sein Gedicht ist
ziemlich gut.   7. Sein Gedicht ist überhaupt nicht gut.   8. Sein Gedicht ist ganz gut.   9. Sein Gedicht
ist sehr gut.   10. Sein Gedicht ist gar nicht gut.

21·4   1. Martin kaufte etwas für sich.   2. Ihr habt nur an euch gedacht.   3. Wir helfen uns, so oft wir
können.   4. Ich verberge das Geschenk hinter mir.   5. Er setzte sich auf den kleinen Stuhl.   6. Wer
wollte sich ein Würstchen bestellen?   7. Sie konnte sich nicht helfen.   8. Wäschst du dich im
Badezimmer?   9. Ich frage mich, warum er weint.   10. Warum widersprecht ihr euch?   11. Mutter
wird sich ein paar Nelken kaufen.   12. Sie finden gar keine Plätze für sich.   13. Karl hat sich an die
große Prüfung erinnert.   14. Wo kann er sich waschen?   15. Wir ärgern uns nicht darüber.

21·5   1. Wir wussten nicht, warum sie nach Hause gegangen ist.   2. Wir wussten nicht, was er im Einkaufszentrum gekauft hat.   3. Wir wussten nicht, mit wem Sabine Tennis gespielt hat.   4. Wir wussten nicht, wie lange sie im Ausland bleiben mussten.   5. Wir wussten nicht, für wen Erik die Blumen gekauft hat.   6. Jemand fragte, wann der Bus abgefahren ist.   7. Jemand fragte, wessen Mercedes der Mann gestohlen hat.   8. Jemand fragte, wohin die Jungen gelaufen sind.   9. Jemand fragte, wofür sich der Wissenschaftler interessiert.   10. Jemand fragte, warum du dir immer widersprichst.   11. Können Sie mir sagen, um wie viel Uhr der Zug kommt?   12. Können Sie mir sagen, wem ich damit helfen soll?   13. Können Sie mir sagen, was geschehen ist?   14. Können Sie mir sagen, wie viel diese Hemden kosten?   15. Können Sie mir sagen, wonach der Polizist gefragt hat?

22 Double infinitive structures

22·1   1. Du hast deine Pflicht tun sollen.   2. Der Mann hat nicht schwimmen können.   3. Man hat sehr vorsichtig sein müssen.   4. Haben sie mit der Katze spielen dürfen?   5. Niemand hat mit mir tanzen wollen.   6. Haben Sie die Berge sehen können?   7. Er hatte ins Ausland reisen wollen.   8. Was hatte er tun sollen?   9. Die Jungen hatten für Sie arbeiten können.   10. Ihr hattet den Hund waschen müssen.   11. Hier hatte man nicht rauchen dürfen.   12. Erik wird ins Restaurant gehen wollen.   13. Wirst du ihm helfen können?   14. Ich werde in die Stadt fahren sollen.   15. Wir werden ihn vom Flughafen abholen müssen.

22·2   1. Er hat das neue Auto waschen lassen.
Er wird das neue Auto waschen lassen.
2. Er hat seine Eltern im Keller flüstern hören.
Er wird seine Eltern im Keller flüstern hören.
3. Wir haben den Düsenjäger über dem Wald fliegen sehen.
Wir werden den Düsenjäger über dem Wald fliegen sehen.
4. Herr Dorf hat einen neuen Anzug machen lassen.
Herr Dorf wird einen neuen Anzug machen lassen.
5. Der Junge hat mir das alte Radio reparieren helfen.
Der Junge wird mir das alte Radio reparieren helfen.

22·3   1. Sie kann seine Rede nicht verstehen.
Sie konnte seine Rede nicht verstehen.
Sie hat seine Rede nicht verstehen können.
Sie wird seine Rede nicht verstehen können.
2. Wir hören den Mann Gitarre spielen.
Wir hörten den Mann Gitarre spielen.
Wir haben den Mann Gitarre spielen hören.
Wir werden den Mann Gitarre spielen hören.
3. Du musst ins Ausland reisen.
Du musstest ins Ausland reisen.
Du hast ins Ausland reisen müssen.
Du wirst ins Ausland reisen müssen.
4. Wer sieht die Mädchen im Fluss schwimmen?
Wer sah die Mädchen im Fluss schwimmen?
Wer hat die Mädchen im Fluss schwimmen sehen?
Wer wird die Mädchen im Fluss schwimmen sehen?
5. Der kranke Mann darf nicht nach Hause gehen.
Der kranke Mann durfte nicht nach Hause gehen.
Der kranke Mann hat nicht nach Hause gehen dürfen.
Der kranke Mann wird nicht nach Hause gehen dürfen.
6. Ich soll eine neue Schule besuchen.
Ich sollte eine neue Schule besuchen.
Ich habe eine neue Schule besuchen sollen.
Ich werde eine neue Schule besuchen sollen.

7. Viele Leute können schwimmen.
   Viele Leute konnten schwimmen.
   Viele Leute haben schwimmen können.
   Viele Leute werden schwimmen können.
8. Er will die Suppe probieren.
   Er wollte die Suppe probieren.
   Er hat die Suppe probieren wollen.
   Er wird die Suppe probieren wollen.
9. Der Wissenschaftler lässt die Software installieren.
   Der Wissenschaftler ließ die Software installieren.
   Der Wissenschaftler hat die Software installieren lassen.
   Der Wissenschaftler wird die Software installieren lassen.
10. Die Soldaten helfen ihnen die Tulpen pflanzen.
    Die Soldaten halfen ihnen die Tulpen pflanzen.
    Die Soldaten haben ihnen die Tulpen pflanzen helfen.
    Die Soldaten werden ihnen die Tulpen pflanzen helfen.

22·4 1. c   2. a   3. b   4. d   5. c   6. a   7. c   8. b   9. a   10. c   11. a   12. d   13. b
14. c   15 c   16. a   17. b   18. d   19. d   20. a

23   Infinitive clauses

23·1 1. eine Sprache zu lernen   2. ihr sechs Euro zu geben   3. ihm ein Glas Wasser zu bringen   4. an der Ecke zu warten   5. mehr Zeit zu haben   6. nach meiner Tochter zu fragen   7. in einer Fabrik zu arbeiten   8. ihn nicht zu sehen   9. schlechter zu werden   10. heute in der Hauptstadt zu sein

23·2 1. eine Schule in Bremen zu besuchen   2. die Fahrkarten zu vergessen   3. um acht Uhr anzukommen   4. sich umzuziehen   5. bald zurückzukehren   6. es zu empfehlen   7. einen Freund mitzubringen   8. einen alten Koffer zu verkaufen   9. die Gäste vorzustellen   10. in der Schillerstraße auszusteigen

23·3 1. zum Einkaufszentrum gefahren zu sein   2. ihnen danken zu sollen   3. sehr kalt geworden zu sein   4. die Polizei angerufen zu haben   5. nicht schneller laufen zu können   6. eine Tasse Tee bestellt zu haben   7. in die Schweiz reisen zu müssen   8. einen Regenschirm mitgenommen zu haben   9. langsam hereingekommen zu sein   10. nicht alleine fahren zu dürfen

23·4 1. den kranken Mann zu verstehen   2. in dem dunklen Wohnzimmer zu lesen   3. so schnell wie ein Pferd zu rennen   4. in einer kleinen Wohnung zu wohnen   5. ohne einen Computer zu arbeiten   6. einen neuen Ausweis zu bekommen   7. elf Kinder zu erziehen   8. einige Pakete nach Afghanistan zu schicken   9. die schweren Koffer zum Bahnhof zu tragen   10. Politiker zu sein

23·5 1. im Garten zu arbeiten   2. den wichtigen Brief zu schreiben   3. die Suppe vorzubereiten   4. den armen Mann aufzuheben   5. noch eine Flasche Wein zu bestellen   6. den unartigen Jungen zu strafen   7. eine Fahrkarte gekauft zu haben   8. von uns Abschied zu nehmen   9. zu weinen   10. deine Kleider auszuwählen   11. beim Militär zu dienen   12. in der Fabrik zu arbeiten   13. mehr Geld verdienen zu können   14. einen guten Job zu suchen   15. Goethes Leben zu untersuchen

24   The passive voice

24·1 1. Die Maus wurde von der Eule gefressen.
       Die Maus ist von der Eule gefressen worden.
       Die Maus wird von der Eule gefressen werden.
2. Der Kranke wird von der Ärztin geheilt.
   Der Kranke ist von der Ärztin geheilt worden.
   Der Kranke wird von der Ärztin geheilt werden.
3. Der Artikel wird von ihm gelesen.
   Der Artikel wurde von ihm gelesen.

Der Artikel wird von ihm gelesen werden.
4. Die Briefe werden von mir geschrieben.
   Die Briefe wurden von mir geschrieben.
   Die Briefe sind von mir geschrieben worden.
5. Die Schüler werden vom Lehrer unterrichtet.
   Die Schüler sind vom Lehrer unterrichtet worden.
   Die Schüler werden vom Lehrer unterrichtet werden.
6. Die Anzüge werden vom Schneider genäht.
   Die Anzüge wurden vom Schneider genäht.
   Die Anzüge sind vom Schneider genäht worden.
7. Das Brot wurde von Herrn Benz gekauft.
   Das Brot ist von Herrn Benz gekauft worden.
   Das Brot wird von Herrn Benz gekauft werden.
8. Eine Tasse Kaffee wird von der Kellnerin gebracht.
   Eine Tasse Kaffee wurde von der Kellnerin gebracht.
   Eine Tasse Kaffee wird von der Kellnerin gebracht werden.

24·2 1. Das Dorf ist vom Feind zerstört worden.   2. Der Bauernhof wird von einem Waldbrand bedroht.
3. Der alte Hund wurde durch einen Schuss getötet.   4. Viele Schweine werden vom Bauer aufgezogen
werden.   5. Die Aufsätze sind vom Lehrer verbessert worden.

24·3 1. Dem Professor wurde von seinem Gedicht imponiert.   2. Der alten Frau ist von mir geholfen worden.
3. Dem König ist von dir gut gedient worden.   4. Das Lied wird von allen gesungen werden.   5. Uns
wird vom Dieb mit einer Pistole gedroht.   6. Der Mann ist von mir in Berlin gesehen worden.   7. Mir
wurde vom Soldaten für das Geschenk gedankt.   8. Das Eis wird von den Kindern gegessen werden.
9. Der Gesundheit wird durch das Rauchen geschadet.   10. Ihm ist von einem guten Freund geraten worden.

24·4 1. Ein Haus muss hier gebaut werden.   2. Ein Haus kann hier gebaut werden.   3. Ein Haus soll hier
gebaut werden.   4. Ihm wollte damit geholfen werden.   5. Ihm sollte damit geholfen werden.   6. Ihm
konnte damit geholfen werden.   7. Das Problem kann auch von ihr verstanden werden.   8. Das
Problem muss auch von ihr verstanden werden.   9. Das Auto wird nicht repariert werden können.
10. Das Auto wird nicht repariert werden müssen.

24·5 1. Das ließ sich nicht leicht ändern.
   Das hat sich nicht leicht ändern lassen.
   Das wird sich nicht leicht ändern lassen.
2. Das Geld kann nicht gefunden werden.
   Das Geld hat nicht gefunden werden können.
   Das Geld wird nicht gefunden werden können.
3. Diese Probleme lassen sich schnell lösen.
   Diese Probleme ließen sich schnell lösen.
   Diese Probleme haben sich schnell lösen lassen.
4. Ihnen wird dafür gedankt.
   Ihnen wurde dafür gedankt.
   Ihnen wird dafür gedankt werden.
5. Der Hund war gewaschen.
   Der Hund ist gewaschen gewesen.
   Der Hund wird gewaschen sein.

25 The subjunctive

25·1 1. müsse   trage   versuche
            müssest   tragest   versuchest
            müsse   trage   versuche
            müssen   tragen   versuchen
            müsset   traget   versuchet
            müssen   tragen   versuchen

2. sehe an	laufe	interessiere
sehest an	laufest	interessierest
sehe an	laufe	interessiere
sehen an	laufen	interessieren
sehet an	laufet	interessieret
sehen an	laufen	interessieren
3. wisse	wolle	gebe aus
wissest	wollest	gebest aus
wisse	wolle	gebe aus
wissen	wollen	geben aus
wisset	wollet	gebet aus
wissen	wollen	geben aus

25·2

1. schliefe	äße	wollte
schliefest	äßest	wolltest
schliefe	äße	wollte
schliefen	äßen	wollten
schliefet	äßet	wolltet
schliefen	äßen	wollten
2. lüde ein	tränke	ginge mit
lüdest ein	tränkest	gingest mit
lüde ein	tränke	ginge mit
lüden ein	tränken	gingen mit
lüdet ein	tränket	ginget mit
lüden ein	tränken	gingen mit
3. dürfte	verstünde/verstände	riefe an
dürftest	verstündest/verständest	riefest an
dürfte	verstünde/verstände	riefe an
dürften	verstünden/verständen	riefen an
dürftet	verstündet/verständet	riefet an
dürften	verstünden/verständen	riefen an

25·3

1. nennte	erkennte	wäre
nenntest	erkenntest	wärest
nennte	erkennte	wäre
nennten	erkennten	wären
nenntet	erkenntet	wäret
nennten	erkennten	wären
2. hätte	brächte	würde
hättest	brächtest	würdest
hätte	brächte	würde
hätten	brächten	würden
hättet	brächtet	würdet
hätten	brächten	würden

25·4 1. Der Reporter berichtete, dass der Kanzler bald gesund werde.   2. Der Reporter berichtete, dass niemand die Rede verstehe.   3. Der Reporter berichtete, dass die Touristen nach Italien reisten.   4. Der Reporter berichtete, dass die alte Frau gestorben sei.   5. Der Reporter berichtete, dass Herr Dorf in Polen wohnen werde.   6. Sie haben ihn gefragt, ob seine Frau wieder in der Schweiz sei.   7. Sie haben ihn gefragt, ob die Kinder Fußball spielen könnten.   8. Sie haben ihn gefragt, ob er genug Geld habe.   9. Sie haben ihn gefragt, ob sie wüssten, wo sie ist.   10. Sie haben ihn gefragt, ob der Junge bestraft werden müsse.

25·5   1. Der Richter hat gesagt, dass der Junge mit dem Hund gespielt habe.   2. Der Richter hat gesagt, dass wir die Uhr verloren hätten.   3. Der Richter hat gesagt, dass sie mit dem Bus gefahren seien.   4. Der Richter hat gesagt, dass Erik das Auto gestohlen habe.   5. Der Richter hat gesagt, dass der Dieb zwei Stunden im Keller gewesen sei.   6. Sonja berichtete, dass sie eine neue Speise gekocht hätten.   7. Sonja berichtete, dass Karl zu spät gekommen sei.   8. Sonja berichtete, dass ihre Tochter gut getanzt habe.   9. Sonja berichtete, dass mein Vater ihr zehn Euro gegeben habe.   10. Sonja berichtete, dass Martin oft an uns gedacht habe.

25·6   1. Wenn ich in meiner Heimat wäre!   2. Wenn er mehr Mut hätte!   3. Wenn wir mehr Glück gehabt hätten!   4. Wenn er nicht in die Stadt gefahren wäre!   5. Wenn du besser gearbeitet hättest!

25·7   1. er verletzt wäre   2. er uns hasste   3. wir taub wären   4. sie sehr krank gewesen wäre   5. sie ihm überhaupt nicht glauben könnte   6. sie ein Ungeheuer gesehen hätte   7. sie ihn liebte   8. sie den Mann nie kennen gelernt hätte   9. ich ihr Diener wäre   10. sie perfekt Deutsch sprechen könnte

25·8   1. Wenn Tina im Lotto gewänne, würde sie sich einen Pelzmantel kaufen.   2. Wenn der Mann lange schliefe, könnte er nicht arbeiten.   3. Wenn sie das verlorene Geld gefunden hätte, hätte sie es dem Polizisten geben müssen.   4. Wenn das Wetter schlecht gewesen wäre, wäre ich nicht auf das Land gefahren.   5. Wenn der Student nicht aufmerksam gewesen wäre, hätte er einen großen Fehler gemacht.   6. Wenn es nicht so weit wäre, würde ich dorthin zu Fuß gehen.   7. Wenn das Mädchen ein Gymnasium besucht hätte, hätte sie an einer Universität studieren können.   8. Wenn die Frau besser arbeitete, würde sie mehr verdienen.   9. Wenn sie uns angerufen hätte, hätte ich sie vom Bahnhof abgeholt.   10. Wenn du wieder gesund wärest, müsstest du wieder einen Job finden.

R3   Final Review

R3·1   1. C   2. B   3. B   4. C   5. C   6. B   7. A   8. A   9. A   10. A

R3·2   1. D   2. D   3. C   4. A   5. C   6. B   7. C   8. X   9. A   10. A

R3·3   1. D   2. C   3. C   4. B   5. A   6. D   7. B   8. A   9. D   10. C

R3·4   1. D   2. D   3. A   4. A   5. D   6. C   7. C   8. B   9. A   10. C

R3·5   1. D   2. A   3. D   4. B   5. A   6. C   7. C   8. B   9. A   10. B